Hey
Hi
Hello

Hey
Hi
Hello

*Five Decades of Pop Culture from Britain's
First Female DJ*

Annie Nightingale

WHITE
RABBIT

First published in Great Britain in 2020 by White Rabbit,
an imprint of The Orion Publishing Group Ltd
Carmelite House, 50 Victoria Embankment
London EC4Y 0DZ

An Hachette UK Company

1 3 5 7 9 10 8 6 4 2

A CIP catalogue record for this book is
available from the British Library.

ISBN (Hardback) 978 1 4746 1668 3
ISBN (eBook) 978 1 4746 1670 6

Typeset by Born Group
Printed and bound in Great Britain by Clays Ltd, Elcograf S.p.A.

FSC
www.fsc.org
MIX
Paper from
responsible sources
FSC® C104740

www.whiterabbitbooks.co.uk
www.orionbooks.co.uk

To: Lucy
Alex
Will
Olie

Contents

The Happy Happy Sound
of Radio 1

Imagine you are a passenger on a scheduled flight on a commercial modern jet airliner.

Imagine that suddenly the entire flight crew is stricken with some mysterious bug and are all slumped unconscious on the flight deck. And *you*, who have never ever even been allowed near the cockpit in your life, must now take over the controls, fly the plane and land it. Safely. Single-handed. A 747 perhaps, or a Dreamliner with several hundred passengers aboard.

You are confronted with a huge array of dials, switches, levers, controls and computer screens. You don't even know where the on/off power button is.

And that is what it's like, being confronted with a live radio desk.

I was the subject of my own press conference, organised by the BBC, to launch my new career as the first female DJ. A question came sailing over, an opening salvo from the press, of which I had been a part. Up till now, it seemed.

'Poacher turned game keeper, are you?'

I expected to last three months, a year, tops. For all I might say about early Radio 1, the later bosses have let me carry on playing records for them for five decades. So thank you.

It was a photo call as well, so a battery of cameramen was lined up to take pictures of me. It was daunting, to say the least. In an outside, daytime location — a formal garden somewhere in central London.

Yeah, the journalists and their reporting team needed an angle, I knew that. But . . . *Poacher?*

I so wished at that moment that I was in The Beatles. George Harrison once got asked at a press conference, 'What do you call that haircut?'

And he replied instantly, 'I call it Arthur.'

OK, it's a fair cop, got some fancy rabbit pelts in the back of me van, I didn't think to say. Nor would I now.

Sure, I'd used the media to criticise the BBC for its (what would be laughed out of court now) sexism. When Radio 1 had been launched three years before, its bosses were quite open about the station being hosted by all-male DJs. I could hardly believe it, but there were to be no on-air female DJs.

Wha'? Why? That was my response.

So I had gone into campaign mode — in teen mags, newspapers or television — to challenge what was to me quite unwarranted and ridiculous bias.

But it didn't quite equate to being a poacher. No one accused any of the dashing new DJs, almost all of them having come from illegal pirate stations to work at the BBC, of being poachers.

Whatever.

Not that I felt any entitlement. *At all.* I had little initial confidence that I would be any good as a radio presenter. But surely, I and any other female had the right at least to . . . have a go. That was all.

Let me try and see, and if I'm no good, I promise I'll shut up and go away. I promise. By then, I'd had ten years of being a journalist and TV presenter — why should radio be the exclusive preserve of males? It was just bewildering to me.

I did talk a bit posh, not that I was. I'd come from the most average, suburban, non-distinguished background you could imagine. But sometime early on, I'd had elocution lessons. Also I smoked more than a packet of fags a day, so I couldn't be accused of having a high squeaky voice. It was quite *blokey*, it's been since pointed out, though I didn't see it like that at the time.

Please let me have a try seemed a fair enough request to me. It took three years to persuade the BBC to let me try my hand.

There's a huge difference between being a presenter/announcer and being a DJ, in radio terms. For one, you have to know how to work the desk. Intimidating, and to a newcomer, terrifying.

What I was also confronted with were a bunch of male engineers in the glass booth beside me, waiting if not willing me to fail.

There were so many technical hoops to jump through. For example, not 'crashing the vocal'. That meant you could talk all over the introduction to a tune but had to judge and time your words to finish — bang! — just as the vocal came in. Supposedly sounded slicker. Kept the pace going. If you timed your words badly and still kept talking *after* the vocal started, that was crashing it. A terrible crime. To fade the tune out and speak over the vocals at the *end* of the track, that's allowable on daytime pop radio. But *not* on golden oldies or AOR radio. That *really* annoys their listeners.

Of course, the people these talk-overs annoy most are the artistes who made the record in the first place. But they were supposed to be grateful to get their record played on the radio.

And radio airplay became more and more vital to get a hit. So the recording artistes were hardly going to complain if the DJs talked over their records. And to be fair, the DJs were bigging up their tunes.

I'd had no pirate ship background, which was where all the first-generation DJs had learnt their craft. And from whom I got my first inspiration.

I knew all about the pirate ship revolution as it happened. I'd met Ronan O'Rahilly, who launched Radio Caroline, in some plush office suite in Mayfair. I wore the T-shirt. White with a red image of a ship and 'RADIO CAROLINE' emblazoned beneath it.

On one occasion the ship was moving its anchoring and sailed right past my flat on the seafront at Brighton.

'Ahoy there, we can see you, Brighton!' declaimed the newly famous DJ Simon Dee. I felt like waving back from my second-floor balcony. Actually, I felt like jumping in the sea and swimming out to board Radio Caroline there and then.

I was hooked. I wanted to be a DJ too. But it didn't seem any more than a dream, until . . . the pirates were moved onto dry land, outlawed and now at the BBC. Aha, I thought, now's my chance. This will be more do-able.

Not so. I had to wait those precious last three years of the sixties till it happened. But then I got chucked in the deep end. Live on national radio. Well, perhaps it was the only way.

And it is a lot easier now, with digital formats. The hazards then . . . for instance, accidentally playing a vinyl record at the wrong speed, 45 revolutions per minute, instead of 33. Playing the wrong side of the record (the B-side instead of the A-side). Finding the right track on a vinyl album. Playing the wrong, unexpurgated version, with swear words left in, unedited. 'Working Class Hero' by John Lennon comes back to mind. Pre-9 p.m. watershed when the word 'fuck' isn't OK. Knowing what various slang words meant when referring to drugs or sex. Viz, Radio 1 played Lou Reed's 'Walk on the Wild Side' for some weeks before someone pointed out what 'giving head' meant. Or that the Stranglers' 'Golden Brown' was about heroin.

From day one, I wanted to choose the records I played. I didn't join a radio station in order to *seek* fame or promote my public profile. I'd already had some of that working as a TV presenter. But it came with the territory, and everyone nowadays has to be a 'brand'.

My thing was my passion for music, and radio seemed the best medium for spreading the word, enthusing about great new tunes . . . or albums.

But being on Radio 1 meant that you had to become a 'name', because that's how they built the station's listening figures. I was used to promoting other people, like David Bowie or later Daft Punk or myriads of others. But now I had to promote myself. Bluntly, the Radio 1 DJs were often treated as more important than the music they were playing . . .

More satisfying, surely, more effective as a means of communication than trying to describe music in words, in a newspaper or a magazine column.

What I had been missing, in those frustrating years of not being allowed near the mics of Radio 1, was this.

The management heads in the early Radio 1 days were technical-grade blokes, some ex-RAF. Their mantra was: Radio 1 DJs are 'husband substitutes', jolly chaps who would keep the little woman at home entertained, the imagined housewife in her frilly pinny, till hubby came back from work and male authority could be restored in the home. In those days a woman was not allowed to open a credit card account, or take on a mortgage, without a male partner. A woman broadcaster would not be welcome, would alienate the listeners. That's what they told me.

It was as though the social revolution of the sixties, young music made by a new generation of young people, had never happened.

Radio 1 seemed then like a day-long version of *Housewives' Choice*. As though women didn't go out to work, have a job, have a career, and also not taking on board that young me, who loved new music, might be listening too.

The strange thing was I had not experienced sexism until I confronted Radio 1. I'd had a decade working on newspapers, writing features, op-ed magazine columns, making documentaries, hosting music shows on TV, and never been told, 'You can't do this job because you're a woman'.

WTF? I was amazed.

Anyway, public opinion was changing. They were going to have to take on at least one female. Because I'd been the one tapping – well, kicking – at their door for so long, eventually they let me have a go.

On the very first live show, I accidentally stopped the record that was being broadcast and cut the station's output all over Great Britain to an agonising and grinding halt. Silence ensued. I thought that would be the beginning and end of my radio career, in one go, like a Broadway show closing on the first night . . .

Learning on the job was difficult and slow, because I had one show a week. A bit like having one driving lesson a month and forgetting half of what you'd learnt by the time the next one came around.

It was this techie side that the blokes favoured. Rather than what was actually being **said** between the records – the presentational style.

What I did feel confident about, if not the technical side, were my choices of music. I soon realised that the daytime DJs were subject to a playlist, not choosing their own music to play.

This would have defeated the whole object to me. It was my obsession with finding new music that was the whole reason for wanting a record show.

I asked the boss if I could join the *Sounds of the Seventies* evening DJs who broadcast their own chosen tunes. Some presenters wanted the massive exposure of a daytime slot, with added fame. I wanted the freedom of the night-time shows. It was one of the best decisions — professionally — I ever made. Even though I'd begun in a 'review' slot, in the afternoons, having heard a few of those early shows back recently, I'm now shocked that I could have been so sharply critical — in a way that no one is nowadays on popular radio. I wasn't into career destroying; it's best, probably, if you don't like it, to not play it.

But my sharp comments had caught the ears of The Who, and they went on a charm offensive to win me round, which worked admirably well, and they became friends for life!

There was no commercial radio in Britain then, so Radio 1 had a massive audience, with the breakfast show reaching eighteen to twenty million or so. But in a small, quite basic studio with a stack of records to play and a microphone, you cannot let those types of listening figures unnerve you. Broadcasting was to me then, and still is, as simple as making a phone call.

To your best friend: speaking to one person:

Hi, have you heard this new one?

Let me play it to you. *See what you think.*

I just wanted to share my enthusiasm. Spread the word. It's really that simple.

To be fair to the first wave of managers and bosses of Radio 1, it was all a new challenge for them too. Radio 1 had been foisted on an unwilling BBC after the pirate ships, of which I was a slavish follower, got closed down.

We pop kids wanted the real thing, back-to-back tunes (or 'choons' as they were hailed by nineties ravers). I would say that the pirates' most prominent years in operation, 1964–66, produced and promoted some of the best quality pop music from both sides of the Atlantic that has ever been. Pick a top 10 from 1966, and I'll bet you would know most of these even now.

Tell you what . . . let's try that right now . . .

Here's a published UK top 10 from May 1966:

1. Paint It Black – THE ROLLING STONES

2. Wild Thing – THE TROGGS

3. Strangers in the Night – FRANK SINATRA

4. Pretty Flamingo – MANFRED MANN

5. Sorrow – THE MERSEYBEATS

6. Sloop John B – THE BEACH BOYS

7. Shotgun Wedding – ROY C

8. Monday Monday – THE MAMAS AND THE PAPAS

9. Rainy Day Women Nos 12 and 35 – BOB DYLAN

10. Hey Girl – THE SMALL FACES

Even if you don't know any of the titles, you've surely heard of most of the artistes.

But the BBC wasn't *allowed* to play back-to-back hit tunes all day long. Radio 1 was chained by restrictions – the number of records they were allowed to play in a day. The pop acts had to audition to check if they could play their hits as well live as they did on the records. The Rolling Stones failed the first time. It's laughable now, but those were the quaint rules.

And what and who were these . . . these, er . . . *disc jockeys* exactly? These ex-pirates who were now allowed to be let loose in Broadcasting House. Designing their own 'self op' studio desks, and worst of all . . . allowed to broadcast *live*, and unvetted? All sounded rather suspiciously brash, and sort of, well, to them, suspiciously foreign and suspiciously commercial.

I reckon the bigwigs at the BBC were secretly hoping this pop music was just a fad and would be dead in the water within a year. That it would all go away, and Radio 1 with it.

The station thrived against all odds. And I am amazed still and thankful that they kept me on, for all these years.

The only strategy for Radio 1 to survive was to make its DJs into big stars and build massive listening figures. Which they did. And it is the presenters that of course are now key to the vital difference of gaining an audience from the alternatives such as the streaming site Spotify.

In no other country are pop radio DJs bigger names than the musicians whose music they play. Household names, national treasures, and in the process, some unsavoury characters who slipped through the net in the early days.

The DJs had come from such different backgrounds. Actors, a chef, a few musicians, some ex-public schoolboys, a smattering of media types.

There were scant university media courses, degrees in media studies. Few reality shows on TV. So Radio 1 was an extraordinary magnet for those driven by a deep need and craving, almost an addiction to fame and recognition. It was said that being signed to Radio 1 was like playing for England. It was also to involve taking part in motor racing at Brands Hatch, roller skating at Thorpe Park, and being jumped over by a stunt motorcyclist. Little did I know . . .

There was, fortunately, John Peel. He seemed to be allowed to be there because he liked playing new music. He also loved football, and I think that reassured the management that he was actually in some senses a 'normal' human being and not a long-haired, potentially anarchic dangerous hippy freak.

I did find out some years later that all the DJs on Radio 1 had been vetted by a branch of our intelligence service, MI5. What did the dossiers have to say? I'll never know.

If John Peel was a freak, then I was most definitely treated as one. Not necessarily in a negative way, more out of bewilderment.

Why would a *woman* want to be a DJ? So, *techie*, in other words. *Just leave all that stuff to the boys who know their kilohertz from their megahertz* was the patronising inference. *Why worry your pretty little head with such technical matters, dear?*

Answer: I want to be a DJ, because I figure it's the best job in the world!

But the wife of a BBC executive, at some early in-house reception (*Stepford Wives* style, except that sci-fi story about housewives becoming fembots hadn't even emerged yet) had drawled to me, with a worried frown: 'Aren't you afraid you'll lose your *fem-in-nin-it-tay?*'

So this was all going to be much more of an uphill struggle than I had imagined, and perhaps explains why no other female DJ appeared on Radio 1 for another *twelve* years . . .

Right Place, Wrong Time?

Now everyone is much more decade-aware, but it certainly wasn't apparent by 1970 that the big happy shiny party that had been the sixties was well and truly over. Any more than that what is regarded as sixties culture began in 1960. (And actually, nineties culture started in the late eighties.)

But you can feel change coming, you can feel something in the air, like that buzzy tune by Thunderclap Newman and Pete Townshend, who got it, smashed it big, one time.

I always wanted to be in the swirl of forward movement, and always believing that things were going to change *for the better*.

Well so far, they had. As a war baby born in the London Blitz, you only know what you are surrounded by. Because of the shortages of absolutely everything, nothing any of us kids had was new. First-hand. I had a threadbare teddy bear, a two decades-old china doll, a second-hand tricycle, hand-me-down clothes and precious but well-thumbed books. We ate what they called mousetrap cheese and powdered egg. But as none of us in the gang I grew up with had seen any different, it didn't matter. We didn't feel deprived, because we didn't *know* we were deprived. (It's so poignant to be writing this now, in the midst of the COVID crisis.)

The adults were always talking wistfully about 'Before The War', banging on about it, like it was some enchanted place, a lost domain. Somewhere where the lead character in *Le Grand Meaulnes* was always trying to find his way back to. Though 'Before The War' in his case was World War One, which swiftly killed its young author, Alain-Fournier. For the small circle of British adults in my domain, there always seemed to have been some lavish party going on, in a vast night club with sparkly-covered white grand pianos, being played by smarmy looking blokes, their hair slicked back with brilliantine, and Marcel-waved women swanning around in fur coats over long satin evening dresses, doing the foxtrot and brandishing cigarette holders. The men looking like bank managers trying to dance like Fred Astaire and wearing evening tailcoats and white bow ties, and comical round rimmed spectacles, which made them look even more like bank managers, overdressed and totally failing to look cool or dashing.

'Before The War' they seemed to spend all their time going to dinner dances and wearing camellias in their hair. My parents and their friends kept showing me now curled-at-the-edges old black and white photographs of themselves and their friends, swivelling round from their dinner table placings in large hotel ballrooms to stare and pose for the commercial photographer capturing their image for the night.

I thought that's what they did all the time. Perhaps they only ever went once. Kinda glamorous, I suppose. All very *Great Gatsby*, all very *The Beautiful and Damned*. I wasn't envious, I didn't want to live in the past. There was no going back. That world was over, finished, lost forever. The evidence was everywhere. Every day I wandered between buildings with their facades ripped down, roofs blown off, revealing fascinatingly the one remaining square of rose strewn wallpaper from a child's bedroom wall, once on the third floor, now exposed for all to see, and open to the elements. A small Victorian iron fireplace, suspended, hanging halfway up a bare brick wall, itself supported by a single iron girder, propped up at forty-five degrees to the ground to prevent the nearly shattered edifice from crumbing into the street, creating more casualties. Similar to the way Havana, Cuba, looks now. But a giant bombsite, that's what my neighbourhood, and most of Britain, looked like. Exciting really. You never knew what you might find next. A bit of old bomb casing, a mine, any form of UXB from a cracked open cellar. Completely normal, if that's what you'd grown up with.

Looking every day into those bombed-out buildings was a blatant metaphor for the bombed-out lives of the survivors of the Second World War. Ex-service men on crutches ventured out from the Star and Garter Home on Richmond Hill, each with one empty grey flannel trouser leg folded and pinned up neatly above the knee, swinging back and forth as they struggled on their wooden sticks, on their one good leg, the half of the other blown away.

The adults who hadn't been killed or maimed in the war, but had known better times, seemed to be trying to wish themselves back into this pre-war rosy existence. 'Look For A Silver Lining', that was a popular lyric of the day, and 'There'll be blue birds OVER, the white cliffs of DOVER' (what good bluebirds would do in terms of broke Britain, I have no idea). The once popular perfume 'Evening in Paris' by Bourjois, or rather its empty bottle, adorned my mother's dressing table. That pre-war empty bottle seemed a perfect symbol of the past. Of the thirties. An Evening in Paris. Not much chance of that now, or even of finding the origin for the more vulgar 'California Poppy' (well I was told it was vulgar, it came from Woolworths). The adults in turn felt guilty, sorry for us kids, poor, deprived, rationed, with only a red tin money box with just a few pennies to save . . .

Oh please! It wasn't that bad! — only materially.

We had never known Before The War so we had no sense of missing out on anything. In fact, we felt almost a kind of cool superiority. There was no need to patronise us kids because we were resilient. We were fortunate enough, unlike millions of others, to have survived the war.

We played on bomb sites, we *loved* playing on bomb sites. Born to the air raid siren, mournfully yet chillingly foreboding, it was the first sound I remembered . . .

Try that screaming, sweeping, yowling intro to 'Blockbuster' by The Sweet to get the full 'Focke-Wulf on a Thames bombing run' effect. We were the Bisto Kids — ragged but defiant. We were unafraid, and unimpressed with anything sickly or sentimental.

And gradually, though very gradually, things did get better. Through the much maligned 1950s . . . which wasn't all grey and gloom. There were coffee bars with cappuccinos in glass cups, the *New Musical Express*, *Eagle* mag's Dan Dare, *Journey into Space* on the radio. And the utter delights of Radio Luxembourg. We became teenagers with rock 'n' roll, Elvis, Little Richard — expressly for us, for young people. Which then exploded by 1963 into an even more deliciously exciting time, with *That Was the Week That Was*, pirate radio, *Beyond the Fringe*, James Bond, miniskirts, and eeeeeeeeekkkk — The Beatles!

It just never occurred to me that things were going to, or could, or would get worse. And I'd always tried to cling a little to that sense of wonder that the unquestioning child is so fulfilled and awed by.

Before all the 'it's all been done before', 'nothing new under the sun' scepticism and cynicism pours its black treacly depression over joy and exuberance.

At the time of the disastrous Altamont concert in December 1969 I don't think the social commentators were declaring the sixties dead. Even at the Isle of Wight Festival in 1970, the atmosphere wasn't pleasant — it was quite scary at times — but we weren't declaiming 'This is the end', even if The Doors were.

And hey, wow, I'd joined Radio 1. My big chance. My chance to change the world! Bring great music to more people, millions of people.

But actually . . . who did I think I was? I had one show a week, was still devastatingly terrified of screwing up every time I went near the decks. I had no say in what went on the station's daytime playlist. I was still the rebel outsider.

It seemed that the teenage battlegrounds or wastelands we had gained — Hendrix, the Who, Velvet Underground — were in danger of being reclaimed, won back by the Establishment. Conventional, safe showbiz. Mantovani, Jim Reeves country . . . middle of the road stuff.

And for me that was a very unwelcome prospect.

Even as a small child I was very resistant to what I thought was bad music and slick marketing. One of the top tunes in those pre-radio playlist days was 'Yes! We Have No Bananas' (revived from the 1920s because now, ha ha, there actually were no bananas). Really?

We'd never had any bananas, so why would we want to hear a song about not having any bananas? And an upbeat version at that, not even a 'Yes! We Have No Banana Blues' (although such a version did exist, but we were never allowed to hear anything so negative in defiant, bright, Brexity, we-won-the-war Britain. I must say at this stage that I am no flag-waving, two world wars, one World Cup aficionado.) Bewilderingly lavished upon us by the music publishers in Denmark Street were more novelty songs about fruit and vegetables. 'I've Got a Luvverly Bunch of Coconuts'. 'You say to-mahto and I say to-mayto'.

Dear oh dear oh dear. *Please, 1970s, don't put us through that again.*

The unemployment figures rose. The highest since the end of the Second World War. Fifty thousand protesters marched against the Industrial Relations Act. The Tory government wanted to repatriate immigrants.

American showbiz stalwarts were furious with The Beatles for gate-crashing their game, *taking over* like that. How dare they?

How very dare they threaten the dominance of the Sinatras, the Perry Comos, the Tony Bennetts? Even Elvis had been effectively de-fanged by his spell in the US army and was never a threat to the American Dream of conventional living, or the American Way of Life, ever again, after that.

And that was just in music. The counterculture in the US was having to square up to the Establishment there too. The young didn't just want to fight the war in Vietnam. They wanted racial equality. They wanted — well in some areas — to grow their hair long and smoke weed. Students had been shot dead at Kent State University in Ohio for demonstrating that they did not agree with the US occupying Cambodia.

It didn't really help though that The Beatles were now, themselves, falling apart. I had not been a fan of the too long and now wobbly winding road. Turns out they weren't, either. Previously impeccable, good taste, Wall-of-Sound Phil Spector, adding schmaltzy *strings*?

Come *on*!

Tin Pan Alley moguls were having their breakthroughs. Break-backs. Clive Dunn with 'Grandad', for example. Though Clive was an exceptionally nice guy 'in real life'.

Excuse me, I'd be thinking . . . but — *no!* I grew up a child music critic, because there was a lot to critique. I was what was politely called 'well covered' i.e 'chubby' as a child, and deeply resented a popular polka song which ran along the lines of one guy saying to another, about a girl, 'You can have her. I don't want her, she's too fat for me.' I really took that personally.

Ghastly gushingly sentimental songs about babies, even twin babies — 'Twenty Tiny Fingers'. That's what Tin Pan Alley thought us kiddos wanted. That and enough Walt Disney to shove down our necks to choke us culturally, they hoped, for ever.

I'm sorry, but I *hated* Mickey Mouse. He looked ugly to me, his head was big for his body, though that's a photogenic proportion still favoured by Hollywood in its casting of real flesh-and-blood characters. To me Mickey's ears were so oversized that he didn't look like a mouse at all.

Donald Duck, what a plain scary pervert *he* appeared to be! I could never understand what he was saying, but it sounded deeply unpleasant by insinuation, and he looked like he could give you a nasty goose with that yellow bill of his. It was bad enough having to suffer all this trash as a child; it must have been hell if you were an adult.

Instinctively I knew I was being marketed at, persuaded to have the hated Mickey's image on my bucket and spade, school satchel, pencil case, gas mask.

Lucky you if you didn't have to grow up with songs that opined 'I'm a pink toothbrush' or 'Gillygillyossenfeffer-somefuckingstupidthing-by-the-sea'. People would *learn the words* to the made-up doggerel. As *entertainment!* And maybe that's where the serious misjudgement was made by the adults. Trying to provide and sell us popular culture. Sharp kids who had wised up a lot earlier than their parents realised. They did then and they always will!

We cannot go backwards, I was thinking, in the early seventies.

Hollywood was trying to get its own back after The Beatles' invasion, by creating massive hits like 'Wand'rin' Star' by the gnarly actor Lee Marvin from the film *Paint Your Wagon*. A musical from the 1950s . . . 'In the Summertime' by Mungo Jerry's jug band, another smash of the time, sounded to me like a throwback to skiffle.

Had I finally got my chance to play what I felt was a great music when the scene had just evaporated? Disappeared down a drain . . . Had I arrived *too late*?

There were other subtle shifts too. Evident through the window of fashion. The glory of miniskirts, Biba's classic simplicity — showing off long legs in pale tights, with high-button collars — were giving way to hippy culture. Young women in long, long skirts, *maxi* skirts, florals (bit frumpy) and the newly moustachioed boyfriend calling their partner 'my old lady'.

My? Somewhat possessive, for the supposedly new feminist movement?

When was that phrase popularised: 'pregnant, barefoot and in the kitchen'?

Females were being encouraged to wear hats again (more like Victorian bonnets), shawls, and an almost demure, denim, down-home look was being *suggested.* Even if they were being invited to live in a commune with all the free love that could be exploited therein. Not so much high heels now, as laced-up boots.

Young women were being caught between two cultures, regarding sex. Your mother would still be saying: 'Don't.' The men — older men, who tended to be the predators — were saying: 'Do.' You *must* endorse free love.

Otherwise you're not . . . *cool*. And who didn't want to be cool?

Then the pill happened, and it was harder for girls to say no if they didn't want to say yes . . . The pill, anyway, was not universally available over-the-counter. The theatre staged happenings like *Oh! Calcutta!* and the musical *Hair* (great songs) that were highlighting the four-letter word and nudity. You gotta be cool and intellectual, that was the pressure.

Having signed me up, I don't think Radio 1 knew quite what to do with me.

There was still that *Housewives' Choice* pro-male bias. A former crooner Jimmy Young read out recipes at lunchtimes. Ed 'Stewpot' Stewart hosted a children's programme called *Junior Choice*. Radio

1 still didn't really have its own identity and had to share airtime with Radio 2. I was the token female; I was also a known music columnist and critic, with strong views. I didn't fit comfortably.

Music was going folky. Steeleye Span, the Incredible String Band, acoustic recordings and real instruments . . . traditional tunes . . . going back to live on the land . . . yeah, but . . . Seemed a bit retrograde to me. I was more interested in what the mellotron could do. Also synthesisers. And what David Bowie had achieved using the very simple stylophone on 'Space Oddity'. I was into these interesting-sounding new bands on the Island label, like King Crimson and Roxy Music.

The mainstream was sounding a bit *worthy* and sort of earthy. I'd never been a slavish paid-up mod, but I was certainly a modernist. I had no desire to live in the country and grow vegetables. My dad had had that pleasure of digging an allotment in Marble Hill Park by the River Thames during the Second World War. (In his spare time from being a firefighter in the London Blitz, that is.) It was an absolute necessity then.

But weren't we supposed to keep moving on, moving forward? I embraced mod cons. And modern futuristic music. Where was that going to come from? Lou Reed's 'Walk on the Wild Side' and Kraftwerk as it turned out. But meanwhile Radio 1 had to keep these massive listening figures up.

We were going out on the road . . .

— 3 —

John Lennon, The Beatles & Apple Records

I would not have achieved my desire to be a DJ at Radio 1 without The Beatles and Apple, to whom I am for ever indebted. I have a maxim I try to pass on to others:

If there's somewhere you want to be, circle your target. Hang in there, do not be deterred. When it's said that someone achieved their aim by being 'at the right place at the right time', I say this: you may need to hang in there and be in the right place for potentially *a very long time* before that magic door opens.

I had been inspired to become a DJ since the pirate days of the earlyish sixties. However, by the end of that decade I was not much nearer my dream ever materialising.

But I was a journalist and I must have spoken of my desires to be on radio when hanging out at Apple. In fact, I would get odd opportunities to pass over some of my cherished taped interviews with The Beatles, for later broadcast.

The recording quality was terrible, because the tapes had only ever been intended as aides-memoire for writing up the interviews for newspaper and magazines.

Full of 'ahs' and 'ohs', 'mmms' and 'oh I see what you means' from me. (Absolutely *verboten* for broadcast interviews; you must ask your question, wait for the answer, keep your mouth shut, don't interrupt and only nod vigorously to encourage your interviewee to keep talking.)

But I had a good rapport, a good friendship with The Beatles, so perhaps I did have a possible potential value to the people in radio. We all need a helping hand, someone putting a word in . . . at the right moment. That's what Derek Taylor did for me. The BBC was now actively seeking a female DJ (after all the negative publicity I had generated — and the feminists were coming after Radio 1, too).

Apple had become, strangely, my sanctuary.

Happiness is a warm gun . . . bang, bang, shoot, shoot.

For years and years after the killing of John Lennon at the Dakota you couldn't. You couldn't mention that song. You couldn't play it; you couldn't even think of it or about it. I certainly self-censored it.

Even now it makes me shudder . . . The poignancy of it.

It had first been heard, off the back of the psychedelic pinnacle of 1967 and *Sgt. Pepper*.

The plunge into 1968 was so swift. It was the worst year of my life thus far. And seemed to echo the upheaval happening in the wider world. The assassinations of Martin Luther King Jr. and Robert Kennedy, the anti-Vietnam war demos in Grosvenor Square in London, students rioting in Paris . . . Apart from Apple. Apart from the solace of being allowed to grace the interior of the most desired four walls on the planet. Inside number 3 Savile Row, London W1 now and again . . .

My marriage was over. I had a five-year-old and a one-year-old. How on earth was I going to manage for money? I had always thought I'd best try to stay at least a little financially independent. I had a job, of sorts — well, a freelance version, which was best for working mostly from home. I was the pop columnist for the *Daily Sketch*. A tabloid, but gentler than the *Daily Mirror* or the *Sun*. At least, it was at that time.

When I finally got the job I'd really wanted at Radio 1, the sometimes previously bullying subs put me on the front page, with the caption:

ONE IN A MILLION

Derek Taylor and I had been friends since he first worked for Brian Epstein at NEMS, The Beatles' HQ on Argyll Street, next to the London Palladium. He'd been a provincial journalist like me, till he met and fell in love with The Beatles and went to work for them. Then he fell out with Brian Epstein, moved with his family to California, discovered The Byrds and revamped the pre-*Pet Sounds* era Beach Boys' image . . .

Now he was back, back back back in the Yoo Yoo Yoo Kay, running the public relations for The Beatles' utopian dream Apple.

Derek's office, positioned on the second floor of the white-walled historic town house, with its velvety green carpeting, was kind of the centre of the universe for me and for many others. I wasn't ligging and taking advantage of The Beatles' wealth and drinking all their free drink and hospitality. I was a supporter. I thought it was incredibly positive that The Beatles should want to share and spread their advantages, create opportunities for new artistes. That's where maybe I could help. Interview their protégés. Get their careers off the ground.

Of course they would be taken advantage of. Of course. But in the beginning, it seemed such a worthwhile venture. Trouble was, everyone thought that Apple was their heaven, their record company, their book publisher, their bank, their film financier, their venture capitalist, their fairy godmother, their money-laden apple tree.

There was an unwritten rule between The Beatles and individual members of the media. One strike and you're out — we'll trust you, but only once, if you betray us. Which I thought was perfectly fair.

Yes, the press and media had helped them to world domination, and they had been far more open in terms of interviews and access than any other entertainers before or since then.

Paul would phone me at home for some pop mag chat.

'Who's this?' I would say, probably after giving out my number, as you did then, as my parents had done.

'Popes Grove six-three-five-six,' my father would always announce dutifully to the incoming caller. We had no fridge, no telly, but we'd always had a telephone.

Even into the twenty-first century, my remaining close relative, an uncle in Chiswick, west London, would say on answering the phone: 'Eight-oh-four-two!'

'Brighton two-five-six-seven-two,' I said into the two-tone green phone handset in the small study office at the back of my house in Montpelier Road.

'Hello, who is it?'

'McCartney,' came the cheery reply.

'Oh,' I said.

Then added my trick question, in case it was an imposter:

'Which one?'

My slightly provocative-to-be-cool defensive shtick.

'James Paul,' answered one of the four most famous people in the world.

He knew that I knew his brother Michael. Five years previously Mike, in the satire group The Scaffold, and I had taken part in a TV pilot which had changed my life.

It was for my first presenting job on a show called *That's for Me.*

I had The Beatles' trust, which was more important to me than is imaginable. Of course I was a fan. Not just of their music, but what they had done for all of us, given a whole young generation hope and belief that we could have our dream realised, too, and believe in ourselves. I still go on and on about this debt we owe those four young men. It just cannot be overstated. It's one of my main reasons for wanting to stay at Radio 1. I want today's musically inclined youth to have the opportunities I had. To assist them if I can, to be able to help them realise their potential. So, to be allowed into their sanctum I needed a role, to justify my existence there. To contribute to the movement. To be part of it.

To change the world. I believed we could, and I had access to the very people to make it happen. I could at least write about the new artistes they were signing and the people that passed through the doors of 3 Savile Row at that time.

Much has been made in the past about money streaming out of those doors, viz. the glorious rockumentary *The Rutles*. Directed by Eric Idle with songs by Neil Innes of The Bonzo Dog Band. George Harrison played a TV news reporter, interviewing 'Eric Manchester', a satirised Derek Taylor played by Michael Palin from *Monty Python*. With an ad libbing vox pop from Mick Jagger, a non-singing role he never bettered. It could have tanked as a smug in-joke, but *The Rutles* became an affectionate Beatles parody classic.

To me, Apple was a meeting place for ideas, more like a literary salon. Perhaps like Paris had been in the fifties. Harry Nilsson, James Taylor and John Tavener were the best-known recipients of Apple's being, in some way or another.

The Beatles said at the time and since that they were not the change; they were part of it. Yes, there were others. The tiny islands that make up Britain were punching *so* above their weight, especially in the popular arts. John Osborne, Peter Brook, Mary Quant, David Lean, Hockney, Bailey and Donovan, the James Bond films, Michael Caine, *Beyond the Fringe* (the other four-headed monster besides The Beatles, of Peter Cook, Alan Bennett, Jonathan Miller and Dudley Moore), Hugh Carleton Greene (the Director General of the BBC for much of the sixties) and Pauline Boty, the pop artist. The will and confidence to shine was so contagious.

But by 1968 this optimism was changing somewhat. Realism was beginning to tug at our coat sleeves. With hindsight, it's easy to see, but the real revolution had been instigated in the late fifties and hatched between '63 and '67. The Beatles are so venerated now, it's hard to describe. But their image was somewhat dented in certain areas of the media beyond those years. And didn't improve for decades.

Despite winning over the whole world, they still seemed to be at the mercy of the media. For years since their moptop peak, sections of the press had been chipping away, trying to bring them down. I didn't want that, or any part of it.

Perhaps that's why they trusted me. But somehow being a journalist still made me feel an outsider, a possible enemy to be wary of. I knew I would never betray them, never let them down, but could they be so sure? The breakthrough for me was becoming a TV presenter. That made a huge difference in perception. Because of that I was accepted by the pop generation, not shunned as a journalistic spy. (The former Iraqi dictator Saddam Hussein regarded all journos as spies.) But it wasn't a full-time job, or a living. I still needed the fourth estate.

In Fleet Street among the so-called 'hard' journalists and newsmen I was sneered at.

'Huh! You just rewrite publicity handouts.'

The raincoat brigade of door steppers were hardly a bunch of flower children, and didn't believe in the youth revolution. Or in getting committed or personally involved in it. With the professional veneer of cynicism that seemed a necessary tool, they wouldn't embrace any of the fashionable new idealism.

Getting the story first was what mattered, for them to keep their well-paid jobs. Though there were stirrings of a new breed from the emerging underground press. I was a great admirer of Richard Neville, the young Australian editor of *Oz*. But then I wasn't quite accepted by his gang, either.

So my home life had unravelled. I needed to work for a living like never before. It would be two more years before I appeared at the divorce court, with the help of The Beatles' lawyer Martin Polden. He gave me a copy of Philip Roth's novel *Portnoy's Complaint* as a divorce present. Martin had advised The Beatles through drug busts and was closely affiliated with Release (a UK charity that arranges legal representation for people charged with drug possession), when he accompanied me, a bundle of nerves in a pale pink coat, to the divorce division of the High Court.

Paranoia was gripping the creatives. The Stones had experienced the Redlands bust the year before. In October 1968 the police raided Ringo Starr's home in London; John and Yoko were staying there at the time. The police found nothing incriminating. But all The Beatles were aware the Establishment wasn't going to do them any more favours. The days of 'those in the cheap seats clap your hands, the rest of you rattle your jewellery' — the love affair with The Beatles in their home media — had seemingly evaporated.

And much of the media had not greeted the launch of the dream palace, the Apple record label, with quite the warmth and delight they'd hoped. The Beatles, in the eyes of much of the popular press had gone, well, seriously *weird*.

No one could argue with the massive critical success of *Sgt. Pepper*. But my, how the four had changed in the eyes of the media, many of whom felt unable to go with them on their real-life mystery tour.

'You are either on the bus, or off the bus', was the ominous Beatle saying at Apple at the time. I knew what they meant. Be loyal or go away. Flower power, LSD, the Maharishi, Yoko Ono, nude photographs, transcendental meditation, flowers in your hair . . . It was all too much, as their own song reflected, for the media to take.

The Beatles had changed as people, almost immeasurably. And unsurprisingly, they were no longer the lucky-go-happy lads from Liverpool. They were part of the world's avant-garde artist community. They were ex-art school students. Lennon anyway. Bob Dylan was a significant catalyst. People went to his concerts, *applauded* his poetry, they didn't *scream* at him.

Paul chose the logo for Apple, inspired by a Magritte painting. I still feel unhappy for them that the world's now richest company should have successfully taken a bite out of their clean, simple and original corporate image design for its own . . .

In 1968 the soundtrack playing out of the speakers at Apple was altogether darker and carrying more ominous words . . .

If some Beatles fans had thought 'A Day in the Life' was strange and discomfiting, what were they going to make of this new stuff?

Hey, Bungalow Bill . . . what did you kill . . . The walrus was Paul . . . number nine number nine number nine . . .

I didn't know now if we at Apple were listening to advance, yet-to-be released tracks from the White Album. I think we were . . . There was much discussion, doubt even, being expressed about it being a double album, about the plain pristine white sleeve. With just their name embossed, you could run your fingers across it very satisfyingly.

It was the sound of The Beatles diverging. You could hear, in retrospect, their separate futures emerging, and it wasn't reassuring to many. The Beatles probably didn't look reassuring either. Those clean-shaven boys with the matching Cardin collarless suits had been replaced by what? Would-be mystics with long, flowing locks, straggly beards, bright nursery-coloured clothes . . . or in Lennon's case, a woman's second-hand fur coat.

What on earth was going on with them? wondered the media, who weren't quite in the loop.

The only public appearance they'd made was for the BBC round-the-world link-up TV show, where'd they'd debuted 'All You Need Is Love'.

They weren't pop stars anymore. They had been corralled by some of the most forward thinkers in the world: Timothy Leary, aristocrats, politicians and would-be revolutionaries including Tariq Ali. Everyone wanted access, especially those with an agenda they wanted The Beatles to espouse. Or adopt, or publicise.

And they didn't have the layers of protection that now almost entomb 'celebrities'. No one 'sat in' on my conversational inter-views with The Beatles or their protégés, as happens now. Though Paul McCartney, still single at the time, breezed into the middle of an interview I was conducting with Mary Hopkin, inquiring if I was still married. And suggesting that I should marry him instead. I don't think he was being entirely serious, so this should not be taken out of context.

When I am the subject of a BBC interview now, I am 'patched through' via a press officer who listens in. To keep the interview on message. Well then, we all know where we stand, it could be said.

Brian Epstein had died in August at the end of that significant summer of love. This in turn, in time, let in Allen Klein, the New York tough guy manager. Klein, once he had his metaphorical feet under the table, wanted a cleansing of almost all the Apple staff. He got it too, and used an intended-to-be compassionate feature I'd written about the press office staff as a lever to fire them. People who'd shown me nothing but warmth, friendship and trust. It was horrible.

Derek, their boss, said it was just a matter of time, that Klein wanted everyone out. But I've never forgiven myself for stupidly and unwittingly giving Klein any help. One was Carol Paddon, another was Richard DiLello. He wrote a scintillating, now classic book about the Apple days, calling it *The Longest Cocktail Party*. One day the movie will get made. The last I heard was that Liam Gallagher had taken up the option on the film rights. Go Liam . . .

Derek's job — to keep the press as well as all the freaks who turned up on Apple's doorstep at bay or on side — wasn't easy. He developed his own almost daily mantras, haikus to deal with the pressures of endless questions and requests. Sort of like: 'The Beatles are here there and everywhere, and will be something, though tomorrow never knows, thank you and goodnight.' But rather more eloquently expressed than that.

'The Beatles are dead, long live The Beatles,' John Lennon announced just to my tape recorder at around that time.

It was confusion and paranoia. It's all so obvious, to us now, listening to those dark, disturbing songs. 'Sexy Sadie', John's attack on the Maharishi, whom they had all spent so much time with in Rishikesh.

You did not necessarily want to be around The Beatles when they were calling someone out. They were battle hardened, but fair. They spoke openly, honestly, didn't give too much of a fuck what you thought. But were never anything but friendly to me. Even when under siege, harassed, which was often the case.

And they could all turn back into charm mode on a dime. John had been ranting to his then assistant, the tall lanky art expert, Anthony Fawcett. I had in my hand the brand-new John and Yoko *Wedding Album*, in its presentation box. I said to John, very, very tentatively, as it felt so unprofessional somehow to do this, 'Sorry, John, I feel terrible to ask you, but would you sign it for me?'

This was inside the entrance hall of Apple. John and Yoko were making their stately way out of the building. If I didn't ask now . . . it would probably never happen.

John stopped in his tracks.

'But of course, my dear,' he said, beaming expansively, now all smiles and honey pie. 'Don't be embarrassed. I used to do it all the time. Ask for autographs . . . outside the Liverpool Empire!'

I'm sure Mark Chapman would have found another occasion to murder John, had it not been after asking for his autograph as Lennon made his way out of the Dakota on 8 December 1980. He waited through twelve hours altogether, outside the building till Lennon returned, to shoot him dead. There was the question of whether this murder would have happened if he and Yoko had gone to a restaurant instead of going home that night when they did. 'It wouldn't have made any difference', Yoko Ono has said resignedly. Meaning that Chapman would have still been waiting there anyway . . .

In the TV conversation we had later that night, Paul Gambaccini said his brother, who lived four streets from the Dakota, told him that people locally knew of this 'weirdo'. Fanatics are doggedly persistent even if they are not with deadly intent.

You don't know, as their stalkee, of the years that have been spent studying you, watching you, fantasising over you. As almost anyone in the public eye, myself included, will have experienced.

John commented openly about how safe he felt living and walking around freely in New York City. I was due to meet him there just two days later, to interview him for the BBC TV programme *The Old Grey Whistle Test*. I had bought presents for Yoko, a brooch, and a child's gift for their five-year-old son Sean.

The trip didn't happen.

When I did meet Sean, it was twenty-five years later. He was a grown man by then, of course, a musician wanting to talk about his band. He had dropped in to an after-party in a Manhattan hotel, for a charity event hosted by Kate Moss. We were cooped up in a quite small hotel bedroom, a group of us having decamped there. The main reception area downstairs with its fairy-lit trees outside, had now been rumbled by fans and the paps.

Standing outside, waiting, in the middle of the night.

Even now myself and almost any other Beatle fan can piece together what was happening when they heard the news of John's death. In the UK it was already the next day, Tuesday 9 December. I heard through my daughter Lucy, a Beatle era child, named in part after 'Lucy in the Sky with Diamonds'. She had answered the phone to Richard Skinner, from Radio 1, who wanted to know if I had Paul McCartney's home number.

It was decided that *The Old Grey Whistle Test,* the TV show for which I had now been the anchor for two years, would broadcast a tribute to John, live, that evening on BBC2. I was as distraught as anyone and everyone else.

Perhaps it felt disrespectful to John, to the outside world, but Paul had gone to work as scheduled. At AIR Studios, then in Oxford Street, above the shops, very close to Oxford Circus. Working on what would become his next two solo albums, *Tug of War* and *Pipes Of Peace.* Keeping up with his usual routine. Having something to concentrate on. Work ethic: it runs right through his family.

Also to be in the safety cocoon of the studio, away from the clamouring press. He didn't want to be at home with reporters at his gate. One of The Chieftains was flying in from Ireland to record with him, but not a lot got done during working hours. . . At the end of the day Paul did go home, switch on the TV and watch the news.

I hosted the discussion with those we could persuade to come and face the cameras with me. It was difficult to find anyone who had been close to, or as the US would say, 'tight' with John. They were all far too upset to speak. We sat in a semi-circle: Michael Watts, an erudite journalist, Gambo, the DJ Andy Peebles, and me. That was it. Andy had been one of the last people to interview John. When he'd boarded the plane from New York, heading back to London, John had been alive. When he got off the plane, John was dead.

Our programme was transmitted from a small presentation studio at the Television Centre, as we had no live bands or musicians taking part. Mike Appleton, the producer, suddenly appeared in the studio from the gallery.

We were running a segment of VT, one of several excerpts from a lengthy *OGWT* interview John had recorded in New York, some five years beforehand. The one where he talked about missing chocolate Bath Oliver biscuits, fashionable at the time. He was inundated with packets of them from British fans after that.

'Paul's on the phone, wants to speak to you,' said Mike Appleton.

I know this sounds ridiculous, but I had no idea what Mike could be talking about. On the PHONE? In the middle of this live TV programme. What? Paul *who*?

I have pieced together some of the details that I didn't know before when writing about that night, which have come to light more recently.

After facing the media early in the morning of 9 December, Paul had had no more contact with them all day. He worked at AIR Studios and set off home to Sussex by car with Linda. He was, it is said, upset at some of the punditry, some of the commentaries that were pouring out of every radio and TV station in the world that day and that night.

Who else besides Yoko would they most want to speak to? Paul McCartney, of course. The other half of the most successful song writing team the world had ever known. Now in demand as now the most wanted for interview by every media outlet in the world. No internet then, no email, just terrestrial TV and the telephone.

Otherwise we could have Facetimed or Skyped Paul, though I very much doubt he would have agreed.

I might have looked composed. Just. I wore a black jumper, trousers, and a blue silk jacket. No jewellery. I hadn't spent much time in make up or done much with my hair, and it showed.

But I wanted to get across to the audience that this was no time for preening or TV glamour, I just wanted them to know I was feeling like they were. And was so concerned as how to express to the TV audience what this shocking, apparently pointless murder meant. With no more facts at hand as to what had happened, WHY it had happened. And then to begin to look back on his life and achievements. We even 'reviewed' *Double Fantasy*, the album he had just finished, and had now been vigorously promoting.

I said to myself before the live show: Don't be mawkish. Hold it together, be professional, don't wobble, don't falter. But at the same time, I wasn't an impassive news reader, trained to show no emotion.

Now I was to be Paul's messenger. Not that I thought of it like that then. I just happened to be on live TV at that crucial time. Could have been anyone else. So, I passed on his words, the conduit, directly through the camera. 'You know how it was,' he said to me. 'Please say thank you to everyone for their support, from George, Ringo, myself and Linda.' It was the fact that now there were three Beatles that got me. The fab four. Now minus one.

Alright they had split up a decade before, but that wasn't the point. They had changed my life, and millions more, for the better. Now neither I nor anyone else would ever have a chance to thank John Lennon for that.

I wouldn't have been the one sending this message from Paul on live TV without their influence on the whole culture.

My own first representative, Bunny Lewis, a very established, powerful if horse trader type of agent, was the then go-to man for radio DJs. But his peak influence had been during the 1950s. He hadn't really 'got' The Beatles. His opening comment to me was: 'You'll never make it as a BBC presenter.' (He also told Dusty Springfield she would never make a success of being a solo singer because she was 'too intelligent' and didn't know the right songs to sing.)

I was wearing a John Lennon style cap on my head at the time. Which probably sent signals to him. Right for me, wrong for him.

Bunny Lewis didn't really 'get' me either. I had wanted to become a DJ and/or introduce programmes to channel new and exciting music. Because I wanted to share it. Not because I'd wanted to be a hired hand, a hack on the box. Oh, call me naive, still, I know! But I liked the medium of TV and the immediacy of radio. No one could rewrite your words or stick crass headlines over what you'd written. Using the broadcast media seemed a much better way than writing about records in print.

From day one, I chose the records I wanted to play, and stuck to it ever since. It became clear pretty early on that the cool stuff got played in the evenings, not during the day. I wasn't there for the 'exposure'. Although it also became obvious early on that that was what was expected of a radio DJ. I preferred the evenings, where I wouldn't have to introduce playlist tunes I didn't like. That would have been like lying to me. Hyping a tune you didn't believe in. I also thought that it would show in my voice if I was being insincere. I'm not a bluffer.

This is how the present-day daytime DJs on music stations deal with this situation, playing a baddie: either back anno the tune, segue into the next, or just not mention it at all. Daytime DJs are much more of the entertainer, and great credit to those who do it, and hold a mass audience's attention. It's a different kettle of challenges to being a 'specialist' DJ.

*

John Lennon and the other forthright three had helped make the media understand that to our generation it wasn't any more about looking decorative, being just a dolly bird or a heartthrob boy. Or being a hypocrite, doing crooked deals; but having the opportunity to speak the truth and have the courage to be honest through the lens of the media.

John even recorded daft trails for my shows, ad-libbing around my name.

'Anne [as I was known then] Nightingale will be twittering on for the next hour . . .'

Dropping the artifice of old school, often seedy and corrupt showbiz, the convenient lies, the traditional pretences.

My first crush, as a tween, had been the film actor Rock Hudson. I didn't know he was gay; I didn't even know what gay meant. And Hollywood wanted to keep it that way.

It was announced he had married his secretary Phyllis Gates (her name is forever etched in my memory). Little did I know that this had happened to stop stories leaking of him being not entirely the heterosexual hunk . . . In his case, getting married stifled rumours reaching the media.

Of course, fibbing to say you were single, even if married, was another tactic used to promote young pop stars. That pretence, though, that's the sort of thing The Beatles helped to blow away.

This is how John Lennon put it to me in Brian Epstein's office in Mayfair.

*

We don't like lying.

Maybe because we've done a lot of semi lying over the years, that has made it important not to lie.

But you know, because you have taken it (acid) and somebody comes and asks yer if you have . . .

It was like when I was married. No one really came and asked me.

I never sort of HID it or anything,

But I did a bit . . . till anyone ASKED me. Well, ARE you?

And I said:

Yes.

It was just the same . . . somebody asked me,

'Have you taken acid?'

YES.

Because if you say 'no' you're a liar, and it's not nice.

(At which point I asked him: Are you put in a position where you've almost got to, where you can't actually do the right thing?)

He answered, referring to Paul's recent public admission of having taken LSD:

To do personally what's right is not always what's publicly right.

But you just gotta do it.

No messing.

Because otherwise you're not nice to live with. It's lousy. We all sort of got a shock when it happened.

I turned up at Paul's the day it happened, the day it came out, but I didn't know.

He was exhilarated, because it was a load off his chest.

Like having your first drink . . . in the family circle. It was a relief that we weren't doing it in secret anymore, you know . . .

WHAY HAY!

His life was the ultimate price paid for Beatledom. George Harrison was nearly killed by a fanatic too, the intruder inside his own home, Friar Park in Henley Upon Thames, the night before

Millennium Eve 1999.

Pete Townshend told me soon after that George's injuries had been far worse, far more serious than had been made public initially. That horrific event must have sapped George's strength to fight off the cancer he had already been diagnosed with two years previously. He succumbed to it just two years later.

To have two out of four Beatles, the founding member John, and George, the youngest. determinedly sought out and attacked by fanatics, one immediately fatally, still appals. To an unimaginable degree for their enduring families.

But was it their such extraordinarily powerful imagery, however positively intended, that drew to The Beatles those with such extreme mental health problems?

I can only figure out that was the case.

At 3 Savile Row the name of the game was for The Beatles to prove that they could create success for artistes other than themselves, via Apple.

The first break out hit was with a talent show contestant from Wales, Mary Hopkin. With an old Russian folk song which had been an earworm for Paul since he'd heard two folkies perform it in a club. 'Those Were the Days' became its new title.

Paul tried to persuade Mary how easy it would be for her to write her own hit songs. Somewhere in London and I just cannot remember where, I watched as Paul said to Mary, 'Look, it's easy.' He flipped open the lid of a grand piano which was conveniently poised on a dais nearby. With his left hand he rumbled out some Jerry Lee Lewis-style boogie chords, and sang:

'Ahhh, the big black piano is sitting in front of meeeee.'

I can hum the tune to this day.

'You see?' he said, turning to us. 'How easy it is to write a song?'

Mary and I, the only people present except Linda, who was

snapping away from the back of the room at the pair of them, looked sceptical.

Then I realised that Paul McCartney probably didn't know or realise that not everyone had his facility to compose instant hit pop songs.

He probably thought that anyone could, if they put their mind to it.

At the height of Beatlemania, The Beatles were producing two albums' worth of songs a year. Not including singles. It was their policy not to duplicate releases of singles on albums, as they believed that short-changed the fans. It was a phenomenal output, and the singles maintained that gut-punch excitement all through their career.

A single bass note, then *feedback* FFS, to open a record! Still does it for me.

That note, that feedback, that tune I FEEL FINE and yes, suddenly it was Christmas 1964 and I did feel fine and still feel the thrill of just BEING ALIVE in the time of The Beatles.

That summer they'd brought a frisson of excitement, warm wind blowing in through open windows, as I blasted out over and over the finger-tingling start. The blistering mystery chord on the twelve-string Rickenbacker from George. Paul with the bass note, John's rhythm and George Martin's added piano,

BWANG . . ..
It's been a Hard Day's Night chookachookachooka.
And I've been working like a dog chookachookachooka

The speed, the energy, the attack, were enough to lift you right off your feet.

Only four years before, and now The Beatles were if not starting again, certainly scaling a different spikier summited mountain. It was all a bit, 'yesterday all my troubles seemed so far away, now it looks as though they're here to stay' troubles . . . in Paris, in the US over Vietnam, in Grosvenor Square, London and around the corner, and for them in their own new basement studio inside 3 Savile Row.

Building your own modern efficient recording studio had proved a little more difficult than the fab four had anticipated. And they weren't used to having a non-Beatle sitting in with them — John's new friend, Billy Preston. The multi-talented American keyboard player was the only musician, a special guest that day, who lifted the atmosphere from a tense gloom, when I visited.

The argument over who split The Beatles up has raged almost continuously for nearly five decades. Was it Yoko, or was it Allen Klein and the business interest clashes? Paul, still in 2018 prepared to meet the (selected) media to promote a new album, said it was business.

Yoko has taken the flak for breaking up The Beatles ever since 1970. Those elements and a lot more besides, were the reasons why.

George told me in an interview for Radio 1, around seven years after the split, that he found playing in the same four-man group had become restrictive. The Beatles had been together, literally, man and boy in his case, since he had been fifteen years old. He'd managed to bring in Eric Clapton to play on 'While My Guitar Gently Weeps'. Eric had been reluctant. As he'd remarked 'no one else but The Beatles play on their records'. Well certainly not lead guitar!

And then as if that hadn't been enough of an indication . . . Harrison joined the Traveling Wilburys. A total dream supergroup with Bob Dylan, Tom Petty, Jeff Lynne and Roy Orbison. A perfect line-up for George, though they never toured. The very name sounded like a dry, wry George joke.

And he'd said while giving evidence during the trial of his

attacker at Friar Park, 'He wasn't a burglar, and he certainly wasn't auditioning for the Traveling Wilburys.'

*

After John left the UK to live in New York, the remaining ex-Beatles were not averse to playing at the odd wedding. Well. Two. Ringo's, and Eric Clapton's to Pattie Boyd, George's ex. Also playing with Paul, George and Ringo at the bash at Eric's were Mick Jagger, Bill Wyman, Elton John and David Bowie. I was invited. No Uber then, no internet, no mobile phones. On the day . . .

My car broke down.

I didn't get there.

I know.

— 4 —

Marc Bolan

Marc Bolan, at his home in west London, Bayswater area, 1973. Buses can be heard going by outside the window. Interior. Day. Afternoon.

MARC: (*into mic, obligingly*) One, two, three, four . . . one, two, three, four.

ANNIE: You've got a quiet voice (*adjusting mic control*).

MARC: Mmmm. I don't wear a Cross Your Heart bra. (*He was mockingly referring to a high-profile TV commercial for which I'd recorded the voice-over.*)

ANNIE: Well, the whole campaign didn't work, then. It was aimed at you — today's person.

MARC: Me, the youth market! So . . . what do you want, my dear?

ANNIE: I don't really . . . throw questions. Are you doing a day of interviews? Because if so, at the end of the day, the poor person ends up repeating themselves. (*Yes, I was that patronising!*)

MARC: I did the first interviews for the last nine months last week, for the music papers.

ANNIE: If I'd been you I would have been sickened, watching the dreaded *Top of the Pops*.

MARC: I've been away, don't forget, I haven't seen it for four months . . .

ANNIE: (*plunging on, regardless, bee-in-bonnet*) Well even if you've been away you must have been aware, of the vulgarising, and the cheapening of it. (*I was referring to the glam rock wannabes on Britain's then top pop TV show.*) Didn't you feel . . . disappointed?

MARC: No. Why? Why should I? They make me look quite good (*chirpily ironic*), quite tasteful!

ANNIE: Who did?

MARC: All those . . . monkeys. Made me feel, in a way, like Elvis when he had all those millions of copyists. I don't include David (*lowering voice respectfully*) . . . David Bowie in that circumstance, or anyone like that – musicians. It [glam rock] did what it was supposed to do, for 'the business'. It brought back some kind of movement. As opposed to the James Taylor kind of thing.

ANNIE: (*drily*) People applaud James Taylor tuning up.

MARC: Do you not think people have always tended do that, with someone that is their fave? The man they may feel . . . knows where *they're* at, and *they* know where *he's* at, and they're *all* at, you know what I mean?

ANNIE: Anyone now called a singer-songwriter – doomy!

MARC: And folk. I used to be 'folk'.

ANNIE: I heard some Tyrannosaurus Rex being played a couple of weeks ago. (*The change of name of Marc's band from Tyrannosaurus Rex to T. Rex was ostensibly so that radio DJs would be able to pronounce it correctly, but also benchmarked Bolan's change from the 'Bopping Elf' to full-blown pop star and sex symbol.)*

MARC: I find them really easy to listen to now. I didn't two years ago. I sounded so . . . (*searching for the right word*) . . . little.

ANNIE: You what?

MARC: So little . . . so young — and my voice! The range of my voice! A little, *tinny* voice.

ANNIE: How long ago was the first T. Rex hit?

MARC: Three years.

ANNIE: Every time I see you, you look different. You seem relaxed now, maybe it's because you're tired.

MARC: I decided that if I was going to talk to people at all, I just . . . want to make it . . . pleasant. A year and a half ago I was doing a lot of it [interviews] and it really got on my nerves. Couldn't cope with it.

Always the same questions. I find it funny now when people say: 'Marc, do you think you're gonna last?' Because it's three years later and I'm still here. Then it was: Slade or T. Rex? If someone said that to me now, I'd laugh. I can't believe people . . . *still* with stars under their eyes. And a bloke with a lump of glitter stuck on the side of his face! (*The doorbell rings and Marc moves across the room to the front door, and says, over his shoulder:*) Chicory Tip, you know — next thing.

ANNIE: Oh, I hope not.

MARC: (*opening the door*) And there he is . . . Mr Chicory.
 (*Chris Williams, then Marc's publicist, enters the room.*)

MARC: (*turning back to me*) How do you think . . . it's not an ego thing (*yes it was, Marc*), but . . . how *do* I seem different to the last time?

ANNIE: More relaxed and wound down. (*There is a suspicious amount of clinking glass sounds on the tape. Marc was plying us both with booze.*) You're getting old, that's what it is!

MARC: (*twenty-five years old, sighs*) I wish it **was** that. Yesterday we rehearsed all day, that's why I feel relaxed. Four days ago I was fucked up. I was bored. I can't really go out that much. So I sat here for about five days. Sat and watched telly in bed. Wouldn't answer the phone. (*He brightens up.*) But I'm reading . . . a lot of Jack Kerouac. I've bought all his books. He was my first influence. The book [*On the Road*] didn't happen for him till '57. It took eight years to get published, and when it was . . . he hated it all. That bebop thing was dead. 'Wow, man' and 'blow, baby' and all that stuff — 'rock it, cat!' (*To the publicist:*) Chris, have a drink!

ANNIE: Who was your contemporary writer hero, or didn't you have one?

MARC: What I read most of all when I was a kid was Greek myth — Robert Graves, and Kerouac. Then it was William Blake, Ginsberg. I read 'Howl' the other day. There are some fantastic images there. Very valuable. It's like good David Bowie work, or good Marc Bolan work.

I was talking to Lulu the other day and she said she wanted a hit record. It seems so easy when you are really involved with music. But if you're not on that level . . . then you don't get that vein of gold, that golden ladder.

Smokey Robinson said: 'Look man, I make two-minute records,' and that's all I'm doing. I want to sell to the kids, and I don't really care if people think I'm a good poet or not. I'm making tunes, and the ones that are bad are never hits.

I write twenty-five songs and select the one I think is the strongest. I've always been incredibly prolific.

I've written four songs this week.

I wrote three yesterday.

I just get in the mood.

I've always got lots of ideas but I'm not always near a guitar or a tape recorder. I would write a song now, but it's a question of am I or not interested in sitting on my own, that or this day. Or the phone rings, I forget it immediately.

ANNIE: Can you remember it afterwards?

MARC: No.

ANNIE: Arrh. Is that awful?

MARC: Plenty more where that came from. It's confidence. Paul Simon says there was a year when he didn't write. There's the fear of drying up. The point is: you've got to have something to say. You learn the chords. I've been writing for nine years so I should know my trade now.

I can play you any chord that sounds like (*FX brrrriiing – phone rings*).

ANNIE: I was thinking more of lyrics.

MARC: Lyrics the same. It's very easy. I don't use very ordinary subjects, like girl and boy subjects. I find it very hard to write moon and June songs, cos how many times can you write about the chick you love? And try and make it sound different every time?

ANNIE: (*there was a big Cole Porter revival going on at the time*) 'You're the Top'. Was that the greatest song ever written?

MARC: That's Porter, isn't it? There's a great book of his lyrics.

ANNIE: You've got *the* book? (*A huge art deco coffee table book with a silver sleeve had just been published. I really coveted a copy.*) I'd like that for my birthday, please. (*How emboldened! I must have been drunk by now.*)

MARC: When's your birthday?

ANNIE: April the first.

MARC: Appropriate day! OK. (*He did send it to me for my birthday, too. How could he not?*) Did you know he was crippled? A horse fell on him . . .

ANNIE: The moment of conception of a song, how does that happen?

MARC: I don't think there is one. I tend to need to do something exciting. It's always melody first with songs. You can always knock out lyrics. You can come back to lyrics. Any time.

Take any Beatles song. The lyrics are not very important, it's the melody. All I do, I try to get one nice image and just repeat it a couple of times and then put in what they call 'a hook'. I try to think of something nice that is out of the ordinary. ('*Solid Gold Easy Action*' *comes to mind.*)

My place is to do . . . what Hendrix, people like that, did. Whether people think it's progressive music, I never believe in that as a term, just *better* rock 'n' roll.

The only totally commercial record I've put out is 'Hot Love'. And it goes on for five minutes with the la la bit at the end. A joke, really, at the end. They said: 'You'll never get away with it − *five minutes*,' and it sold ten million. But I was so aware that it had to be *the* hit, and it's the least interesting song, to me.

ANNIE: Will you sit down and start working before you get the melody?

MARC: I've found it hard sometimes to write up-tempo songs, and then everything I write will be twelve-bar blues for about two weeks. And then everything I write is (*sic*) love songs. Then they're all space-age poetry. Then they're all singles, and then I write all album stuff, not right for teenage consumption.

A lot of it is very rude. Not rude to me, but like, bold. Tits and bums and stuff. A single can turn on a kiss and give you an energy buzz. There's nothing like driving along in a car in the sun and hearing a record you really dig. With no other pretensions other than that it's a great little boogie.

They're important, but they should be forgotten and a new one take their place. 'Rubber Bullets', that's a nice record, but in four weeks' time I won't remember what it was or who it was by. (*10cc – it became their first number 1, in June 1973.*) I'm lucky in one way, a bit like Elvis. They're Bolan records and they mean more, as opposed to '. . . that song'. I'm very lucky like that.

ANNIE: You don't feel trapped by that?

MARC: No, I can buy things I want, go where I want – go to Barbados this minute if I want. And I don't really feel I have to talk to you, unless it's nice. I don't feel I have to do concerts if I don't want to – the only thing is walking about, and I never walked about much – I've got plenty of cars I can go out in.

ANNIE: I didn't actually mean trapped like *that*. I meant trapped *musically*.

MARC: Oh. No. I don't have to pander to anyone, only myself, I don't sit there and think: has this got a catchy feel? I don't think you can.

ANNIE: Or if the way you write suddenly changed and became more . . . serious?

MARC: Well then, I would have to. I know that. You know that. I'm not a Donny Osmond. I'm a musician, even though through the experience I've become a teeny bop idol and I enjoy that.

ANNIE: Still?

MARC: Oh yeah. I think everyone does. I've never met anyone who doesn't. That's why everyone goes back on the road eventually. You might not want to be screamed at, but you certainly want the roar of the applause.

We're all ego maniacs, that's the truth of it, and we're all very nice, really.

We're basically for the chicks.

Marc died in a car crash on 16 September 1977 in Barnes, southwest London, two weeks before what would have been his thirtieth birthday. His anniversary is celebrated every year by a Marc Bolan fan club. Tribute band T. Rextasy play all the Bolan hits, and everyone is clad in top hats and feather boas. I became involved in one of these events in Germany in the mid-nineties, persuaded by a guy I was seeing — himself a huge Bolan fan. He introduced me to Marc's most fervent followers. Once they knew I'd actually met and known Marc I was given special status. This reverence by association made me feel really uncomfortable. Chief fan the Silver Surfer (a character from the T. Rex song 'Teenage Dream') asked me the question fans always ask: 'What was Marc really like?'

I replied, inadequately: 'He was great. He used to click his tongue and say "Chk! —dynamite!" a lot.' Trying to add a little nugget of Marcdom.

The following year there was a similar party in London. The Silver Surfer turned up again, in full effect . . . And asked me again: 'What was Marc really like?'

What could I say? Same as last year, and sadly, still dead.

How chuffed Bolan would be to know that his songs are now never-to-become-dated, solid-gold classics. Kate Moss asked me to DJ at one of her themed birthday bashes, this one tagged glam rock. Kate (in a star-scattered shimmery Chanel jumpsuit) and her friends threw themselves into the spirit of the night. Well, you had to. No dressing up, no entry. Sequins and feathers flew every-where, and the tiny dance floor in Soho was a ballroom blitz. A make-up artist was on hand to paint glitter shapes and stars on all our faces − no one had seen so many spangles since the seventies. I had sparkly tears in my eyes bopping to 'Children of the Revolution'.

I, a fan too, miss Marc to this day. I also almost had tears in my eyes when I realised, after about two hours, that us team of DJs was seriously running out of genuine glam rock dance-floor friendly hits at this party. The legacy and the look have carried on, but glam rock was a short-lived craze. Marc Bolan, David Bowie and Roxy Music came out of it with the greatest glory, as well as The Glitter Band and The Sweet. For me. Matter of opinion. But Bolan was the unwitting originator, who began his career with an album entitled *My People Were Fair and Had Sky in Their Hair . . . But Now They're Content to Wear Stars on Their Brows.*

— 5 —

Song Contest, Anyone?

Put on your own song festival? Well, why not? A competition to see who can write and arrange the best song, words and music, with a star to sing it, a clutch of musical experts to judge?

Eurovision had been going since 1956, really an exercise in overseas outside-broadcasting skill and panache, among the EBU (European Broadcast Union) countries. Their theme or signature tune has always sounded like some creaky Ruritanian national anthem. Fill of pomp and self-importance, and very, very dated. But kinda cutesy quaint at the same time.

The idea had begun inspired in Italy, 'land of song', especially popular in the 1950s with 'Volare', and Americanised versions such as 'Ciao, ciao bambina'. Italy still has a pop chart with more indigenous hits than any other European country.

It all began with a song festival in Sorrento. And another, further north in San Remo, a seaside town on the Riviera near to the French border, where their song festival continues to this day.

I'd been sent to San Remo in my early days as a TV presenter, the year that Dusty Springfield took part (see later chapter). I met and was photographed with almost all the international stars taking part, from Gene Pitney to Petula Clark and Timi Yuro. The event was really for the benefit of songwriters and music publishers, to sell their wares, as much as for the stars who sang the songs.

So . . . thought Associated-Rediffusion, the TV company that had created *Ready Steady Go!* . . . let's do our own version, a British song festival, right here in the UK, on ITV (as the BBC has the rights to broadcast the Eurovision version).

And it was decided that the British Song Festival would be held in my adopted hometown of Brighton.

It was, it's safe to say, an unmitigated disaster.

Rules of entry got, er, bent, so that one song had already been performed in public. The event had been organised by middle-aged music publishers, hoping to have winning hits with old-fashioned ballads. But the teenage audience were more into screaming for the then pop heartthrobs such as Billy J. Kramer (of the Dakotas) and Paul Jones of Manfred Mann.

I was a co-host but was always unclear what my role was to be. Actually no one had any idea what anyone else was supposed to be doing. It was live and had never been attempted before.

I shared a dressing room with Marianne Faithfull, though hardly saw her there at all. She was newly pregnant and being hotly pursued by the intrepid *Daily Express* showbiz reporter Judith Simons, known to all as Fag Ash Lil on account of her equally intrepid chain-smoking habit. There was a drama a day, with tantrums, storm-outs and disqualifications.

I had to make a 'promo film' trailer for the event to camera, poised aboard Volk's Electric Railway, clattering along on the beach front in a bright-yellow painted miniature train that ran — still does — a mile from Black Rock to the Aquarium and Palace Pier. I had to deliver my lines between stops, no retakes possible, and could not screw up.

I did photo shoots on the beach in a navy bikini, and more in front of the Royal Pavilion. I'd been lent a very glam sugar-pink evening gown with sequin top to wear for the final. I had my picture taken with Lulu, one of the participants. Lulu's song was announced the winner. Then was . . . unannounced. There had been a mix-up. Sorry folks. Sorry Lulu, there's been a mistake. You are not the winner. The proper winner was adjudged to be a song sung by Kenny Lynch. All this confusion unfolding on live TV.

The world's press was there. *Variety*, the US showbiz bible, attended, and delivered its career-killing line about my televisual delivery, 'The girl's a looker but not a sayer.' You never ever forget reviews like that. I rather hoped they were reviewing the dress, not me. But I'm sure my part in it all was abysmal. The British Song Festival was a write-off.

It never happened again.

Except . . . it sort of did. Nine years later, in the early seventies, the actual, actual real Eurovision Song Contest came to Brighton, to the same venue. I was not taking part and very relieved not to be. But I was busily involved, meeting the publishers, mingling with the managers. Hearing the songs, interviewing the singers. Who came from myriad counties, with myriad customs and taste and appearances. Eurovision had had to break its rule that the winning county must host the following year's contest. Luxembourg had won two years in a row. Said they didn't have the cash to put on the event yet again.

It was all nearly as bizarre then as it is now. As the UK representative chanteuse, we had Olivia Newton-John, who had lived most of her life in Australia. Israel, geographically challenged as a country actually *in* Europe, situated as it is in the near Middle East, took part. (But then Australia, the other side of the planet from Europe, is now included. Go figure, it's all part of Eurovision's delightful eccentricity.)

Even so, it was bewildering to behold the Yugoslav entry called 'Moja Generacija', a Serbo-Croatian creation and composition. No, *not* a cover version of the Who's 'My Generation'. I met, interviewed and misunderstood the author. Also another entrant, an unknown singing group. They wore knickerbockers and weird little hats.

I mostly likely thought that the UK had it in the bag, with our international superstar rep Olivia Neutron-Bomb.

I told the rather out-of-touch-looking knickerbocker group, in as loftily kindly a way as possible, not to get their hopes up. They didn't stand a chance.

The UK host nation jury concurred. Awarded them NUL points.

They represented Sweden.

They won.

They've sold, since, 385 million records.

They were . . .

ABBA.

— 6 —

On the Road

There had been the disc jockey before the first wave of us at Radio 1. But in many people's minds, I think this figure had been seen as semi-anonymous, shut away in a booth in the corner of a *discotheque*. Someone to put one record on after another. Someone hired to keep the punters on the dance floor.

Yeah, they might dress up in funny clothes, have a light-up revolving bow tie . . . that sort of caper. They might even have their own travelling set-up, the mobile DJ with own van and twin turntables. Someone who might play at your wedding reception. A step up from the conjuror or magician at a posh children's birthday party.

But nothing cool, nothing fancy and nothing *starry*. Not a showbiz money-making attraction.

But now . . . ah, the Radio 1 DJ . . . this was something else. Cash could be raised, the entrepreneurs realised, from the DJs making personal appearances. These new guys, with huge followings on air, could be money-spinners. And soon, as the one female in the gang, shouldn't I be drawn into this, too? So I was, but very, very apprehensively.

What exactly should we *do*, at our personal appearances? Were we performers? I didn't sing or dance or play an instrument.

But we had to be, somehow, entertainers . . .

Some of my colleagues modelled themselves on, or had been or were inspired by, redcoats. These were the uniformed staff at holiday camps, who indeed entertained their captive audiences.

So you had to be, I presumed, hale and hearty, cheery, ultra-friendly; you had to host competitions, keep talking, give stuff away, sign autographs, and make like you were a star. It was the acknowledged breeding ground for comics, but I wasn't that either.

All I could do was play records in front of people. And not well or confidently either. While the audience shouted at you, repeatedly, not that you could hear because of wearing headphones, but it turned out to be, in most cases:

'I SAID . . . COULD YOU PLAY . . . SOMETHING *DECENT?*'

Or:

'OI! . . . THIS IS ABSOLUTE *CRAP*. HAVEN'T YOU GOT ANYTHING THAT'S *IN THE CHARTS?*'

And:

'CAN YOU PLAY A RECORD WE CAN *DANCE TO?*'

Comments and uninvited requests made to DJs while they are playing have grown into their own culture over the years. Even when DJs first became cool superheroes like the house music giants of the US or the late and so much missed 'The Guvnor' Andrew Weatherall in the UK, they all have stories to tell. About what's being shouted in their ear while they are trying to effect a tricky mix.

One of Weatherall's most well remembered: *'CAN YOU PUT MY COAT UNDER YOUR DECKS?'*

And another, experienced by him when a member of his audience, after having studied him all evening, observed into Andrew's ear: *'YOU'RE FATTER IN REAL LIFE, AREN'T YOU?'*

Interesting that, forty-five years on, the modern equivalent of the mobile DJ has evolved into the highest-paid showbiz attraction on the planet. Calvin Harris, David Guetta and a few others have earned, it is estimated, in the region of *forty-five million US dollars. A year . . . each.*

Nothing, but nothing, like that was coming my way. My venues were Young Farmers' boozy get-togethers, or questionable clubs in Birmingham with shiny tiled walls and very little soul. And not always a guarantee of getting paid at the end of the night.

I just didn't really . . . *get it*, understand somehow. See how to cash in or monetise the potential of the personal appearance. I think I had severe imposter syndrome. Scared of being found out. That I didn't have a fucking clue.

Radio 1 also saw personal appearances by its DJs as a way of promoting the station. Commercial radio had now started up, in direct competition to Radio 1. So, the BBC had to up its game. Protect and project itself, through its newly created in-house stars.

Outside events were to be jacked up, broadcast live around the country. A chance to meet the fans, build the presence. The BBC engineers and 'OBs' chaps loved any challenge like that. Any event Radio 1 put on would be outdoors so anyone and everyone who wanted to show up, could.

These events would be massively bigged up on air beforehand. A sprinkling of current pop star names would fill the bill along with the top-name DJs. It was a bit like having a cabinet of politicians descending on a key marginal swing seat before a general election . . . What could possibly . . .

The Radio 1 Roadshow became a summer touring fixture, visiting holiday resorts all over the UK. Starring the jocks with daytime shows. A definite split was appearing. We called it third-floor and fourth-floor mentality. The evening and weekend DJs and their/ our producers resided on the third floor of a sixties building called Egton House. Situated to the right of the stately ocean liner-like building that was and is Broadcasting House where the proper Establishment broadcasters held office. (Now that part is called officially Old Broadcasting House. The new part, which looks like a giant bright blue 'U' is called NBH.)

In this evolving hierarchical system, the grand old BBC looked down generally on the vulgar upstart Radio 1, but secretly envied the brash new pop success for its huge listening figures.

Within Radio 1's own ecosystem, the fourth floor at Egton House was home to the producers and DJs who were considered more important. The third-floor lot, such as me, less so. Somewhat like that classic Two Ronnies and John Cleese sketch depicting the British class system. 'He looks up to me because I am upper class . . . he looks down on me because I am working class' kind of thing.

We thought that some of the occupants on the storey above us lot were getting a bit up themselves. 'Fourth floor' we would mutter under our breaths to each other, with a barely perceptible raised eyebrow. It became a bit pejorative, though we all smiled sweetly at each other. Office politics happens in all major organisations, I'm sure.

The road events were mainly fourth-floor projects.

It should be understood, then, that the blokes at Radio 1 were somewhat infatuated with their . . . *cars*. Cars were the most outward status symbol which the successful DJ could show himself off with. Perhaps motors, two or four wheeled, were part of the wider popular culture at the time. The success of Steve McQueen films such as *Bullitt* and *The Great Escape*. It continues with rappers and their fascination with Lamborghinis and other 'whips'.

When I arrived to do gigs I was often asked, and judged by, not what kind of music I was going to play, but what kind of car I drove. Much later on I'd have a tour manager/driver and would dream of driving 400 miles on my own, hopping out of the car, doing a club gig and driving back again. But I did. It was absolute insanity.

I'd be barrelling down the M1 southbound at 4 a.m., hallucinating. The shadows from the lit road signs on the opposite motorway lanes threw giant black shapes across the lane I was driving on. I was so tired and stressed I thought they were solid iron bars deliberately strewn in my way, that I would have to make my car somehow jump right over. Pink Floyd's spooky, rhythmic 'One of These Days' blaring out of the car stereo just heightened this sense of fear and apprehension. That repetitive *dum de dum, dum de dum, dum de dum WHARRRR* was really the wrong thing to be playing.

In subsequent years, watching Steven Spielberg's dialogue-less *Duel* wasn't a good idea either. It's about a lone driver being pursued by another, a stranger, trying to kill him.

Now when driving alone on a motorway late at night, I was convinced if a truck followed me off the road to a service rest area, that the truck driver was going to leap out of his cab, hit me over the head and kill me with a giant spanner. For overtaking him, then staying in front of him in his lane, driving too slowly on an incline or some other unspeakable driving misdemeanour.

There seemed to be so many things — about broadcasting, DJ'ing, driving, life — to learn. And having to find out by yourself, because no one ever told you anything.

And I never drove anything to swank about. One of my less wise second-hand purchases was some British model, with dull, mustard-coloured 'coach work' — referred to by a serious male petrolhead friend as 'the heap of sand'. Even members of my own family would say 'can you drop me off round the corner' rather than be seen in this shabby-looking product of that ultimate failure of car manufacture, British Leyland.

Despite the obvious allure of foreign makes from Italy, France and Germany, my dad, a dedicated car owner/driver from boyhood, would always insist: 'Oh you must buy *British.*'

Radio 1 began getting involved not so much with music events as with *motor racing*. And motorcycle racing. Yes, these sports were popular, but then so was football. Maybe Old Trafford was too big, or too disinterested to hold a Radio 1 event, though I did take part in a Radio 1 show at Wembley Stadium with Elton John.

I became involved with the motor racing events.

How could I not be?

Couldn't let the side down.

I found myself wearing a safety harness and careering round Brands Hatch motor racing circuit, with an instructor urging me, 'Keep your foot *off* the brake,' as we were approaching one of the track's famous sharp bends at speed. While all my internal survival instincts were screaming at me: 'SLOW DOWN!'

On the open road in my own modest vehicle I would try to practise 'clipping the bends' on a twisty, snaky section of the A23.

I'd wanted to be a DJ, not a racing driver. I became even more involved with motor sport through a documentary TV series for BBC, themed around the build-up to major sporting events. Filming in the pits at Silverstone during the British Grand Prix, for instance, and including motorcycle racing at Thruxton. Even more hair-raising moments, perching on, clinging for dear life onto the back of a world champ's bike, doing 'the ton', 100 miles an hour.

That was one thing, being a passenger. But now we were required to participate. To get behind the wheel and race, ourselves.

7

Bob Marley

It was the second year in a row of sweltering hot summers in England. In a desperate attempt to keep cool, I would go for a dip in Brighton in the early morning, dunk my cheesecloth top and denim jeans in the sea, slide them on, still wet and salty, jump in my car and drive to London. To keep from overheating on the journey.

Ridiculous idea. It didn't work, and there was no cooling air con flowing through my blue Ford Cortina. But I regarded this action of going to work in wet clothes as a rather punk thing to do, even though I wasn't wearing black bin liners, which would have been more authentic but even less practical.

The huge clash of cultures was about to erupt. Half the country was planning street parties for the Queen's Silver Jubilee, dressing up in Union Jacks, red, white and blue plastic boaters perched on their heads, and stringing up, across the pavements, bunting that hadn't been out of the attic since VE Day in 1945.

The other half of the country was simmeringly resentful, about almost everything. Lack of jobs, strikes, the government. And the Pistols had up their sleeves the highly successful piracy of the Jubilee celebrations with their Thames riverboat outrage — plenty to get riled about if you were a member of the Establishment.

Nineteen seventy-seven was the year Gary Gilmore, the spree murderer from Waco, Texas, was executed by firing squad in the USA. He chose that over being hanged. Gilmore donated his corneas and other organs to the living. This gave rise to one of my favourite ever punk anthems '(Looking Through) Gary Gilmore's Eyes' by the Adverts, the song being about life seen though the dead murderer's eyes.

That song and the pungent *um–cha*, *um-cha* rhythm of reggae were taking over British popular music, and not before time. It was also the year Elvis died.

Even the punks who were dominating the music scene couldn't not love reggae. It unified the unwaged, the unloved and the unwanted. And the spliff-heads. I had been playing reggae since my first days at Radio 1 in the early seventies.

Having bowed under pressure to take on a female DJ, I think the all-bloke powers at Radio didn't really know how to 'schedule' me, or where to place me. An early controller had said to me: 'We don't really regard you as a real disc jockey, we only took you on because you're a journalist.'

Strange reasoning, and a back-handed compliment if ever I heard one. But hey, they had not yet fired me during the first of the Nights of the Long Knives, the culling that was to happen not infrequently at Radio 1 ever since. No one ever wanted to leave the station voluntarily, then.

Daytime presenters had to play tunes as designated by Doreen Davies, the 'godmother' head of the playlist committee at Radio 1. Daytime DJs weren't trusted to play what they liked, and anyway, they might all play the same stuff if left to their own devices.

But as I wasn't a 'real' disc jockey they let me review new records. There was another devious reason for this. It was a dodge round the 'needle time' restrictions. Radio 1 was only allowed to play a certain number of records per day. This was to preserve the sanctity of musicians and 'live' music, so the people who played on the original records now had to go to BBC studios and try to reproduce and replicate as faithfully as possible the sound on the record.

Which is probably why The Beatles and many others failed their first recording tests with the BBC. Ludicrously time-consuming, and it seems insane now, but that was the rule. I do not include the John Peel sessions which proliferated later.

But everyone knew Bob Marley and the Wailers. 'Stir It Up', a cover version hit by Johnny Nash, and the much more main-stream appeal of 'No Woman, No Cry' — irresistible, and Bob's first hit outside Jamaica.

Eric Clapton had further raised Bob's profile by having a number 1 hit with his rock-reggae cover version of 'I Shot the Sheriff'. And Marley was now signed to Island Records, with pluggers and publicists to elevate him to superstar status.

For Chris Blackwell, Island Records' owner (the blueprint for Richard Branson), Bob Marley was the real shit, the real deal. Blackwell had been importing Jamaican records to the UK for many years before reggae took off. And here was a Jamaican singer who could cross over to the massive mainstream market and sell millions. And who could write hit songs. And was good looking and cool.

But there was rather a lot more to Bob Marley. He was called 'the Natural Mystic', a kind of prophet himself. His Euro facial features were as a result of his mixed-race background. His mother, a Jamaican named Cedella Booker, was just eighteen years old when he was born.

I reviewed away, playing what I wanted of an afternoon, and much of it was music from Jamaica on the Trojan label. Mint copies of these 7-inch vinyl singles I played then are now worth fortunes, comparatively. I was also writing a music column for the *Daily Express*. In fact, I got signed up the very day after the Sex Pistols' infamous TV clash with their own columnist Bill Grundy. It was a pretty right-wing leaning paper even then. So I got perverse pleasure in writing about obscure musicians, whose mostly revolutionary, subversive, anarchic sentiments would never have got past the subs, had they'd known.

Bob's father was fifty-year-old Captain Norval Marley, a white quartermaster with the British West Indian Regiment. Bob rarely saw his father as a child. He was housed hither and thither within Jamaica. Quiet, studious, and feeling a misfit because he considered himself neither black enough nor white enough to be accepted.

Meanwhile Rastafarianism was growing in Jamaica, as a result of Ras Tafari Makonnen who changed his name to Haile Selassie on being made Emperor of Ethiopia in 1930. For the former slaves in the West Indies, Haile Selassie became a messianic figure, believed to be a new black king and figure of deliverance.

Bob Nesta Marley became a follower.

He embraced Rastafarianism, and he'd recently been shot at during a highly politically charged peace rally in Jamaica. I was invited to interview him in June 1977. This was the release time and date of what was to become one of Bob and the Wailers' most excellent and classic works: the album *Exodus*, named 'Album of the Century' by *Time* magazine.

This has proved the most difficult of all my original cassette tapes to conjure back to life. Being a journalist does really involve sometimes being a bit of a chameleon, but there was no mistaking that here was I, the middle-class suburbanite from Twickenham, trying to connect with Bob from Trench Town.

Everyone in east London might now affect a bit of a Jamaican twang and use the word 'skanky' at every opportunity when hanging out in Shoreditch, but Bob had the deepest patois I had ever encountered. I was too embarrassed to admit that I found him hard to understand. Like I am with certain Glaswegians and Geordies, for example. It's not their problem, it's mine. A lot of people, and many Americans, don't understand my accent. So that, and the bad quality of the microphone, probably built into whatever rubbish cheap tape recorder I had at the time, and the VERY LOUD MUSIC being played in another part of the room, have not helped when bringing back Bob Marley's precious words.

I have tried every combination of headphones: Sennheiser, Technics, iPod; digitised the tape, played it back through my mixer with all the treble up, the bass down, and the bass filter onto max. But it's still a nightmare of *crrssshhhkkkkkrreeeeeeaccw*, hiss, crackle and *screrrggh*.

I thought I'd start at the beginning. Innocently.

If this was a film script, I'd start it this way.

West London, 1977. Interior. Day. A downstairs room opening onto a patio area in a spacious house, rented by Bob Marley. Various young ladies ebb and flow into the outside area where I've pitched my tape recorder.

Bob is tapping at a football. With his toe. The one he had injured several times and that would lead to complications.

ANNIE: (*a bit nervously, gushing at him*) Sorry about the tape recorder — but I can't do shorthand! And anyway, if you ever want to complain you've been misquoted, there's always the tape, ha.

Ha.

Anyway, let's ramble on and forget about it. I didn't know you were so into football. Would you go and play for (*racking my brain for a credible team name*) . . . Chelsea, for instance, if you could?

BOB: (*laughs*) I wouldn't say I wouldn't do it.

ANNIE: So, have you always been keen on sport?

BOB: I like cricket as well.

ANNIE: What do you like best? Batting?

BOB: Bowling. I like bowling.

ANNIE: I don't imagine you have much time—

BOB: We had coaching at cricket at school.

ANNIE: When you were a kid, did you think . . .? What did you think you would grow up to be?

BOB: Well, I became a welder (*laughs*).

ANNIE: Did you grow up in the country?

BOB: Yes, with my grandfather, he had a farm. Then I was in Kingston when I was about twelve years old. So then I left school and learnt a trade — welding. It wasn't so bad.

ANNIE: How long for?

BOB: About four years. At that time my grandfather liked calypso and the rhumba, and the family played church music . . .
   (*So far so reasonably intelligible. Then: BOOOM:*

I don't wanna wait in vain for your love
I don't wanna wait in vain for your love
From the very first time I rest my eyes on you, girl . . .

From the back of the room Bob's latest single and future classic, 'Waiting in Vain', comes blaring out of the speakers. REALLY LOUD. My little tape recorder can't handle it.)

BOB: (*trying to ignore his own hit record*) . . . and there were dances. Desmond Dekker and I, we were working and singing together. (*Now he realises we have a problem and shouts out:*) **TURN** THAT SONG DOWN. TURN THAT SONG DOWN! TURN THAT SONG DOWN. HEY, TURN THAT **DOWN**!

ANNIE: (*gratefully*) Thank you. Cos you know what happens, with these little machines. You play it back and all the music drowns everything. (*It certainly does. And twenty-first century technology has not helped a whole lot, either. Back in 1977, I sparked up a cigarette.*)

Do you want one of mine? (*Yeah right, as if the king spliff builder would have been interested in a Benson & Hedges.*)

BOB: No, no. During that time, I was singing and learning trade and ting. And the music comes on the radio station, and we have music on all day.

Yeah, mon. Me, I liked calypso, but I couldn't play it. I liked it a lickle bit diff'rent. Fats Domino, Little Richard, Nat King Cooowl . . .

(*He mentioned another name, but his own music had mysteriously got louder again on the hi-fi. So this other crucial influence on Bob Marley is now lost for ever.*

But the American singers influencing Bob Marley were being picked up from a radio station in New Orleans. This influence was to be crucial in the development of Marley's music.)

New music was coming, and I liked that.

ANNIE: If you take any modern music from anywhere in the world, Jamaican music seems to have developed more drastically than anywhere else.

BOB: Reggae music, that is *it*!

ANNIE: It's been through all these name changes as well.

BOB: Yeah, ska, rocksteady, blue beat. It was all changing. I don't remember where reggae come. There was a time when the music was skank. But then reggae become more popular. But I don't remember who invented reggae. But the thing is, skank was fast, reggae is slower. Like for instance when I play skank, I have to make it slower speed, it's my job writing to reggae.

ANNIE: Are you surprised at how popular reggae has become internationally?

BOB: I like music I can dance to. Reggae is that.

ANNIE: How long have you been in London for?

BOB: I've been in London for four months. I'm mixing here. It's different vibes. We go for different vibes. So I've been mixing at Island in Basing Street, in Hammersmith. With a Jamaican engineer.

ANNIE: So you won't lose the atmosphere of the original? Are you going back to Jamaica now?

BOB: No, I'm going to America.

ANNIE: I've heard that you're not bothered about being a big star, not concerned about your 'image'?

BOB: I'm nat-ral, man. Not this star business. Sometimes it's nice being near to the people, when I feel I like it, you know what I mean?

ANNIE: Yeah. (*Unconvincingly. I decide to change the subject.*)

ANNIE: Do you like touring?

BOB: I really love touring, but not for ever, certain amount of . . . period of time. (*Now he changes the subject. Throws me a curve ball.*)

Rastafari! Rastafari, that is the most important thing!

ANNIE: Right. (*Floundering. Out of my depth.*) And . . . you feel . . . you are . . . doing that through the music? There's a lot of things I would like to ask you about this but I don't know very much. I've read a bit . . . where did it all begin?

BOB: What?

ANNIE: Rastafarianism.

BOB: It started with Haile Selassie. (*As if on cue the hi-fi blares loud again.*)
Um-cha, um-cha . . .

Don't wor-ry about a thing
Cause every little thing
Gonna be all right . . .

Well, I wasn't at all sure that this interview was gonna be all right, but how could I mind this song being played? The chorus of 'Three Little Birds' remains one of the most uplifting songs ever written. But now Bob Marley himself had raised the subject of Rasta, I had to grasp the nettle. And look back two thousand years or so!

The perceived knowledge of Rastafarianism is that it began in the 1920s and 1930s among the disadvantaged of Jamaica. It was a religion inspired by Haile Selassie, Emperor of Ethiopia from 1930 – 1974, seen as a messiah, Jah Rastafari, who would lead the people of Africa and its descendants to peace and prosperity.

But there are conflicting views of its origins. Some look to King Solomon and the Queen of Sheba. Others to the Hindu god Shiva. There are also suggestions that the roots of Rastafarianism and the wearing of dreadlocks are in the Old Testament (the Book of Numbers). Dreadlocks were also taken up by a spin-off cult of

Judaism, the Nazarites, who were told not to cut the hair on their head and were instructed to avoid corpses and graves.

I wish I'd known this before interviewing Bob Marley — ah, the benefit of hindsight.

BOB: Yes, the Emperor is Christ come back.

ANNIE: So, do you believe that Jesus Christ was the son of God?

BOB: I don't really . . . try. Certain thing are beyond explanation.

ANNIE: I just don't want to get this wrong (*I still don't*). Um, when did that happen, in his lifetime?

BOB: Who? (*Now I seem to have confused him!*)

ANNIE: The Emperor . . . in his lifetime . . . is that when Rastafarianism started?

BOB: (*He must have felt I was like some irritating schoolchild, but he carried on, patiently.*) In the Bible. Revelations, chapter five . . . (*he pauses*) . . . Actually, I'm not sure which chapter it is, but it's Revelations. It say: 'When God come on Earth he will return in two thousand years.'

Now it's one thousand nine hundred and seventy-seven . . . so, it's proved. (*Maybe I looked a bit dubious about this approximation. Bob continued.*)

It's kinda, uh, it's kind of deep inside I, to know certain things.

ANNIE: So when did you first have this . . . understanding?

BOB: It was in 1966. I was in America and I had a vision of Haile Selassie.

(*Bob Marley's mother had by now remarried and had gone to live in Wilmington, Delaware in the US. She sent Bob an air ticket for him to visit. Still nowhere near successful as a singer, Bob took a job in the US building Chrysler cars.*)

ANNIE: What were you doing at the time? At the moment you got the vision?

BOB: I came in from work. At twelve o'clock I usually drop asleep on the couch. I had a vision. This man came into the house and gave me a ring to get married with. He said to me: 'Long time ago your father said to give you this.' The vision said the ring was from my father. The vision was the Emperor.

ANNIE: Is he still alive? Your father?

(In fact, Bob Marley's father had died when Bob was ten years old. He had married Bob's mother, but he had not been around much during Bob's childhood.)

BOB: No, he dead. So, after that in Jamaica I respect Rasta a lickle bit.

ANNIE: Is Rasta something you would like to happen to the whole world?

BOB: It *must* happen. It is *going* to happen. Christ's government must rule! It's hard for me to express, but I have to learn and learn. Rastaman is something strange to society.

ANNIE: A lot of people seem to be frightened of Rasta.

BOB: I was, one time. But it's not a joke. Some people have been killed for being Rasta.

ANNIE: What are the most important things?

BOB: Well, we know His Majesty lived.

ANNIE: What else is important in Rasta?

BOB: The religion. And, well, you mustn't eat the meat of an animal with a cloven hoof or those that chew the cud. Because it is unclean. (*A Bible reference, Leviticus 11:4 and also laid down in the Hebrew dietary laws of the Torah.*)

If you eat meat you must know where you're gettin' it from. You can eat certain meat, but not from a horse or a donkey, but if you want to eat meat from a sheep then you can. But for me I don't really like eating meat. Rasta men don't eat pork or lobster.

ANNIE: You eat fish, don't you?

BOB: Yes, but not plaice or flat fish.

ANNIE: You've got a lot of people right here in this room. Are they all friends of yours? Is this usual, all these people here?

BOB: Well I don't know. I can't speak for all Rastafarians, but I love people, there are no barriers.

ANNIE: What about relationships, wives, children, how does the Rasta feel? I mean, you've got nine children [by seven different women], is that Rastafarian?

BOB: Maybe you can have up to twelve. I have no wives, I never wanted to get married. It's not about signing an agreement.

(Although he did marry the rather fabulous Rita in 1966. Said to have been to help her secure future residency in the US, Rita had witnessed the stigmata on the hand of Haile Selassie when he visited Jamaica in 1966. She joined the crowds at Kingston airport. Haile Selassie raised his hand in greeting, and she saw the image of the nail wound on his palm.

This was said to have had a quite profound effect on Bob's recognition of Rasta. Rita's sister, the Ranking Miss P, became a cherished colleague of mine on Radio 1, and had her own Sunday night reggae show in the 1980s. She was incredibly careful to hide her real identity as Bob's sister-in-law, not wishing to cash in on his fame.)

ANNIE: Are lots of Rastas married?

BOB: I don't know, I know a lot who aren't.

ANNIE: (*getting a bit* Newsnight *here*) Well, as most people in Britain only know about Rastafarianism because of you and what you say in interviews, they might think that it is typically Rasta to have several children by different women?

BOB: (*showing the only male pride he displayed during our interview*) Not everyone is as strong as me, in that sense.

ANNIE: It must be all that football — and all this food! (*Marley had his own travelling chef who went on tour with him and prepared special Rastafarian food.*)

ANNIE: Do you drink alcohol, or is that banned by Rasta?

BOB: I like to drink — a wine sometimes. (*Checking himself.*) But it's not right to get drunk. You don't get inspiration from being drunk.

ANNIE: What about sharing wealth?

BOB: Yeah and living in a commune type of thing.

ANNIE: Would you like to go and live in Africa?

BOB: Yes, eventually. If I don't do that, I'm not nat-ral.
   (*I was beginning to wonder if Rastafarianism was adaptable, and personally interpretive to its followers.*)

ANNIE: (*admiring Bob's shoulder-length dreadlocks*) The beautiful hair of yours, I love it. Does it have significance?

BOB: Yes. When you take a vow to be a Nazarite, which is Rasta, no comb or razor shall come upon you until your days are fulfilled. If you see a dead man lying in the street, you must cut it off.

ANNIE: What, *your* hair, *your* locks?

BOB: Yes, you must stay away from the unclean, you must cut off your hair.

ANNIE: (*wondering what would happen to the bodies if Rastafarianism took over the world*) But on a purely practical level, someone has to bury the dead? Surely?

BOB: Hmm, yes, it's kind of ticklish.
   Dread is a fear of the dead . . . dreadlocks.
   It's also a way of saying what you are.

   A statement.

And that, perplexingly, was the extent of the Natural Mystic's statement to me.
   His music, very fortunately, lives on.

8

The New Band Name

As the sixties had boomed with hit singles, for the next generation it was all about albums, and the 'business affairs' personnel taking serious interest in the amount of record sales long-haired hippies were now racking up.

The entire Virgin empire was built on the success of one long-playing record, a continuous instrumental piece called *Tubular Bells*. By a reclusive, penniless doctor's son, Mike Oldfield.

There were many other unlikely sources tapping into this new 'revenue stream' — a term no hippy would have ever used. Making money was for 'breadheads', the worst insult then available with which to malign rock musicians.

I'd known for years a session chap — quite skinny, dark hair. Was often at BBC music events, live studio shows that hosted current pop bands, where I would be on hand as the interviewer. His name was Jim, or James, or Jimmy.

'Hey, we've just formed a new band,' he said, on one of these occasions, with a great deal of excitement in his voice.

'Great! Congratulations,' I said politely.

The thing is, or was, people like this Jim or James were forever breaking up or splitting from their old band and forming a new one every other minute, or so it seemed. Very regularly. All too frequently. That's how Pete Frame's famous rock family trees came about. If you hadn't been in seventeen band line-ups and a couple of supergroups by the time you were twenty-three years old, then really . . . were you getting anywhere at all?

Take Humble Pie. I had met them, interviewed them, seen them play live, reviewed their album, and was the proud owner of one of their limited-edition promotional ceramic ashtrays. *Ashtrays?* How quaint.

Humble Pie was made up of Steve Marriott, ex-Small Faces, Peter Frampton from the Herd, Greg Ridley from Spooky Tooth and Jerry Shirley from the Apostolic Intervention. (The what? *Apostolic Intervention,* yes.)

Members of the Apostolic Intervention had appeared in bands, apparently, such as Little Women and the Wages of Sin.

Almost all the members of Humble Pie left this band to go solo or join other outfits. Then one of two former members who had left Humble Pie would re-join, reform the band with more new members. And so it went on.

We music journalists were required to record all these band name changes and personnel updates with strict and due reverent accuracy. Perhaps, though, our buzz from having exciting information like this was beginning to be tinged with a little . . . doubt. That each member would not leave within a short period and form yet another outfit. Which they would want to announce with the same level of expected front-page newsworthiness each time.

'I'm really excited about this one,' went on this Jim/Jimmy guy.

'And we've got a great name too!' he went on. 'Would you like to hear what it is?'

I wasn't intending to be blasé, but there were new names cropping up, dozens a week. And then folding again before you had time to say: 'Groovy, baby.'

So why would the new name of a session player's latest get-up be so rivetingly interesting? It would probably have a *colour* in the name, like:

Black Sabbath,
Pink Floyd or
Deep *Purple*.

Or sound psychedelic, or surreal (there have been many Surreal Madrids, of course), or have the word *exploding* in it.

So I politely restrained myself from saying: actually I don't desperately this minute need to know the name of your new group.

And said instead . . .

'Oh, go on, then . . .'

Well anyway, there was no stopping my session player guitarist friend from imparting his good news: 'We are going to be called . . .' he announced, '*Led Zeppelin.*'

And I replied to Jimmy Page, for it was he . . .

'Um, I don't think you will get very far with a name like that.'

9

Ian Dury and Catshit Mansions

'Oi, Spyder. You there, mate?'

Ian Dury called it Catshit Mansions. His home, a flat in a grim four-storey block. Right in the shadow of a gasworks and over-looking the world-famous cricket ground the Oval in Kennington, south London.

I had arrived, bowled up, ha ha, with a camera crew on behalf of ITV's then early-evening news magazine *Thames at Six*. It had not been an easy commission. Persuading the editor to send out a crew to interview a polio-disabled cockney ex-art teacher dressed like a Teddy boy. Who I was convinced was going to be a world-renowned pop star and poet.

At almost any other time during pop music's history the chance of recognition for someone such as Ian would have been pitifully bleak. He certainly wasn't *X Factor*-type material. He had huge talent for sure. As a musician, as a lyricist, as a visual artist. But he couldn't have been groomed into an Adam Faith or a Cliff Richard-style early sixties male pin-up. Disability was an even greater handicap in those days. Ian wore callipers to prop up his legs. He called himself a 'raspberry' (as in rhyming slang, raspberry ripple — cripple). And he used his condition to raise awareness with his angry outburst in the song 'Spasticus Autisticus'.

Although the right age for it, he had missed the Merseybeat sixties boom. He wasn't glam, he wasn't prog rock.

Britain in the mid-seventies was not exactly brimming with opportunity or cash for the young.

Entrepreneurship, the slick yuppies . . . the growth of Thatcher's beloved financial services boom in the City of London . . . the red light blinking on top of Canary Wharf. The show-off champagne drinking in wine bars of the eighties was utterly unforeseeable.

Ian didn't fit in with any of that either.

There was, though, a sliver of hope. A slim crack of opportunity for a sort of anti-showbiz genre. It had a very anti-showbiz name as well: pub rock. Not at all a glamorous image. But there was an energy, an ambition to channel the abundance of musical talent. There was the band Hatfield and the North, a play on a road sign name, the green-backgrounded white letters presaging the proximity of . . . our pride and joy, the spine of England's mainstay highway, the M1. Any musician, DJ or entertainer spent a huge amount of time trundling in a Commer van up and down the M1.

On Fridays most likely, on the way to a gig up north, listening to *Roundtable* on Radio 1 where DJs and others would or could often flippantly destroy the budding careers of hopeful artistes and bands whose latest tunes were being 'reviewed' by the likes of Emperor Rosko and on occasions Keith Moon, Mick Jagger, Debbie Harry and myself.

'I heard what you said about our record,' the hopeful musicians would say, accusatory, hurt eyes saying it all, on meeting them later.

Ian's first band was called Kilburn and the High Roads. Inspired by a London street name. There was Dr. Feelgood from Canvey Island in the Thames Estuary, to the east of the capital. And Elvis Costello, a blisteringly good songwriter, son of an Irish bandleader with a hugely talented band, the Attractions, was leading this movement.

Pub rock was a direct reaction to slick and big-budget pop music which major labels found themselves saddled with. Empty, soulless, rudderless music going nowhere.

The pub rockers were a grimly determined small bunch of uncompromising musicians. They were good, musically and technically. They played in small venues where they could maintain contact with the audience, the very opposite of stadium-bound bubblegum pop. They were not, to start with, of much interest to the then giants of the recording world: CBS, EMI, Polydor and the rest. They had Charlie Gillett on Radio London to champion them, and John Peel, and . . . as far as I could, myself.

The pub rock bands had integrity. But integrity don't pay the rent. Joe Strummer's 101ers were over in Maida Vale, named after their squat there. Borders of Kilburn. London north-west.

The Sex Pistols and punk were the catalyst. Suddenly there was an opportunity for a mid-thirties front man to have his moment. Through Stiff Records. The label was the lighting of the blue touch paper for Ian. And like Factory Records shaped alternative music to a huge degree. Stiff wasn't (then) part of a huge corporation.

It was a shopfront in west London. The name was a joke too. A stiff was a flop, a record that didn't sell. But Stiff knew the value of marketing and attention-grabbing. They made a clock out of an old vinyl record, and stencilled in white on the clock face, 'Kill Time and You Murder Success'. Or their better-known T-shirt slogan, 'If It Ain't Stiff, It Ain't Worth a Fuck'.

Very collectable.

Ian was outside his upper-storey flat. Well, he was hardly an upstanding home*owner*. It's much more likely he was a squatter. He was at ground level to greet us. Only problem was, he didn't have a key to let himself, or anyone else, in.

In that unmistakeable salted-caramel voice that had no problem reaching the back of the stalls in any theatre without a microphone, he shouted, again, very loudly at the building, 'Oi, Spyd, hurry up, geezer.'

We all looked up at the windows hopefully.

'Must be akip,' observed Ian, giving the crew a charismatic, daring — he hoped reassuring — grin.

'Spyder! Where are ya? Door keys. Need the keys, chuck 'em out the winder. Pron'oh. Gotta TV crew waiting down 'ere.'

Ian was not yet sufficiently famous to feel comfortable keeping a camera unit waiting. It was the mid-seventies. There were no mobile phones. Maybe Ian's flat in Catshit Mansions didn't even have a doorbell.

Eventually a window on an upper storey bang-slammed open. Ah, Spyder at last.

But no, it was . . . a woman. An angry woman. Her bescarfed head bobbed up like a papier-mâché puppet head in a Punch and Judy show.

'What's going on down there?' she yelled. Then answered her own rhetorical question. 'I know what's goin' on. I'm gonna report you lot. What you're doin', it's against the law.'

Ian looked, it has to be said, a bit sheepish.

'You're runnin' a record comp'ny in 'ere. Arncha?' She was in full, shrieking, let-all-the-neighbours-know mode . . . 'Makin' *records*. Disturbin' the peace.' It was a damning-sounding accusation, as if on a criminal parallel with gunrunning or class A drug dealing. I looked pleadingly at the cameraman. Please, please hoist that camera on your shoulder and press the record button. Capture this on film.

Though a seasoned news cameraman he was not sufficiently motivated to realise this was a true punk rock moment: Ian Dury, hanging around outside and locked out of a block of flats in south London, being shouted at by an angry resident — not the usual experience for the rock star interview. Usually these were held in plush hotels or well-appointed record label offices with drinks and eats aplenty. The last one I had taped for Thames TV was with Paul McCartney and Denny Laine from Wings. They had obligingly come to the Thames TV studio. Turned up on time. No problem.

Eventually Spyder, a peculiarly piratical-looking figure — black hair, long black clothes and, I recall, quite Magwitch-like — appeared at another window above and chucked the keys down into the street. Spyder was a former cat burglar. Probably didn't need keys.

'Sweet, Spyder,' shouted Ian, and we trudged up the stone stairs to his lair. Spyder and, on other occasions, Kosmo Vinyl, and later the mysteriously named minder the Sulphate Strangler became Ian's official entourage.

Ian, I felt, was an important discovery. I was going to shout from any rooftop, be it Catshit Mansions or the BBC, to get his talent noticed.

I'd managed to play 'Razzle in My Pocket', with dubious lyrics about nicking a porn magazine from a newsagent, on Radio 1. It was the B-side to 'Sex & Drugs & Rock & Roll'. (Certainly, a track with a title like that would have got me into a lot of trouble. I had a bad name already for playing supposedly provocative material.)

'Sex & Drugs' was not at all recognised at the time for its lexiconic quality, which would see it adopted into the English language. Endlessly borrowed and adapted to this day. Liam Gallagher proved what a decent human being he is by agreeing to present me with a Guinness Book of Records award in a dismal BBC basement at ten in the morning, *on his birthday*. He was happy to pose with an S & D & R & R banner (made by my daughter) for the photo shoot.

But the tune didn't even appear initially on Ian's first and classic album *New Boots and Panties!!* We finished the interview, cramped in a small but highly decorated room, mostly orange.

The crew left, relieved to be out of these dubious surroundings, somewhat hurriedly. Ian invited me to Spyder's own flat in the same block for a drink. Or two. He was charming and endlessly entertaining. Then he said in a gruff voice, so deep I couldn't understand him, 'I think we should . . . *errrlllrrr*.'

'*Seyoww sorreh?*' I went, in my still cut-glass, elocution-ised, posho received pronunciation. 'Eye couldn't *quaite h'yar yoo*.'

So he said it a second time, but somehow it had lost the impact. 'I said,' he repeated, 'that we should elope.'

Maybe I hadn't heard him right the second time either. Anyway, Gretna Green did not beckon; we became lifelong friends instead.

Ian treated his fans, if not his fellow band members, with great respect and lavished on each one a piece of his own art, a bespoke drawing, a cartoon, a sketch, with every autograph. He gave me a pair of green plastic scissors moulded like crocodile's jaws which he hand-decorated with the colours of Jamaica, sort of reggae scissors. As a present for my forthcoming second wedding. (Not to Ian, obvs.) This time he'd come round to my house in Brighton. After a gig.

'Did you get lost or anything?' I asked when he eventually arrived, very late.

'No, I asked the fans at the gig,' said Ian. 'They all knew where you live.'

Which was a bit alarming.

Ian attended the wedding with Kosmo Vinyl. Kosmo worked with the Clash and Ian and was a lightning spirit with the brightest neon orange-red dyed hair I've ever seen on anyone.

'I love being on tour and staying in hotels,' he would say. 'You move on every day, can't get into trouble for leaving the dye all over the pillows.'

Baxter, Ian's son, who appeared next to his dad as a five-year-old on the cover of *New Boots and Panties!!*, has called his own son Kosmo. Lovely bit of symmetry, especially as Baxter is now receiving acclaim for his own talent as a recording artist. At the age of forty-eight. First time I heard his track 'Miami', I had that compulsive must-play-it-over-and-over-again feeling, which only happens once or twice a year. To me anyway. Jarvis Cocker made it his tune of the year in *Mojo* magazine.

Ian and Kosmo's other wedding present was to hire a rockabilly band of great repute, Whirlwind, to play live at the after-party. This was all in collaboration with Johnnie the Monk.

Johnnie the Monk might sound like another of Ian's co-conspirators. But he was a real monk. He had been Johnnie Porterfield. I met him in the Colonnade, the bar in Brighton next door to the Theatre Royal. I had dragged David Bowie there in 1969 to tell him he was the future of music.

I doubt Kosmo Vinyl or Ian Dury or the Whirlwind musicians had previously visited Worth Abbey in Sussex. Its traditions could be traced back to St Augustine's monastery in Canterbury, larged up by the Pope back in AD 957.

A mere thousand-odd years later Johnnie Porterfield had now become Fr Anthony, to mark his calling to the cloth. He was a Geordie who'd taken a circuitous route from being a music hall end-of-pier singer, through theatrical restaurateur.

During the wedding proceedings, he was overseeing — sort of MC'ing — where and when the band should appear. Having told them to get in place asap, he turned and whisked away in his full-length black cassock.

'Who the fuck was *that*?' undertoned one Whirlwind member sotto, he thought, voce to another.

The priest copped the question.

'Fucking Father fucking Anthony, that's fucking who,' came back the full baritone in broadest South Shields.

Ian and his band the Blockheads were the finest funk band in Britain, if not further afield. Ian had teamed up with Chaz

Jankel to write music to Ian's often plaintive poetic lyrics. The sound was underpinned by the phattest bass playing by Norman Watt-Roy and drummer Charley Charles. Plus Micky Gallagher on keyboards and Davey Payne who could play two saxophones at once. Our paths were to cross many more times.

I couldn't have been more delighted when the band started chalking up big hits like the now classic 'Hit Me with Your Rhythm Stick', 'What a Waste', 'Sweet Gene Vincent', 'Clever Trevor' and 'Billericay Dickie'. 'Reasons to Be Cheerful' is still a headline beloved of magazine subeditors and media producers in every bleak post-festive season in January, when mainstream media seems bereft and bare of any fresh, optimistic ideas. And during the pandemic in 2020, too.

Ian took to being a bona fide pop star like a very enthusiastic Aylesbury duck to a massive great lake. He sure lived out the lyrics to 'Sex & Drugs & Rock & Roll' and alcohol rather too much for some of those around him. I was a step away from his dark side. Or possibly I was regarded as a Media Friend, so he hid that away from me.

Every Christmas Eve during my five-year tenure as host/anchor for *The Old Grey Whistle Test*, the TV show became a live celebration broadcast from some well-known London venue. That year we needed some divertissement to lift us from the shock and the grief of John Lennon's murder just sixteen days beforehand. In fact there was hesitation that we should even be broadcasting a rock 'n' roll show at all, so soon, be it Christmas or not.

By 1980 Ian and the Blockheads were the dogs b., proper stars. I was thrilled for them. This was very much a prime slot, on stage at the Dominion, Tottenham Court Road, where I had once, as a student, seen Judy Garland perform at a matinee. I really overdid the seasonal costume and looked like something dragged off the top of an over-decorated Christmas tree: a shiny silver metal bow in my hair, red kilt, aubergine hair, white trimmed leather cowboy kerchief round my neck overlaid with a gold chain necklace. Yes, really.

The entire audience were Blockheads, fans of the band. I picked my way across the stage, among the leads and cords — stages are dangerous places (see later).

'Oi oi, thanks for coming out tonight,' exulted Ian to the audience. 'I thought no one would turn up . . . we thought you's all gone home for Christmas.'

The audience roared back their acknowledgement. The auditorium was packed, a giant swaying mosh pit, of mostly young men who looked like Kosmo Vinyl. Short, sort of mod haircuts, sharp clothes. It didn't feel any safer on the stage than down in the crowd.

I knew and was to learn from previous, and then further, experiences of introducing the leading attraction. Get on and get off, quick. The crowd hasn't come to see *you*, they've come to see the band and to tell their mates they've been on telly. So don't hog the stage.

Another Radio 1 event took me to Barrowlands in Glasgow, introducing Radiohead, Blur and other then upcoming bands. The first few rows of the audience set up a steady chant when I appeared.

'Fuck OFF, fuck OFF. fuck OFF,' they went. Well, I did my introductions and did indeed fuck off stage as quickly as possible, just a bit surprised by this sudden Scottish hostility. To my amazement, the same lads now chased me down a corridor that led back to the auditorium.

'Annie, Annie, can I have your autograph, please?' they shouted.

'But you just told me to fuck off!'

'Ah, that was just a wee joke. We love ya really.' No wonder the aggressive action of the headbutt is known as a Glasgow kiss.

*

Back at the Dominion, Ian grabbed my shoulder and planted a chaste Christmas kiss on one cheek. The metal bow slid further and further down my head. Ian also affectionately tried to wind his scarf round my neck. If I'd slipped or tripped, he could have garrotted me there on the spot. I had at the same time to announce, on cue to camera, that this show was being broadcast live on BBC2 and on Radio 1, a simulcast that rarely happens nowadays.

The night was suitably uproarious. The stage ended up looking like a war zone. Streamers cascaded endlessly from somewhere above; huge metallic garlands were twisted around every possible protrusion. Fake snow plumed upwards in clouds every time the drummer hit the skins. Glitter guns pelted the stage from every possible angle.

Your everyday production for EDM shows in Vegas, but this was recession-hit Britain in 1980. By the end you could hardly make out Ian or his special guests at all, they were so drenched in party gear. There on stage with the Blockheads was the coolest jazz trumpet player Don Cherry (stepdad of Neneh) who had played with Ornette Coleman and John Coltrane FFS. *And* Wilko Johnson, the hero of Dr. Feelgood, who seemed like he had some kind of self-operated personal hovercraft beneath his feet. Nobody before or since has had that unique capacity of gliding. Back, forth and sideways across a stage without ever missing a beat.

Most Christmas TV shows are now recorded months in advance. When I appeared on *Pointless*, finally broadcast over a year later, it had been recorded the same day as another Christmas edition, taped in the summer on the hottest day of that year. Sprigs of fake holly and cotton wool snowmen were strewn along the corridors of Elstree studios. No matter how long this extremely popular show lasts, I'm not sure I would appear again. Or that they would ask me!

I have declined *Celebrity Mastermind*, *Celebrity Big Brother*, *Celebrity University Challenge*, *I'm a Celebrity*. I do not do well in competitive circumstances. And the more mainstream the TV show and the earlier in the day or evening it appears in the schedules, the greater the amount of online trolling. It comes with the territory.

'Ew, she doesn't look like she did in the seventies . . .'

To which someone did pipe up on Twitter, I guess in my defence: 'Well, what did you expect her to wear . . . a twinset and pearls?'

Then: 'Ugh, she looks really *weird*.'

You have to learn either to suck it up, or preferably not read it at all. It's ever been thus. A London cabbie once said cheerily to me: 'I think you're all right, but my wife can't stand you.'

LOL.

But on 24 December 1980 the Christmas spirit was genuinely adrenaline-filled and totally live. You could not fuck up. There was no question of a take two. Ian Dury told the audience he hoped the band was 'tight enough now that we have been on tour solidly for the past five weeks'. You could hear just how well rehearsed they were. Crackingly good.

I followed Ian's career as he escalated from pop to rock star, to respected and revered musician, and then he became an actor too. Another visit to another of his homes. This time he wasn't squatting. It was prime location west London, overlooking the Thames at Hammersmith. Cross Hammersmith Bridge in all its gold and green finery, westwards, and look to your right, the rowing eights almost always skittering up and down the river, and you'll see Ian's former mansion flat jutting out from its Thames-front terrace.

'Sometimes,' Ian said me, 'the fog that comes up from the water is so thick you can't see across to the other side of the bridge.' I think we made jokes about it being the bridge over troubled water or the stairway to heaven.

When I heard in the nineties that he had liver cancer I felt furious on his behalf. Hadn't this guy had enough to deal with, to conquer, to overcome, with his polio disability? I know life is not fair, but this seemed too unjust.

So I last saw him at yet another abode, in Fitzjohn's Avenue, Hampstead. He was as bright and sociable as ever, but it was clearly a huge effort to keep up this almost onstage persona for very long. His health was fading.

The disease got the better of him. I don't know if he ever came to terms with it, but I certainly didn't. I attended his funeral, a very impressive humanist affair, suitably wildly theatrical, with a horse-drawn glass carriage and a colourful cross-section of characters, from the MP Mo Mowlam to Robbie Williams — Ian had struck up a friendship with the singer when they had been on a UNICEF mission together.

I was asked to DJ at the wake, which was held at the Forum rock venue in north London. This was a big responsibility. What was I going to play, knowing that Ian had been such a master musician? How on earth could I do him credit? I was knee-knockingly nervous, worrying about offending Ian's colleagues by playing anything really crass or inappropriate. The Blockheads band were running the show, and my huge respect for them made me even more nervous about what to play. My new friends and tour henchmen, Vegetable Vision Noah and Adam, came to give me moral support. I can't really remember what the set list was. Possibly mostly dub reggae. I felt honoured to have been asked, and there were many others who wanted to pay their respects to Ian by DJ'ing that evening. I was content to play a minor part. Nearly everyone there, I recall, got bleakly stoned or smashed. It was grim really, not an event anyone wanted to happen.

The next time I met up with this crowd was at the London premiere of the biopic of Ian's life, with Andy Serkis playing his part. It's hard to judge a dramatic characterisation based on a person you have known well in life. Andy gave it everything.

As a film it made the grade, survived the critics, had a BAFTA nomination and won a lot of other awards. Love to know what Ian would have thought. Used his favourite word, maybe: sweet.

What might have meant more to him was the revival of his song 'Spasticus Autisticus' at the opening ceremony of the 2012 Paralympics.

He had written the original as a protest song, about what he regarded as the patronising attitude of the 'Year of Disabled Persons' in 1981. The song was banned by the BBC on release . . . or rather, just not given daytime airplay. Who did they think was going to be offended by this?

It was a battle cry for anyone with a disability. Maybe it takes a personal incident to bring home the anger that Ian felt. I broke an arm and a leg in 2013 in an accident. I was being transferred from an X-ray department back to a hospital ward (a regular occurrence) where I was an in-patient, by wheelchair. A radiologist leaned down to me and said slowly and very carefully as though a kindergarten teacher to a three-year-old: 'We've taken a PICTURE of you, and we are going to give it to your DOCTOR.'

I was incandescent with rage. I wanted to leap out of the wheelchair and say: 'Isn't it amazing? I'm in a wheelchair, but I'm not entirely useless. I may have a leg in plaster, but I am able to function mentally, *believe it or not*. Actually, I'm a doctor, too. Of letters. As if you need to know that to give me a modicum of respect.'

And for all the other patients who've been talked down to, in this thoughtless, ignorant and cruel way . . . 'How dare you fucking patronise us.'

Big up Ian, you geezer.

10

Keith Moon

Keith Moon's hotel room. London, 1976. Interior. Day.

ANNIE: Tell me about the automobile in the swimming pool affair. Was it your twenty-first birthday party, or someone else's?

KEITH: No, it was mine. In Flint, Michigan. It was the Lincoln in the swimming pool. I knocked out my front teeth and slipped on a piece of marzipan, running away from the police.

ANNIE (*incredulous*): *Marzi*-pan? (*Lady Bracknell-style*) On the *ground*, that you could *slip on*?

KEITH: Well . . . it was a birthday cake. I'd thrown it up in the air . . . (*He adds helpfully:*) After I had ripped off my clothes. Lying about in me underpants, the police running after me. The manager had seen the birthday cake. It was *huge*, five *drums*, which I threw at all these guests . . . record company executives — wankers in suits and ties who were all waffling . . . '*Wunnerful area of the Ewnighted States here*' . . . so I threw the birthday cake at them. And, er, whipped off me clothes.' (*Keith could and would switch accents from West End actor posh to Wembley working class in the same sentence. He breezes on:*)
And the manager of the Holiday Inn called the police.

I ran away from the sheriff, knocked out me tooth, jumped into the Lincoln, and drove it into the swimmin' pool. They locked me in my room, with the deputy sheriff outside my door. The band had to fly off the next day to get to the next gig. (*He pauses.*) 'Very *bad* plannin' — a gig, the day after my twenty-first birthday? Will they never learn?

ANNIE: Har har.

KEITH: So the dentist came round, fixed me up, and the sheriff was quite amused by it all. Astounded really, because nothing much ever happens in Flint, Michigan. There again there was no *real* damage, and no one was hurt, it was all paid up [paid for]. They had a private plane to fly me to the next gig, because the others had all left. So they drove me out in the police car to the airport.

As I got on the plane the sheriff said: 'Don't you *ever* get your ass in Flint, Michigan *again*.'

Keith 1, the Who nil. But the band and its management were to take — had to take — drastic steps regarding Keith's almost routine after-gig behaviour. The Who were banned from major hotel chains in the US. So where were they to stay during their many and mammoth tours? The management struck a bargain with the hotel chains, completely unbeknown to Keith. The damage-limitation plan was for Keith to be booked into a room that was due for refurbishment. That way it wouldn't be quite so terrible if he did unscrew every piece of furniture, so that it collapsed when any weight was put on it. Or it would not be so appalling if Keith planted explosive in the toilet, or flooded the bathroom, or threw the TV out of the window — his signature favourite after-show antic.

But the plan was effective only if Keith never found out that the rest of the band members had far superior rooms to his. And it was essential, then, that no other member of the entourage should ever open their hotel room door to Keith, for fear he'd discover that he had been assigned the most rubbish quarters of the entire entourage. If he had found *that* out, Keith might have destroyed whole cities in his towering wrath.

— 11 —

The Jump

Radio 1 had one more trick up its sleeve regarding putting on a live event to entice the punters. And glean us maximum publicity.

Once more it involved a racetrack destination. But with a unique twist . . .

At the time, the mid-seventies, the world had looked on in wonder at the daredevil exploits of an American stunt motorcycle rider called Evel Knievel. He was a flamboyant, swashbuckling hero whose outfits out-sparkled even Elvis Presley's. In the colours of the American flag . . . Stars and Stripes . . . with a semi-billowing attachment, à la Caped Crusader. A true patriot. He and his bike jumped over things. Like a row of buses, or across things like cliff edges, ravines or plunging escarpments. The fairly impossible, in other words. A true-life Spiderman on wheels.

And rather as Cliff Richard had once captured the hearts and minds of a certain section of British pop followers as the home-grown UK version of Elvis, we had now our own British motorcycle stunt jump rider, too. His name . . . Eddie Kidd.

He too jumped over rows of buses. And cars. He also stunt doubled in the James Bond movies *The Living Daylights* and *Goldeneye*.

Another real-life daredevil superhero.

Now he was going to jump over . . . us. The Radio 1 DJs.

As we lay flat, unprotected and helpless on Brands Hatch race-track in front of the packed grandstand.

Hmm. What did I think of that?

I thought it was an insane idea.

But . . . I was still the one female DJ on the team. I could not chicken out.

Besides . . . they said, at Radio 1, that the jump would be . . . perfectly safe.

Oh, OK then, I said. Being amenable. Up for it. A good sport and all that.

And anyway, as I read in the blitz of publicity surrounding the impending event, we would all be insured. For millions. *Millions.*

So that made it sort of all right, then.

I had in my mind beforehand that Eddie Kidd would prepare for the jump over the DJs, a dozen of us, from a huge, specially built ramp. Many, many feet or metres high. And that there would be a massive overhang, like a high-diving board over an Olympic sized swimming pool. So that if anything bad happened, his engine failed or whatever, Eddie would have flown past us, and bounced perhaps a little unsteadily, but safely, back onto the track ahead of us, and out of harm's way.

That is how I imagined the set-up.

I mean, Radio 1 wouldn't want to lose all or indeed *any* of its star names for such a pointless one-off stunt, would it?

So I rocked up on the day to Brands Hatch, quite unperturbed.

Till I saw the set-up.

I was absolutely aghast.

There was no big jumping-off platform. No diving-board type overhang, high in the sky.

Just a couple of short wooden planks propped up at an angle by what looked like nothing more sturdy or substantial than a wire coat hanger.

What?

This puny edifice was going to constitute the entire trajectory for Eddie Kidd to jump over what looked for all the world like a dozen human life-sized sausages lined up on a barbeque? Surely not! But it surely was.

We drew straws to see who would be positioned furthest away from the coat-hanger jump-off, and therefore the most dangerous spot, the most likely place to be mangled by Eddie's engine if something went wrong.

Tony Blackburn got the short straw. The crowd cheered. He made light of it, but I could not believe that all of us were not quaking in our boots.

It was all being commentated on, filmed and photographed. I am not sure if I knew that at some time quite recent to our event, another stunt rider had been killed in the US trying to jump over buses.

Well, it was too late to back out now anyway. Here we were, lying flat on our backs, on the cold hard surface of the racetrack. We couldn't see what was happening, as we were all in this prone position. I could *hear* Eddie revving up. *Vroom, vroom*, as you would expect. The crowd roared.

Eddie and his bike burst into action . . . and for some reason, didn't mount the rickety plank at all, but made a quick sprint, straight past us, his wheels never leaving the track. The sound of that souped-up engine buzzing in our ears.

Maybe it was a warm-up, maybe it was just to whip up the excitement. He turned, drove back along the track back to the start position.

And this time . . . *yes* . . . he took off, sailed up off the planks, he jumped. He was airborne, as gracefully as a steeplechaser over Becher's Brook in the Grand National. And landed, safely well in front of the brave (or foolish) boys and girl from Radio 1.

Everyone cheered. Congratulated Eddie Kidd. Money was raised for a deserving charity.

Afterwards, I remarked to one of our team: 'Well that was a bit scary. But you know what kept me calm? Knowing that if the worst *had* happened — at least our loved ones would be looked after. You know . . . the millions we've been insured for.'

He turned to me, incredulous: 'Insured? For millions? Whatever gave you that idea? Of course you weren't! Who on earth do you think would have insured you?'

12

The Old Grey Whistle Test

Yes, I was the only *woman* who presented the show solo. I didn't make any bones about it at the time . . .

I had written my own news stories, magazine features, fronted documentaries and become Radio 1's first female DJ and broadcaster . . . that was my CV. After a so valuable apprenticeship on local and regional newspapers. It was an interesting, challenging job to do.

It might seem strange, but I'd experienced few barriers or sexism in journalism, even though when I was involved with it, there were certainly some vipers to avoid.

I had become a regular TV presenter in the mid-1960s with a series called *That's for Me*, an arts and entertainment programme intended to be an 'elder sister' show to *Ready Steady Go!*, choosing the pop music guest acts. The shows were live, with no autocue, and script changes that I was to absorb, process and memorise perfectly while in the make-up chair, minutes before transmission. Then deliver live to camera. It was terrifying. Very steep learning curve.

I had done countless one-off appearances. Music panel show such as *Juke Box Jury*. Young people's discussion programmes . . . *A Whole Scene Going* . . . *Ready Steady Go!* . . . A filmed documentary series for BBC TV. Gaining experience of the medium, in and out of the studio. Always learning . . .

I had been part of *The Old Grey Whistle Test*'s wider team since the mid-seventies. There were *OGWT* spin-offs such as *Rock Goes to College*, *In Concert*, *Sight and Sound*, *Late Night in Concert*. Mike Appleton, the overall producer, said he preferred hiring radio people as presenters because they knew how to keep talking if something should go wrong. They were all blokes, the rota of presenters on these shows, come to think of it. Only one female ever after me, Ro Newton, who hardly gets mentioned.

Mike Appleton was a visionary. He'd run *The Old Grey Whistle Test* as an almost guerrilla operation within the BBC. A big, unflappable friendly bear of a man who never lost his cool or his sense of humour. He'd begun on the arts series *Late Night Line Up*, featuring Joan Bakewell. Then music shows from a ludicrously small studio called Pres B, normally used for weather broadcasts. This strand began as series called *Colour Me Pop and Disco 2*. Mike had as his ally none other than David Attenborough, then controller of BBC2. Attenborough encouraged maverick Mike's music shows to spin on live into the late night and be open ended. He also employed music journalists. I was that as well.

Yet *still*, despite being involved on camera with that team for more than *eleven* years, people say, oh weren't you just Bob Harris's sidekick? When he went on holiday?

Actually, I point out, no. I wasn't. He would be the first to agree. I am not directing any ire at him. *Just the perception.*

This was a kind of inherent sexism. The presumption that no woman on her own could have single-handedly hosted the most iconic music TV show, through its, in my view, most interesting period. Oh, you couldn't have done that on your own.

I'd done nothing else as anyone's assistant or girl Friday. Or sidekick. It was a lone job really. A double header is more difficult. It's easier to make direct contact through the camera, to the audience, rather than picking up cues from an onscreen partner.

I wasn't a TV presenter to be decorative or a celebrity and nab a property developer husband or a pop star millionaire. I did the job because I thought I *might be able to*. I had the desire to communicate, had perhaps the required level of experience and knowledge. I wanted to convey my passion about music to the audience that I knew was out there. Wanting something perhaps that went a bit deeper into music culture than *Top of the Pops*. Which was doing fine, but by the nature of its title, had quite severe limitations in its format . . .

No one — I hope — comments on British TV news anchors such as Fiona Bruce (ex-punk), Cathy Newman, Kirsty Wark or Emily Maitlis for being women. They are just damn good at their job.

Hosting a show such as *The Old Grey Whistle Test* meant taking a lot of stick from the audience. As any TV presenter has to. You take the hit, as the front person. Fair enough.

A member of the audience will not know why you have that particular array of guests and clips that week. Maybe an intended studio guest pulled out at the last minute. An overseas star didn't get their work permit through in time. A bass player walked out of the band and couldn't be replaced in time . . . The singer had laryngitis. Maybe somebody *died*. It happened. Not only John Lennon, on my watch.

We could not always get who we wanted on the show. Not by a long chalk. And the show ran in long series, from September to June. We had to be prepared for anything. And paper over the cracks. The show was produced as live, and completely live on many occasions.

It is this underlying perception of being patronised — that a mere female couldn't possibly have hosted that show, been the main anchor for five years — that has persisted.

Strangely this misconception seems to have grown rather than lessened over the more recent and supposedly more enlightened years. Which is why I raise it.

Do the naysayers think I didn't know one end of a Stratocaster from the other? Or whether the star guest's next album was going to be in the same vein as the last one, or something a bit different?

I saw more than one fawning male interviewer ask that question.

I had been a fan of Richard Williams who had been an early host of the show. He'd captured a brilliant one-to-one session with Little Richard. Then he got somewhat hammered verbally by Captain Beefheart. I was due to interview this actual legend the very next day. Not for TV. But still. So, I took a different tack, and said deadpan to Beefheart:

'Tell me about your mother.'

It worked a treat. He roared with laughter, and we connected. Not that I'd wanted to discuss his early domestic life at all, but just to ask something *different*, something off-kilter, something a bit bizarre. If only I'd taped that one.

Perhaps it was because up until my takeover as presenter it had been mostly male rock bands appearing.

Who had I been interviewing as a journalist for the previous fifteen years, *on my own*, but male rock bands?

Which is why punk was so welcome, so necessary. Stop treating us presenters and female performers as second-rate citizens, empty-headed fools.

The seventies had such a rich scene for musical styles. You know them: hard rock, soft rock, heavy rock, folk rock, heavy metal, glam, reggae, disco, funk, punk. And those are just the broad outlines. Since the *OGWT* had begun in 1972 it had brought in some gem performances from David Bowie and also Bob Marley and John Lennon. Can't argue with that, but for the most part it was long-haired blokes playing long guitar solos.

John Peel had led the punk revolution, really, really led it. Along with the healthy, flourishing music press. No one else had John's courage to risk losing his livelihood, his slot on air because the music he was playing was, in some people's opinion, unlistenable.

But there was a massive audience of young people who desperately wanted more of his music and were turned off by the giants of rock with their Rolls-Royces and country estates.

Things came to a bit of a head over my predecessor presenter slagging off the New York Dolls, and then an unfortunate meeting with some of the Sex Pistols team, who really gave him a hard time. For which I was sympathetic.

But two to three years into the punk revolution and the *OGWT* was not representing punk, nor showing any real enthusiasm for it. So when the opportunity arose to get some punk music on the show, then this was the opportunity not to be missed. We got the Adverts on, who were pointedly caustic, and lyrically superb.

When my predecessor walked away from the job because he and punk didn't get on, the programme team came to me, and I agreed to take over.

I'd worked with them before, on these other shows, and most of all they were a great bunch to be with. Really irreverent, and no one taking themselves or anyone else too seriously. No pampering or star behaviour. The presenter is just one of the team. Try to get your bits right first time, don't screw up. Don't throw wobblers.

And yet people *still* say: 'Weren't you intimidated, taking over?'

Well, I was nervous about getting the pieces to camera right, not tripping over words, but the inference again was: Aren't you intimidated, *as a woman*, taking over from a *male*?

If you met me you would know that I am not arrogant (well, I would say that, wouldn't I? — but seriously I hope I'm not).

But actually, no, why should I be intimidated?

What was this, a new round of interrogation after my Radio 1 early days?

The could-be-tough student magazine interviewers, then, had every right to ask me challenging and fair questions: 'Why should *you* have a radio show? What gives *you* the right to choose what gets played?' I'm sure I did not by any means have all the answers, but they had every right to ask.

I had a different way of communicating, as every single person does.

It's all about reflecting your own truth, looking honestly and straightforwardly into the camera, hoping you've researched enough to be able to impart something interesting, good humouredly perhaps to the audience . . .

More importantly on my first show as its anchor, who would be the live guests *prepared* to come on the new-look show? Did I have the necessary credibility?

Some punk outfits had apparently refused to appear in the series immediately before. Thought the show was too guitar-y, too rawk.

So who would be on my first mission statement show of the new series? I couldn't have been more delighted. It was to be . . .

The Ramones.

The *Ramones*.

Live in the studio.

Who were magnificent. No wonder everyone who saw the Ramones play wanted to start their own band. They played the shortest, sharpest songs ever, and perfectly executed.

The revolution *was* being televised! At last, finally. Well, a bit at a time.

For many of the performers it was their first opportunity to appear on TV. And there were to be no retakes for any musical mistakes. So, a scary prospect for many of them. I knew that and tried to be welcoming and reassuring. Be the ice breaker.

It's a job I've been honoured to have. I felt privileged. I still do. Music was reflecting social change, especially during the years

1978-83. Not just reggae, punk, new wave and no wave, but the 2 Tone label, for example, and the whole electro revolution. A vital period for very exciting new music . . .

For the past year or two I've been working on TV documentaries around the punk and post-punk years and trying to make sure that the women who emerged in that era are as well represented as possible. Siouxsie, the Slits, Gaye in the Adverts, young Tracey Thorn in the Marine Girls, the Raincoats, as well as Patti Smith and Debbie Harry. Sometimes the ephemeral live performances were not committed to film or video. There just were not the financial resources then. Sadly. But when a piece of rare footage does turn up, it's all the more exciting. More and more episodes, more and more performances from that era are being posted onto social media and streaming sites. It's good to know that those musical chronicles remain relevant . . .

— 13 —

Elvis Costello – Shipbuilding

May 1982, BBC TV Centre, Shepherd's Bush, London W12.

The reception desk was through a set of glass swing doors on the right of the horseshoe-shaped building. Studios and offices, where most of the TV shows of the time were made. An array of charming but alert receptionists sat in a row, scrutinising all comers. Whether they be fans in for *Top of the Pops*, or politicians, actors, make-up artistes, camera operators, set builders, news gatherers or blaggers. We had no electronic ID tags then. I must admit I did get a thrill every time I reported in for work there.

This then quite unfashionable part of London, facing a railway line, was the place all the iconic programmes had been made for decades.

Once checked in, and having collected dressing-room keys, I would make my way to an array of lifts. En route to the *Old Grey Whistle Test* camera rehearsals, I stood in front of the stainless-steel doors and stepped in as they glided open. Two grey-haired men in suits wearing serious expressions stepped in behind me.

'We've lost the *Sheffield*,' said one to the other.

This was a serious turning point in the Falklands War.

Opinion is still divided as to whether it was right to defend the Falklanders, or wrong to go to war with Argentina, run by fascist dictator Galtieri, who had made claims to the Islas Malvinas and had invaded the islands, which are 8000 miles closer to the Argentinian mainland than to the UK. I only knew where the Falkland Islands were because they'd issued comparatively valuable postage stamps, acquired by keen young collectors like me when I was knee-high to a space hopper.

The right-wing British popular press, such as the *Sun*, were screamingly pro the Thatcher government decision to open hostilities.

No one seemed to think anyone would come to any harm. It was just sabre-rattling. The British navy would show its might, the 'Argies' would back down, the Brits could sing 'Rule Britannia' once again with feeling and justification, wave their Union Jacks and 'our boys' would all come home, triumphant, safe and sound.

But things didn't pan out like that.

HMS *Sheffield* was the first British Royal Navy ship to be sunk, lost in action, since the Second World War.

Oh fuck, was the collective surprised response, generally. Not a war game anymore, then. The real thing.

British forces had already sunk the Argentine *General Belgrano* with several hundred losses. Controversy still rages as to whether the *Belgrano* was technically outside the war zone, just limping home, and should not have been attacked.

Elvis Costello began working on lyrics to a song about the moral dilemma — and ambiguities — of the war. The shipyards of the Clyde, Belfast and Tyneside being seriously idled by the Thatcher government's policy.

What, though, if you were one of the shipbuilders, out of work? Needing 'a new winter coat and shoes for the wife,' the haunting line from the song that became 'Shipbuilding', sung by Robert Wyatt, and written with him in mind.

In the twenty-teens I made a documentary about the song, the war and the moral issues it had raised. I sat in a small unmanned studio in Broadcasting House, and talked 'up the line' to Elvis

Costello, who was on tour in Newcastle, and had dropped into a similar studio there.

This is his story of 'Shipbuilding' two decades on. He'd been in Australia when the Falklands War happened.

*

ELVIS COSTELLO: We had been fairly gung-ho when we left [the UK] and none of the most tragic events had occurred by that point. But obviously, given that Rupert Murdoch kind of honed his black arts in the Australian media, before he became an American, in that country the level of lurid, inappropriate and downright false reporting in his papers and on his television stations in Australia added to the kind of horror of watching it.

It was already pretty horrifying to see the kind of glee with which the *Sun* and such papers marked things off in the conflict. Almost as if we were watching a football tournament.

You obviously want the guys that are wearing your uniform to come home safely and prevail. I understand that, but there was no debate and anybody that said otherwise was characterised as some kind of 'wet' or 'traitor'.

(Being a 'wet' was one of the more unpleasant terms Thatcher had used towards moderates in her government. I'd thought even then it was an extremely gauche kind of sneer. Something she had picked up from the ex-public schoolboys in her cabinet? No better than a **ner-ner-ner-ner-ner** *school playground taunt. Not exactly stateswoman-like. IMHO.)*

ELVIS COSTELLO: I've never been a great one for the 'which side are you on?' type song. They suit other people. I've never tried to write a straightforward, unquestioning love song. I feel other people do that better than me. And similarly, with this. I didn't want to write a straightforward 'this war is wrong', even though that's kind of what I believed.

I just wanted to extend the thought into something that occurred to me and hence the notion about the shipyards. Because we were in a time of conflict between portions of something which Margaret Thatcher went on record saying didn't exist — society.

(It hardly seemed the right moment to remind Elvis (so I didn't) that I'd once hosted a Radio 1 programme with him and Kim Wilde. Purely on the basis of their parallel experiences as children with famous musician fathers. Kim's dad Marty Wilde, the fifties pop star; Ross McManus, Elvis's dad, trumpet player in the Joe Loss Orchestra, then bandleader, through a similar era.)

ELVIS COSTELLO: And I knew as my family . . . my dad's family is from Birkenhead. That's one of the towns which became depressed due to the absence of the shipyard industry. Others where it was a much bigger employer, like Newcastle, like Glasgow, like Belfast, obviously saw it. The yards were still there in some cases, but things had changed and the projection of the idea, the horrible irony, perhaps a more prolonged war.

It wasn't that hard to imagine there being a need to both provide the means to get the people to the conflict, and the people to actually take part in the conflict.

In my understanding of history, in British history particularly, they nearly always get a working-class boy to do the killing.

*

(Clive Langer had written the melody to what became 'Shipbuilding' and drafted his own words. Then he met Elvis at a party, convinced him to go outside and listen to a cassette demo on Clive's car stereo. Elvis then went

away and tried out his own version. 'The best lyrics I've ever written,' he said. I wouldn't argue with that.)

The song was first released in August 1982 and didn't make a dent in the charts. Hardly going to be A-list playlist material. Rough Trade re-released it the following year, when 'Shipbuilding' peaked at number 35 in the Top 40.

That's the not uncommon story of some later legendary pop records, only ever reaching the lower ends of the sales charts. The furore and the BBC's dilemma over whether to play it reached other heights. Robert Wyatt was by now in a wheelchair after falling out of a building and breaking his back. A wheelchair artiste was not exactly in keeping with *Top of the Pops'* breezy policy of putting on the dancing girls if things looked a bit dicey. But 'Shipbuilding' could not be denied nor ignored. To me, it's one of the most significant popular songs ever written. By anyone.

ELVIS COSTELLO: Both my grandfathers served in the First World War. One was badly wounded. The other spent four years on a German farm, having been captured. It wasn't my direct experience. They had work in the twenties. In fact, one grandfather never was out of work because of the dangerous kind of work he did.

He was a gas main layer, and therefore he was in a reserved occupation in the Second War, given the job of turning off the gas in bombed buildings, when Liverpool was bombed in the forties.

So I am blessed in that I've had a very lucky life, where nothing has been hard. The freedom I've had to do what I do is on the foundation of the work that my parents and grandparents did.

It's not like I'm telling a sad story about, 'Oh, we used to live in a shoebox.' Because I never did. But I am aware of exactly the relationship to the sea. My great-grandfather was killed on the docks in Birkenhead. The travelling in music was set in train on my father's side of our family.

Due to that, my grandfather was an orphan, became a boy soldier, then later a ship's musician. My father became a musician. I became a musician. We're all in a sense in an occupation now. It would be arrogant to call yourself a working-class person, but I am a working man.

*

(A year after the Robert Wyatt version release of 'Shipbuilding', Elvis recorded his own version for his album Punch the Clock. *He added a new solo instrument by the coolest jazz trumpeter Chet Baker, having seen a gig of his in London advertised in* Melody Maker.*)*

ELVIS COSTELLO: The trumpet was the instrument that I thought it should be, because it's the instrument that I should play. I'm the one in the family that didn't learn to play it. That's my big failure.

He [Chet Baker] had ended up doing some impromptu dates in Covent Garden so I just went down there and watched him play a really beautiful set. Then he just got up from the stand after he'd finished, went over to the bar and he was just standing there. People were not bothering him at all, not even talking to him so I went over and introduced myself and of course he had absolutely no idea who I was, and I didn't expect he would do.

I asked him if he would come and play on our record and he said: yes.

We agreed a fee, you know, because he didn't have a manager. I asked him how much he wanted.

He said, 'How about scale?' Union minimum.

And I said, 'How about double scale?'

He was happy to take the minimum and he just came to the studio and played what he played.

Maybe it was an inevitable process [the war], but the way in which it was done was with very little humanity, and respect of the work that people had put in.

People talk about the sacrifice, and our heroes, our brave boys. All of those clichés which are used to try and bring people to attention to the service of servicemen and women, that are now serving in the wars currently, there's another kind of service that's gone on generation after generation.

Who the hell built the ships? Those people did. They were serving too.

14

Montserrat – Emerald of the Caribbean

It was called the emerald isle of the Caribbean. Was. Because of its brilliant natural greenery. And because of Irish settlers there, who continued to celebrate St Patrick's Day annually.

I am fascinated and drawn like many folks to areas of great natural beauty. Where flora and fauna flourish. Where the ground is rich in minerals. Where the best grapes grow, the tastiest fruits. And rare orchis flower . . . And where my favourite, bougainvillea, tumbles over walls. Which in turn attract the most exotic and spectacular butterflies, insects and wildlife. All those life-affirming natural resources.

One problem with all that: *why*? These places are invariably on fault lines. Where the earth's tectonic plates move and grind over our imperfect and unstable planet's crust.

The most conserved beautiful places are so often the most dangerous. From volcanic eruptions, pouring forth the nutrients in the hot magma from the earth's core. (About which we still know so little.) But also, the most vulnerable to earthquakes, hurricanes, tornadoes and tsunamis. The ring of fire around the Pacific Ocean . . . Hawaii, Indonesia, Thailand, California, Japan, New Zealand; then also Italy and Sicily. Turkey, the Canary Islands. And notably the Caribbean. Also, there are dangerous volcanoes all over the world from Alaska to the Philippines to Mexico, and much of the rest of Africa and South America.

And to think that, apart from Vesuvius, we've only known about huge natural disasters — the effects of tsunamis and exploding volcanoes — for the last two or three hundred years.

But now we do know — and still build cities on fault lines, like Los Angeles on the San Andreas line streaking down the California coast, even knowing about the huge earthquake disaster in San Francisco in 1906 . . . No new home buyer in the LA region (where they still talk about the Northridge quake in the Valley in 1994) wouldn't not look into earthquake possibilities or take out earthquake insurance if they could afford it. And there's a wealth of the tech giants in Silicon Valley . . . *why there*?

Densely populated Japan has suffered huge earthquakes and tsunami disasters.

So why do we, or they, do it? Plot up in these regions? Because traditionally folk migrated to and built their cities near and around outpourings of such rich natural resources to grow the most profitable crops, some of the best wine, figs, olives, bananas, melons, peppers, and find the purest water. Not to mention the healing qualities of volcanic mud.

Those sharp outcrops from crystal-clear seas where tropical fish swim in abundance, such spectacular backdrops for holiday destinations . . . It's paradise, isn't it?

Is that why George Martin decide to build the world's most exclusive recording studio on Montserrat? The island lies in the Antilles, nearest to Antigua.

The almost perfect natural arc of the Lesser Antilles islands themselves resemble a tall palm tree trunk bending over, yielding to a high wind, a hurricane. Whipped up from the cold waves of the Atlantic, the Antilles seem to be protecting the intense blue tranquillity of the Caribbean Sea to the west.

Yes, some of the most spectacular scenery on earth. But at a price. Grab the tasty lobsters, live off the ripe fruit. Be a beach bum.

But don't be surprised if the great angry monster that lives in the top of that perfect triangle of a mountain above suddenly rears up, breathes fire, smoke and lightning into the sky, and hurls rocks and thick black magma to rain down on the land below.

A pyroclastic flow, covering and suffocating everything in its wake. That surely was the folklore of the Caribbean islands. Before we knew about tectonic plates.

I don't know how much research George Martin had done when he, a keen yachtsman, decided to drop anchor beside Montserrat. And to add to his Oxford Street, London premises, an alternative base for his company, AIR Studios, on this tiny tropical island. It was a bit of a thing at the time, building remote recording studios; there were a couple in the south of France, and Compass Point studio on the pink sanded land of the Bahamas, near Nassau, had done rather well. Chris Blackwell's studio had created successes for Grace Jones and Bob Marley . . .

And really Montserrat's dominant but dormant volcano Soufrière Hills had not erupted for centuries.

Yet not that far away, the neighbouring island of Martinique had experienced the worst volcanic eruption disaster of the twentieth century.

Thirty thousand residents had been wiped out in less than twenty minutes when a volcano erupted onto the city of St Pierre. Of only three people who escaped, one was locked inside, as it turned out, the safety of a stone-walled prison cell.

And that mountain, Mount Pelée, had not erupted for centuries either.

George Martin went ahead anyway and built his studio complex on Montserrat, near enough to be convenient to the capital Plymouth, to the nearby harbour/port, and to the tiny airport, beside the slim airstrip/runway halfway up the side of the mountain.

No jets, mind. No holiday packages. None of that. The landing strip could only accommodate the smallest of airplanes, mostly flown from Antigua, less than an hour's flying time away.

And whether he was expecting it or not, the world's rock stars flocked to this tiny island, so totally free of distractions: the media, accountants, lawyers, problems . . . reality, really. The musicians could record in the two-storey white stone complex by day, or swim, or go fishing or out in a boat, or get stoned, or drive up into the rainforest in a Mini-Moke (mini open-top jeep). At night, a long table was laid out for dinner on the floor above the studio overlooking the swimming pool, and open to the elements. Breezily further away the blue horizon shimmered. The wine flowed, and jokes were cracked.

Paul McCartney was one of the first visitors and AIR Studios clients to record there. It was a safe refuge for him after the death of John Lennon. And he had partnered up with George Martin as producer again. Macca took his family and then began inviting other players. Maybe it was more of an enticement than trafficy Oxford Street AIR in London.

One of his most prized guests was Carl Perkins.

Carl Perkins! One of those musicians The Beatles, before they were The Beatles, had idolised. The band would take a Carl Perkins record round to anyone's house that had a record player, in the whole of Liverpool — three bus journeys away, if necessary. Just for the chance to play the same Carl Perkins' record, over and over again, ear to the speaker. Trying to catch the words, guess them, write them down, learn these rockabilly lyrics and inflections, and then master the music for their own fledgling beat group.

Tunes like 'Matchbox', 'Blue Suede Shoes', 'Honey Don't' became part of The Beatles' early repertoire, and songs they sang on their endlessly required BBC radio sessions.

Carl's invitation to Montserrat was gladly accepted. Although he had been a real teen idol and musical inspiration to The Beatles, life had not been quite as bountiful to him as his contemporaries, Elvis Presley and Johnny Cash.

He'd been in that triumvirate until a car crash which injured him badly and killed his brother. By the time Carl recovered, that fifties rock 'n' roll boom had peaked, moved on, and he had been left behind.

Another of Paul's guests to Montserrat was Stevie Wonder. There they recorded 'Ebony and Ivory'. Stevie was a regular prankster to Paul and was famously so late for Sunday lunch at the McCartney's home on the island that the occasion turned into a late singalong dinner instead.

The local Montserratians, hearing about these superstar arrivals, believed they were coming to perform a live concert there. But the sweeping Southern-style villa that housed the studio did not have room for a concert venue. It had barely enough studio space to house a whole band. Sometimes one member or another would crouch on the stairwell to record their part.

By the time I'd been invited there, AIR Montserrat was already a success. The clients, when not in the studio, sat around what must have been one of the most photographed pool sides in the world. I still recall the ceramic tile pattern on the perimeter wall. The diving board became a place for rock bands to perch on, for endless snapshots.

So enamouring were the surroundings that Elton John met and proposed to the studio engineer Renate Blauel. And married her briefly before realising this was rather an error, as he was gay . . . Ruth Clapton, daughter of Eric, was conceived there. I made lifelong friends with her mum, the then studio manager Yvonne.

A potent community, in a small space.

The point of Air Montserrat was that it had, at the time, the best studio equipment in the world. With George Martin, The Beatles' producer, in situ, on a remote tropical island? Irresistible.

And so it was to Dire Straits, Michael Jackson, The Rolling Stones, Pretenders, Ultravox and The Police, who made their fifth and last album *Synchronicity* there. Having witnessed so much of The Police's early career, filmed a world tour with them, kept in touch with them, their road crew, guitar techs and drum techs, the whole touring family, it was a fascinating album to listen to. On a Walkman.

Looking out over the island, with the same view, from the terrace above the pool, at Montserrat studios, where they had recorded these songs. Their music in my headphones. The same music that they'd made in this very spot. A bit like looking through Gary Gilmore's eyes. Well, not quite, but . . . weird.

The *Synchronicity* track that felt most Montserratian was 'Wrapped Around Your Finger', quite a nasty little number about remote coercion, or revenge, something similar. A couple of lines that seemed to fit the location, about the deep-blue sea and vanishing in the air . . . But it wasn't so much the words, it was the melancholic descending arpeggios of Andy Summers's guitar playing/effects pedal that remain, for me, so poignantly evocative . . . of that soon-to-be doomed island.

I had to be somewhat diplomatic about what I was listening to, on my headphones. I was here on Montserrat to report on the making of another album, by a different band . . . Duran Duran.

I don't think anyone there gave any thought to the mountain above, away in the hills. Only Jimmy Buffet, who recorded on the island too, and wrote a tune about a volcano erupting. Cheerful catchy calypso style, George Martin commented: a bit too prophetic . . .

I was transfixed by the native iguanas, crested like miniature green dragons. They would stalk about, entering your rented accommodation as they wished, doing as they pleased, going where they wanted to roam. Fair enough, it was their natural habitat, not ours. I was fascinated by the trees in bright red leaf, and the black volcanic beaches ground over millions of years into a sort of dark crystal dust.

For Duran Duran this was their 'difficult third album'. Chris Blackwell had said about artists arriving to record at Compass Point: don't come here looking for inspiration. Make sure you've brought it with you. The same seemed to be true of AIR Studios, Montserrat.

In fact Duran brought Compass Point's most famed engineer/producer Alex Sadkin to oversee their work on Montserrat.

The result was a number 1 album back home and fairly terrible reviews. It took another bumpy decade and some harsh reality to give the Birmingham band back some down-to-earth focus that produced their track 'Ordinary World', which re-established them and their self-esteem.

Life on Montserrat continued with the international visitors making the scary plane hop from Antigua. Until the arrival of Hurricane Hugo in September 1989.

It was named the worst hurricane to hit the Caribbean in a hundred years. Montserrat was slap bang in the centre of the storm and took the full force of 145-mile-an-hour winds.

The hurricane ripped the roofs off 90 per cent of all structures. Homes, churches, schools, hotels, shops. The storm ripped the water supply tanks from their outdoor installations and threw them down a hill. The harbour was torn to bits, and the airport control tower toppled. All communications were lost. There were fatalities, despite the hurricane shelters I'd seen on the streets of Plymouth. The population waited to be evacuated to neighbouring islands. But not everyone wanted to leave their home.

The Brits who had recorded at AIR Montserrat went into action. And took over the Royal Albert Hall in London with a concert for Montserrat. Sadly ironic that the Montserratians who had hoped for a concert from these stars on their own island were unlikely to get to London to see them at the Albert Hall either.

McCartney played, Mark Knopfler, Sting, many more, and Carl Perkins. The last major performance he ever gave. George Martin donated annotated signed copies of the original score of The Beatles' 'Yesterday'. The event raised a million pounds to help the Montserratians shore up their lives.

The rebuild began . . . There was criticism that the British government — Montserrat being a British protectorate — had not done enough to help. Locals also pointed out that they would rather stay on neighbouring islands to get work than be shipped to the UK, where they were concerned they would, if not adequately skilled, end up 'on welfare'.

Worse was to come. So much worse.

Just six years after the devastation wrought by Hurricane Hugo, the volcano blew. The Soufrière Hills, which had been dormant for four hundred years.

The pyroclastic flow poured down the mountain, metres-deep lava. That enveloped and destroyed almost half the island. The southern half, the half where the studio was, by the circular houses set in green lawns where we had stayed, and the capital, 'the 'city centre' of Plymouth, was now buried under metres of grey-brown ash. 'The Pompeii of the Caribbean' it's been called by the gawper tourists who have found a way back there with video cameras and drones. All the crops and island produce were covered. No yacht could sail in, no ferry could putter into the rebuilt jetty. That was gone.

Any hope that AIR Studios could be renovated, revived, was now most definitely over. The finessed electronic equipment in the control room, all rusted. And ruined. The piano keys and strings covered in mould. The swimming pool filled with brown sludge. Its once visible turquoise walls now murky green with algae.

Some Montserratians migrated to the UK. I met one of their daughters, a manicurist in west London.

'We'd love to go back there to settle,' she said. The safer north of Montserrat is being redeveloped. But the whole southern half remains under lava. A huge, totally desolate exclusion zone. The volcano remains active, puffing and venting steam from its slopes and shooting out rivulets of liquid fire, molten-red lava pouring, like a gigantic neon light show, from its peak. A disturbing, unearthly sight against the darkness of night.

I've always been fascinated by volcanoes. Marvelled at the beauty of Mount Fuji in Japan; been awed at a ring of them among the Andes in Chile. Fried an egg, tourist style, on the hot stone mountainside on Tenerife. Hung around the brooding heights of Etna.

And I took a night boat trip around the spectacular Stromboli, one of the volcanic Aeolian Islands off Sicily. Somewhat flippantly. The nightly eruptions from Stromboli are so regular that I did wonder if the locals perhaps made sure we got a good eye view by augmenting any natural display with manmade fireworks. So the tourists wouldn't be disappointed.

Then Stromboli showed it really wasn't kidding; it barrelled forth a much more violent sudden eruption, and killed an afternoon hiker, in 2019.

Like a sign, saying:

Danger. Keep your distance.

— 15 —

Karl Hyde Part 1 – a Hieroglyph Named Freur

Interior. Day. Small audio recording studio cubicle, London W1. I sit opposite Karl Hyde from Underworld. We are recording a radio interview in the mid-twenty-teens, to recall our first and subsequent meetings from 1983 onwards . . .

ANNIE: Karl Hyde from Underworld, one of my dearest friends in life generally. Can I take you back to when we first met, because it became quite a long story, that I didn't expect it was going to at the time. Would you like to say the name of the band that you were in when I met you?

KARL: Well, the name of the band that we were in was a group called Freur.

ANNIE: You were supposed to *say* it as a kind of *sound*, rather than a written-down word?

KARL: Yeah, it was one of those things where when a band spends for ever trying to find a name. And we did that.
 Then one day we gave up. And said to Rick [Smith], who's still my partner, 'Anything you say from now on: the first thing you say . . . is the name of the band.'
 And he went '*Freur!*' We went, oh God! OK. And that was that.

ANNIE: And there was a sort of icon . . .

KARL: A hieroglyph. A way of notating it graphically, because we didn't have a normal name. The record label — we were signed to CBS at the time — they were fantastic. They had these blocks made with the hieroglyph so that when we appeared in the charts, they could print this hieroglyph. And when the newspapers printed our name they printed this funny little squiggle. Which actually came out more like a smudge than a squiggle!

ANNIE: Well, I'm glad you said . . . I didn't want to say the word 'squiggle' because it sounds a bit disrespectful compared with hieroglyph!

KARL: No, it was a squiggle.

ANNIE: So this was in the eighties?

KARL: Yeah, it was, well, '82 we signed to CBS. Went off to Germany to work with the legendary Conny Plank. Which, strangely, didn't work out. We came back and they let us record the album ourselves with Rick producing it. That was the first full album that he produced, at Mayfair Studios. Spending thousands and thousands of pounds — fresh off the dole!

ANNIE: Fresh off the dole? And you'd been at art college before that?

KARL: Mm, I'd spend five years at art college. It was quite a radical course really. For anyone who knows that area, it was based on the philosophy of the Black Mountain College. So people who were working in cross-discipline at the Black Mountain College . . . people like John Cage and Robert Rauschenberg, Franz Kline . . . and it was a very interdisciplinary philosophy. So there were no boundaries.

And we ended up in this place in Cardiff called the Third Area. So we were in a part of the college where they basically put the misfits. Who became performance artists and film-makers. I was working with early video, as an installation artist.

We had our own theatre with quadraphonic sound and synthy EMS synths like Brian Eno used. We kind of thought it was normal to be working with quadraphonics and tape recorders. We didn't know that it was such a special course. So that's what I evolved out of.

ANNIE: Into the brutal world of pop music . . .

KARL: It was rubbish (*laughs*). It was really rubbish! But fortunately, Rick, who was in the band that I formed at that time, after leaving art school — he'd had enough. He went off and started experimenting with electronics. I asked if I could join *his* band. He left *my* band and I joined his band.

ANNIE: That became Freur! At some point, either your manager or you, or someone said: would I like to come on tour with you and be the sort of touring DJ with you? I don't know whose idea it was.

KARL: It could have been the manager, or it could have been the label. The label were pretty cool. It was people like Muff Winwood at the time who was looking after us, along with Dave Novik. They really were cool people, and it was a really bonkers and fabulous idea. It was like wow, yeah, that's kind of nutty. Let's do that.

We were fans of yours for years, so it was like wow, oh OK, 'Do you think she'll say yeah?'

Well no, of course she won't. And then . . . you did!

ANNIE: Well, I was thrilled as well. I'd never done that before . . . So off we went, all over England and Wales.

We got as far as Loughborough University. This was the crucial night. You were setting up on your part of the stage. I had my DJ booth at a sort of angle. And I leaned over to you to say: 'Will you be ready in ten minutes?' or something like that, 'Or, shall I play a couple more tunes?'

But, in leaning over, I didn't realise . . . I'd run out of stage. There wasn't anything [underneath] and I plunged downwards.

And thought . . . this is like *Alice in Wonderland*. Alice falls down the rabbit hole.

And that, we're only at the beginning of the tour. I hope I don't break anything. It wasn't like thirty metres down, but I did hit my back on a fire extinguisher on the way.

What was so fortunate was that it was Loughborough, which is a sports university and had a 24-hour sort of A & E, because they had so many athletes there. So thank goodness for them!

KARL: Yeah, you picked the right place to have an accident!

ANNIE: They patched me up, and the greatest thing was the next day when we set off. I was allowed to sit in the front of the van! Because I'd had this injury . . .

KARL: I've held a grudge against you ever since!

ANNIE: You gave up your seat on the front, the sort of bench seat at the front. That was very good of you, Karl, and I appreciate that!

KARL: We had that big Chevy Blazer 4 × 4 that we were driving around in . . . a big American truck. Yeah, a big old American jacked-up truck.

ANNIE: Well, to me it was like the real thing, rock 'n' roll tour. You, at the time, were wearing very interesting stage-wear . . . Would you like to reminisce about that?

KARL: When Freur formed, remember at that time there were bands like Joy Division and Echo and the Bunnymen. It was a whole very black scene. At the time I found it slightly dour and a bit serious. On reflection I see the other side of it, but at that time I was really sick of it all being a bit black and down.

We'd been on the dole for such a long time that we decided we'd go in the completely opposite direction and just wear the brightest colours we possibly could — freaked-out hair, lip gloss, diamante jewellery. Pearls and heels . . . we were just having fun. We were boys dressing up. Which was always interesting when you went down the pub like that. But it was fun, you know. It was fun.

ANNIE: I remember a red shiny . . . what was that material?

KARL: Oh plastic, yeah. It was like a leatherette. Very tight leatherette. It was kind of quite . . . a bit S & M in a way, I suppose it was, crossed with a bit of lizard and it was just fun. 'Let's see what the maddest stuff that we could wear as boys on stage is.'

ANNIE: I wish we had some photographs . . .

KARL: Oh, they're all over the internet!

ANNIE: You had long hair and you all crimped your hair and you crimped my hair as well. So I felt more part of the band and that was very thrilling as well.

KARL: You were always part of the band.

ANNIE: So then . . . Freur eventually was no more? Freur finished?

KARL: Yeah, it did. We had a lot of things that just didn't go right really. What was it they said? We were ahead of our time, or just crap? It was one of the two. I can't remember which one . . .

ANNIE: Well, maybe it's that kind of, you know, the path that has to be taken before you become international superstars.

KARL: It was really important. We made a lot of mistakes in the eighties that stood us in fantastic stead at the beginning of the nineties. Without the mistakes that we made — and we made lots — we would have made some terrible mistakes and thrown away a career at the beginning of the nineties.

ANNIE: So would you say the eighties were pretty tough? I mean, I am not such a huge fan of the eighties.

KARL: I hated them.

ANNIE: You hated them?

KARL: I hated the eighties.

ANNIE: In my sort of 'what are your favourite decades' the eighties is not near the top for me.

KARL: There was some music that I liked. The early electronic pop. I liked early Soft Cell, Human League, BEF. There were some interesting things. And that winter that we went to work with Conny Plank in Cologne, he loaned us a car.

He said, 'Look, I've put a cassette in the car, there's this new band and I just want to know what you think of them. They're calling themselves the Eurythmics. Just let me know what you think of them. I've just finished their first album.'

We were . . . 'Oh, they're very good actually. Yes. They're very, very good.' And, 'Yes, I think they'll go far.' And of course at the end of the eighties we fast-forward to where we became a band called Underworld that signed to Sire Records, that was kind of a hybrid funk pop group, we supported the Eurythmics on their farewell tour of America, which was also the end of us. We imploded on that tour.

ANNIE: Well, rock 'n' roll is full of these kind of stories. So, anyway, in the bit of the story that I know about, so, Freur was no more. Then you were living in somewhere like Bexhill for some reason.

KARL: That's right, yeah.

ANNIE: And you used to phone me up when I lived in Brighton and you were all sparky and bright and 'Hello, how you doing?' What I didn't know, and you told me a long time afterwards, was that you were practically starving, guys.

KARL: We had the gas turned off. We traded in the jacked-up Chevy for a series 7 BMW. We were back on the dole. We didn't have a penny and we were driving round in this series 7 (!) and then the heater matrix blew so we had no air con in the car so in winter we had to drive round wrapped in blankets with the windows down so the windscreen wouldn't steam up.

We came home one day, and the gas had been cut off, the meter had been taken because we couldn't pay the bills. So we huddled round one of those portable gas heaters.

Fortunately, one of the guys in the band, Alfie, had signed up to one of those mail order catalogues and he got one of those free slow cookers that takes for ever to cook. What do they call them? Pressure cookers? So that's how we ate.

We ate with one of those and lived on coffee. But you were the only connection that we had to a world that we looked like we were never gonna be part of. You were always incredibly kind to us. Just to hear your voice on the end of the phone cheered me up frankly.

And I lost it at that point. I really lost it. I got quite bad depression and completely lost it, and it was things like hearing your voice on the end of the telephone, that sort of made me think, OK, there are some nice people and they do like us and maybe it's worth carrying on.

ANNIE: Of course I had no idea that you were in this state. You were still being very cheery and cheerful. If I had known, as I have mentioned to you before, then I'd have said, right, come and live with me in my house in Brighton.

KARL: No, we couldn't do that.

ANNIE: Well other people did! So you might just as well have done. I just still feel bad that I didn't know that you were going through such a terrible time.

Now the next time I saw you was I bumped into you in the tube in Notting Hill Gate and you went, 'We've just formed this band called Underworld.'

And from then on everything seemed to go right.

— 16 —

Lucy in the Sky

Full of Elgar's echoing pomp and circumstance. Home of the Proms, the pop classics concerts broadcast every summer where you can 'promenade', i.e. take up standing-room-only space on the flat floor area of this vast hamburger-shaped building in Kensington, west London. Right opposite, Queen Victoria, or rather a seated statue of her, looks on, you feel, sternly. Making sure no shenanigans should go on inside to desecrate the memory of her adored Albert.

But beneath that dome of respectability there have been all sorts of goings-on at which she would have raised her sceptre, if not her orb, in horror.

Well, the Orb, actually, for a start. This collective of space-orientated futuristic creators of ambient dub music held a memorable gig there in 1998.

I have never inhaled so many fumes from weed just by sitting in an audience, anywhere. Clouds of aromatic smoke rose from the floor of the hall and permeated all around the draped curtains of the private boxes which turn this grey dome into one the most beautiful concert spaces in the world.

But the RAH had seen worse there and so had I.

Every documentary about the 1950s paints Britain and London as a drab, dreary place, blanketed by austerity in the first post-Second World War decade.

Oh no, it wasn't!

Not where I was coming from. By the late fifties there were jazz clubs, coffee bars, the club on Eel Pie Island (so fortuitously located on my doorstep in Twickenham), riverboat shuffles, wild house parties, Thames water pageants . . . and the beginning of rave culture.

None more so than at one particular event at the Royal Albert Hall at the very tail end of 1958. For the past fifty years the Chelsea Arts Club had held New Year's Eve costume balls there.

These had seemingly become more and more decadent over the first half of the twentieth century. The words 'art' and 'bohemian' seemed to attract a very cosmopolitan underground crowd. More the kind you'd expect in Paris or Berlin than post-Blitz London. The themes of the arts ball would be different every year, and London art colleges were invited to each make a tableau, a float, to parade around the Albert Hall on New Year's Eve.

Well, every kind of person showed up. Wearing exotic 'costume' or very little. Though midwinter, the crowd was sprinkled with very scanty bikini wearers, and many of the girls in the crowd were barefoot and bare-chested. I tagged along with my art school friend Janice.

I was quite demure in just sloppy sweater and black tights, with no skirt over the top. It was the greatest chance to parade publicly in make-up, dresses, corsetry, false eyelashes, fishnets, high heels . . . Anything went. And that was among the males.

The part of the evening that bewildered me the most was the Trashing of the Tableaux. We paraded our floats around the hall, having spent weeks of pre-Christmas evenings creating them from paint and metal and paper. But after one circuit among the 5000-strong revellers, they were gleefully set upon, smashed and torn to pieces by a less than arty-looking rugby player gang. There was actual fighting on the dance floor. And open displays of homosexuality. Illegal for many more years to come.

So much of a tut-tutted debacle was it, that this was the last ever Chelsea Arts NYE ball at the Royal Albert Hall. It was later described as being like a giant acid house party. It sure was a curtain raiser to rave.

RAH has been the backdrop to so many varying events in my life. In the nineties I was asked to step onto its stage to introduce a surprise guest spot from a solo Chrissie Hynde. All I had to say was: 'Ladies and gentlemen, will you please welcome Chrissie Hynde.'

I had introduced rock and music acts probably dozens of times before. Roxy Music at the Hammersmith Apollo, Tom Waits at the Shepherd's Bush BBC Theatre and different bands every week in the *Old Grey Whistle Test* studios. It was kind of my job.

But walking out into that huge Albert Hall auditorium, encircled by backlit silhouetted punters, encased in their draped and swathed boxes, was quite a daunting moment. As appearing at Shea Stadium with the Clash was.

The vertically upward array of stacked rows and rows of seating, the tier upon tier of faces rising up and up and up almost to the sky in front of you, take your breath away. I found MC'ing at Wembley Stadium, with a much larger, but looped U-shaped audience, far less intimidating.

Anyway, I wrote Chrissie's name, that I knew so well, on my hand, in biro, just in case I had a whiteout at the wrong moment. It was fine and she was great.

My most significant trip to the Royal Albert Hall centred around The Beatles' song 'Lucy in the Sky with Diamonds' – from *Sgt. Pepper's Lonely Hearts Club Band*. The LP that was The Beatles at their most psychedelic?

Possibly because the initial capital letters of 'Lucy in the Sky with Diamonds' spell out LSD, right?

Well no, actually.

The cynics still don't believe the protestations. Height of psychedelia, of course the song title *must* refer to acid.

Not according to John Lennon. Who wrote it. So he should know, and he told me so. Lennon was living in Weybridge, Surrey, at the time of the song's creation. What you might call an upscale suburb of south-west London, close to the Thames. His son Julian, then three, was old enough to go to kindergarten/nursery school. He had come home with a painting newly created that day.

As toddlers will, he held it out proudly to show his parents.

'It's Lucy,' he said, 'in the sky, with diamonds.'

For John, ever alert to inspiration for a unique or magical-sounding phrase, it registered straight away as a song title. Julian was later to inspire another Beatles classic, 'Hey Jude', written by Paul McCartney to console Julian when his parents split. And indeed, a third, 'Goodnight', after they had.

It didn't take much to deduce that Julian had painted a picture of one of his school mates, named Lucy.

As John recounted to me. So . . . horse's mouth. He also said to me, laughing about it:

'When it was pointed out that the title spelt out LSD, we went through all our other songs, to see what they spelt out!'

This point is still not taken on board by Beatles superfans, and Beatles completists, to this day. It is so much more convenient to believe that this was another secret conspiratorial message from The Beatles, advocating dropping acid.

Well, I would not take bets against the abstract, surreal lyrical references to newspaper taxis and marmalade skies being trip-inspired. But Lewis Carroll, Lennon said many times, was the source of much of his surrealism, though it was Paul McCartney who added the newspaper/marmalade lyrics.

This episode triggered one of the most significant confrontations The Beatles had with the media. Paul was asked by a TV reporter how he felt about spreading the word to a whole generation over taking the drug.

He batted this right back, stating that it was the mass media broadcasting the information who were at fault, not The Beatles.

They would have preferred to keep this activity to themselves. But once directly confronted . . . they refused to lie.

'*You* are the ones spreading this,' said McCartney, really riled, to an ITN reporter. One of the very few times he has ever lost his cool in front of news media.

The child who had inspired this controversy was then four years old and of course completely oblivious.

Lennon also pointed out to me, which was not so widely known *then*, that *Sgt. Pepper* had been inspired not so much by drugs, but by the Beach Boys' *Pet Sounds*.

'The Beatles were always influenced by other people. There was never a time when they were not. When I made "Cold Turkey" I was influenced by "Amazing Grace".

'Well . . . when I was about halfway through making "Cold Turkey", and the Great Awakening [version recorded circa 1969] . . . and the Lee Dorsey record "Everything I Do Gohn Be Funky".

'Whenever I make a record, I've always got a preconceived other person's record to imitate. Or one of our own. I'll go into the studio and do "Strawberry Fields" again, or "Walrus" again. So I've got something to anchor with.

'It never turns out like the original. We never ended up sounding like the original, like Elvis or Chuck Berry.'

This interview happened several years after *Sgt. Pepper* had been recorded. Since then we'd had the White Album, *Abbey Road* and 'Get Back'. And The Beatles had broken up.

Or were on hiatus. And John was by now ambivalent as to the importance of the *Pepper* album. He felt that the White Album, or his tracks on it, were his best work with The Beatles.

But this hadn't answered the question, as to who was the real Lucy who had inspired the painting, and the song? I had a vested interest in this. I had named my daughter Lucy partially after the song. Partly the song, and partly for my Russian friend and mentoress Lusia.

For me it became a quest to find the real Diamond Lucy. The song became a solo classic, later an international number 1 for Elton John. But no one had ever seemed to seek out the little girl who must have inspired it.

It should not be, I decided, too difficult to find her. Check out the school where Julian had attended, go through the register for the years 1966—67 and track down any Lucys who had been in Julian's class.

But it was not so simple, some two decades later, when I set about my search.

The school, Heath House in the Portmore Park area of Weybridge, was run from the fifties till certainly the late sixties by two sisters, sounding straight out of a Jane Austen novel, named Miss Delta and Miss Sylvia. It was a private fee-paying school with an open-air swimming pool and what was called the 'jungle gym'. There were two 'classic' old cars in the school play area which the children were encouraged to climb in and out of.

John often collected Julian on the school run in his psyche-delic painted Rolls-Royce. The comedian Charlie Drake sent his sons Christopher and Stephen to Heath House also. The uniform was most notable for its bright red blazers.

But by now, in the eighties, the building had been demolished. So . . . how to find the authentic Lucy?

I slapped my hand to my head.

Use the *media*, dummy!

I charged enthusiastically into the daytime Radio 1 studios and launched the topic with the then presenters.

The search for Lucy was now *on*. Official. An appeal for her to come forward was now being broadcast all over the UK. What I hadn't anticipated was the legions of Lucys who came out of the sky and the earth and the woodwork, with and without diamonds, *all* claiming to be The One.

'It was *me*.'

'I was Lucy in the sky!'

'Actually I was!'

At the time of the painting, there were several credible witnesses. Pete Shotton, John Lennon's best mate from Liverpool and Quarrymen days had been at the Lennons' house, Kenwood, and seen it. Paul McCartney knew the true provenance, too, when the band recorded the song early in 1967.

But by now, in the mid-eighties it was harder to verify. John had died in 1980, Cynthia had moved away from the Weybridge area. Julian was grown up. But he was obviously the only person who would be able to identify the true Lucy muse.

Being the son of a Beatle, to have a successful musical career is probably one of the more difficult things to achieve. Zak Starkey, Ringo's son, being the most successful, feted within his oeuvre as being the natural heir, not so much to his father, but to Keith Moon. Which is why Zak became the drummer with the Who in their latter days.

Keith coincidentally had also lived in Surrey, close by the Lennons' home at St George's Hill. At Tara, the 'airport lounge house' as his wife Kim had called it, in Chertsey.

By 1984 Julian had honed his own craft as a songwriter, released a successful album called *Valotte* and scored a memorable hit with 'Too Late for Goodbyes'. He'd become a big name in the US. He was due to play at the Royal Albert Hall.

A young woman called Lucy O'Donnell had heard about my search for the song muse Lucy, and got in touch. She was the daughter of GP and writer/broadcaster Michael O'Donnell. She lived in Weybridge and had been at Heath House school with Julian.

She was a lovely, vibrant young woman, flaxen haired with expressive brown eyes, and only too keen to talk about her memories of early schooldays with Lennon Jnr.

Ms O'Donnell was understandably more than a little miffed and anguished that so many other girls had claimed to be Lucy of The Beatles song. She was relieved to be able to discuss the matter; keen to be recognised, to be acknowledged.

'All my life I've been saying that I was "the" Lucy, but people wouldn't believe me.'

Her sister Fran said, 'In the family we all knew she was the Lucy in the song. We had the record at home. But we didn't have to play it all the time. My parents were more jazz heads.'

Outside of the family, what Lucy O'Donnell found even more annoying were those who dismissed the lyrics as 'just a drug song'. She felt understandably slighted by this.

There was only one thing for it.

To reunite her with Julian.

'But suppose he doesn't recognise me?' said Lucy. 'We were very small children then. I'm sure we must both look completely different now.'

I contacted Julian, who is as direct and honest and decent as the day is long. A bit too honest for his own good, I warned him when we had finished our first interview. He's an Aries like me. We tend to be somewhat direct. I advised Julian not to be as open with other journalists as he had been with me. Off-the-record confidences are by no means always respected by certain members of the media.

Julian was extremely dubious about meeting Lucy O'Donnell.

'How will I know if she's the right one? What if it's another imposter? This could be very awkward.' He was right.

I was getting somewhat OCD. The idea of finding Lucy had begun as a journalistically motivated story. Now, completely convinced that Lucy O'Donnell was the authentic Lucy, I just wanted to help her prove the veracity of her identity.

This was a piece of Beatles history, after all.

By now I was as anxious as Lucy that the meeting with Julian, which he agreed to, should go well. I arranged to take Lucy backstage to meet him at the Royal Albert Hall.

The last time I was ushered into a RAH box was at a Teenage Cancer Trust charity concert. Paul McCartney was on stage and sitting behind me were the comedian Peter Kay and J.K. Rowling. Both very accommodating and welcoming to me, neither of whom I'd ever met before.

By the end of the evening, Roger Daltrey, the organiser, asked me to invite J.K. aboard ongoing TCT activities. I asked J.K. (or should I have called her Jo?) if she would write her email address for me. The only writing material we had between us was a gold eye shadow pencil. She wrote on the edge of a programme card and handed it to me. For such an inventive wordsmith her email address was hardly going to be j.k.rowling@hotmail.com, was it?

It was some made-up word, as expected, really from the creator of Hogwarts and Dumbledore. I read it back to her, to check, and she said: 'No, you're reading that upside down!'

So now I appeared to be illiterate in front of the world's most successful author.

Julian Lennon has hazel eyes, like his mother's, but looked not unlike his dad at a similar age. It was also hard for him to shake off the inevitable comparisons with his singing voice with his father's. Lucy O'Donnell and I sat stage right near the front, on the floor level of the auditorium, and watched his show. I couldn't really relax. I was apprehensive: if Julian really thought she was not Lucy in the sky with diamonds, it was going to be a very difficult occasion for both of them. A horrible let-down for her.

We waited for the customarily polite amount of time before making a post-show visit, weaving our way backstage, a labyrinthine route up around the side of the building.

I made the introduction. And then I didn't really know if I should hover or leave them alone to chat. It was a quite tense moment.

There was no immediate recognition from Julian.

But then Lucy spoke up: 'Do you remember the teacher with the Mr Spock ears?'

Julian's eyes lit up at this. 'Yes,' he said immediately, and with some relief, 'I do.'

That was enough to trigger his memory and convince him that she was indeed *the* authentic, genuine Lucy. So Ms O'Donnell could feel exonerated, and content at last to know that she had in fact been recognised as the muse for a timeless Beatles classic.

Job done. That should have been the happy conclusion to the story. But in 2004 Lucy became ill with lupus, a particularly pernicious illness of the autoimmune system. Julian had by now set up residence in Monaco. He heard of Lucy's situation through his new personal assistant, Annie Fowler, a friend of Fran O'Donnell.

Hearing that the now married Lucy Vodden was unwell, Julian sent her garden gifts; they had both become fans of plants and gardening. In Lucy's garden at Surbiton the flowers were a welcome distraction from her worsening condition. Lupus took Lucy's life in 2009. She was forty-six years old. Although they had now been in touch again, Lucy never saw Julian again after the Albert Hall reunion.

But that was not to be the end of their connection. Julian's at that time recording partner James Scott Cook had written a song simply entitled 'Lucy'. He and Julian recorded this as a digital single released a few months after Lucy Vodden's passing. Fifty per cent of the proceeds were donated to the Lupus Trust of America.

Lucy had inspired his father; now she inspired Julian to record another song. I discovered recently that the cover art was a reproduction of *the* picture, believed to be the original of Julian's painting.

WHAT? Whaaaat? Really?

Somehow in my quest to find the real Lucy muse, it never even crossed my mind that Julian's original painting might have survived for now more than fifty years. How many children's nursery school pictures, pinned to the kitchen fridge with a 'fun' magnet, last more than a few weeks?

I checked with Lucy's sister Fran.

The picture was lost for a while, she said, and was acquired by a collector. Later it appeared again at an auction and was rumoured to have been bought by David Gilmour of Pink Floyd.

It's on Google, said Fran.

It sure is, a yellow backgrounded page with a vague outline of a woman's head, wearing a necklace. To the right . . . clusters of stars. Ah, the diamonds, then . . . Eyebrow-raisingly precise drawings of five pointed stars from a three-year-old. Julian might well have been guided by Miss Sylvia or Miss Delta. It's charming and ethereal. That's hardly the issue.

Yet where is the original now?

The trail goes cold. At least publicly. There was a reference to Lucy in the Pink Floyd song 'Let There Be More Light' from *Saucerful of Secrets* in 1968, the year after 'Lucy in the Sky with Diamonds' was first released.

It includes the lyric:

For there revealed in glowing robes
Was Lucy in the Sky

Followed by the now seemingly cryptic:

> Oh oh did you ever know know
> Never ever will they . . .
> I cannot say

So just where is that child's simple drawing, a unique and most valuable piece of Beatles' memorabilia, now?

Well if I was David Gilmour and I'd rescued the picture from an anonymous bidder, I'd probably want to keep schtum about it too.

To quote the original Beatles song:

> Look for the girl with the sun in her eyes
> . . . and she's gone

— 17 —

Uri Geller

I'd not had any views one way or the other about the famous spoon bender, Uri Geller. Until one Sunday when I was on a train to Radio 1 to broadcast my radio show, live as usual. I read in a newspaper that Uri was going to conduct an experiment the following Sunday. Whereby he would magically, if you sort of tuned in to him, and believed him, he would, with his unique powers, start up your clock or watch again if it had broken or gone kaput. I had a good watch at the time which had stopped, been repaired, and was broken again, it seemed permanently.

So with nothing to lose, at the appointed time, 3.30 p.m. on the following Sunday, I was again on a regular journey just sitting on a train on my way to the Radio 1 studio.

I followed Uri's instructions. Hold your watch that won't work in your hand, he commanded, study the photograph of him in the paper, and concentrate. Well I did, I held the watch tight, and I swear, it started again.

I was amazed and couldn't wait to get to Radio 1 to see if anyone else had tried the same thing. I wanted to use the airwaves to let Uri know that his experiment had worked, for me anyway. And wondering who else might have tried his psychic test. I was telling the story in the middle of the show, when the studio phone rang.

On the line was a photographer who has been taking part in the experiment with Uri. The photographer said he normally never ever listened to Radio 1. But something made him touch that dial on his car radio, tune in, and he heard my story. At the very moment he was driving back from a secret, ancient place where Uri had stayed to conduct the experiment.

'Oh Stonehenge, you mean,' I said, chatting to him while a record played.

Now the photographer sounded amazed.

'Yes,' he said, 'it *was* Stonehenge, but it was a secret destination. How did you know?'

'Oh, I just guessed, it seemed obvious to me,' I replied.

I asked him to get in touch with Uri Geller and let him know about my watch now keeping more or less perfect time again. That his experiment had worked for me, anyway.

A few days later I was invited to Henley-on-Thames to meet Geller at his house. He was most friendly to me, seemed a genuine good bloke.

And sure, he bent a spoon and gave it me. I guess he had a supply to give away, and gave them away as souvenirs, like autographs, or selfies.

I'd never been very interested in 'magic tricks' or enter-tainers specialising in the supposed 'paranormal'. But to me Uri's powers seemed to extend potentially way beyond showbiz acclaim. I always thought that had he not wished to be in the entertainment world he might well have had more credibility; been regarded as a mystic and given more respect for his talents. He intrigued me.

In the privacy of his own home, with no one else present, he told me of his next planned experiment: to make Big Ben stop dead, just by concentrating, using his mind powers. There was no one else with us, no witnesses when he told me this.

Around two weeks later BBC *Newsbeat* called me to say Uri Geller wanted to get in touch with me again. That afternoon he had driven round Parliament Square in London to do a sort of a recce, a rehearsal in his mind for stopping Big Ben, a sort of practice run. And . . . Big Ben promptly — stopped.

So this became a major news story. Uri Geller claimed, that through his mental prowess, he had stopped the most famous clock in the world.

But how could he prove that this was a deliberate action and not a mechanical malfunction of the meticulously maintained world-famous landmark?

The only person Uri had ever told about his plan, he said, and therefore could be witness that he *had* planned it, that it wasn't just a freak accident, that he forced Big Ben to stop ticking, was . . . me.

That was in the mid-1980s. More recently Uri circled Westminster again. The government adviser Dominic Cummings attracted a lot of attention, saying he wished to recruit more government advisers from a wider gene pool than conventional civil service bods, asking people 'on the frontiers of the science of prediction' to apply, whether or not they regarded themselves as 'super-talented weirdos'.

Who better to apply? Uri Geller did so immediately and, irrepressibly (and perhaps indiscreetly), let the media know straight away.

Uri Geller, now relocated from Henley-on-Thames to Israel, pointed out that he had in the past worked for the CIA, Mossad and the Pentagon.

And that working for the FBI he had used his mind powers to erase KGB computer files, tracked serial killers and attended nuclear disarmament negotiations. Quite the CV.

The Request Show

There had been a request show before mine on Radio 1; it had been named *The Dave Lee Travis Request Show*. He, Dave Lee, was then called up for other duties, so it was passed on to me, supposedly temporarily. I wanted to continue calling it *The Dave Lee Travis Request Show*, sort of ironically. It was just to be a three-month filler, after all.

No, you can't call it that, said the BBC, just go and play some good tunes.

But as it was still to be titled *Request Show*, then, how best to make sure I could gather in, reap in these requests? It meant someone having to go to the bother of finding a sheet of paper. And a *pen*, and an *envelope*, and a *stamp*. So there had to be an investment of someone's time, resources and *money* as well. And then, having to find a letterbox to post it in, too. Bit of a faff, really. And . . . post it to *where* exactly?

We had a postcode that I thought might be memorable enough to spur people into writing in. W1A were the first three digits.

So let's call it *The W1A1AA Show*, or *The W1A4WW Show*, I suggested. The BBC bought this idea for a while. (You can probably see where this is going . . .) Years later we had the exquisite pleasure of the mockumentary satire TV show *W1A* — all about the BBC itself. Mocking itself. The meetings, the endless rounds of meetings, the subtle buck-passing and back-stabbing, the middle management with titles like Head of Better and the divine marketing genius Siobhan Sharpe, who was there to tell the BBC hierarchy: 'No one watches television any more. Like. *No one*. Get over it.' It's still the first part of the postcode of the BBC. I doubt the writers knew I'd had the same idea for a programme title some time before.

But it was a way I thought of conveying an easily remembered address. So difficult to imagine now, a world without email, texts, WhatsApp, Snapchat, Instagram, Facebook, Twitter . . . and the rest. Anyway, the show was just to be a stop gap, while Radio 1 thought of something better to put on, on Sunday evenings, after the Top 40 chart show.

So that immediately created a feeling of freedom. This is only temporary, so let's kick ass, have fun, play what we *really* want to hear — that's *me* in the studio, and *you* the listener. We can maybe do something between us, under the wire, but in plain sight. Almost a conspiracy.

This meant a chance to really *connect*. As I'd always dreamt of, joining the medium of broadcasting for, in the first place. We soon had to drop the W1A part of the title, but the basis was still to be listener requests. It also meant I could play all the best new tunes as well. The listeners needed inspiration to ask for *current* good music, this was not going to be a Golden Oldies show, I was adamant about *that*.

Somehow me and the audience found each other, We bonded. We had a rendezvous at 7 p.m. on Sunday evenings. It was a perfect slot for me at the time. I inherited a huge audience from the Top 40 show. It was up to me and my programme that followed to try to hold on to as many of the listeners as possible. We knew some would 'defect' to TV or family dinner, but would there be a hard core who would stick with me all the way through?

My contract was renewed for another three months. I didn't expect it would be extended further. So we could stay and play, sort fast and loose. For a bit longer.

What began to emerge, though, was a very specific kind of listener. They wanted new music, sure, but they also wanted quirky music; to hear half-forgotten tunes, strange album tracks . . . tunes you would never hear anywhere else on the radio, except maybe on John Peel's shows. But we played the big hits too. Just not the naff ones.

It turned out there was a whole *generation* of people out there who were beginning to stay tuned in. They were knowledgeable about music, they were choosy, and they had a great sense of humour. They were broadminded, open to innovation . . . and they liked hearing about each other. Listeners became regular contributors; it became like a club. They were discerning . . . what a rich seam I had almost accidentally tapped into. It was what I had really joined the BBC for, a place to discover and share music. But I never imagined I'd find a such perfect slot as this.

I kept repeating to the listeners: look, this is *your* show, so take advantage.

And the response was becoming greater week by week.

The listeners had wide musical knowledge. They would send me a page-long list of tunes. I would scan them and think: 'Wow, I could play *all* of these, make up a whole show from the wish list of just one person.' Not that I ever did. But there would be inevitably one track in the list that I didn't know, hadn't heard before. And because the requester's other choices were so impeccable, well then . . . chances are that this odd one out would be pretty terrific as well. This inevitably proved to be the case. So I was broadening my knowledge too.

Just who were these people who were writing in? Well, they were people who already had a pen and paper in front of them.

They were schoolkids, and sixth-formers and students at polys, unis and art colleges, institutes of technology . . . listening to the radio doing their homework, or revising on a Sunday evening at the end of the weekend — as they should have been doing the previous Friday.

We had no format, no 'top of the hour' jingle, no obligatory album track of the week, no regulations, no script. No pre-vetted play list. It just evolved.

Play what you like, they said (not thinking the show would last).

All right! I thought, here goes. So I started playing what I thought were good tunes, and asked people for more, and then they started to arrive by the sack load. This was like a different lifetime then; there can never have been such a vast change in personal communications than in the years spanning the request show. People had to write letters and post them. Now there are hardly even any post offices.

The listeners thought that because there was such a volume received at Radio 1, that any individual wouldn't have much chance of being noticed. Unless they illustrated their letter with something weird and crazy. In fact, I read every single letter and card, because I wanted to know *who* they were, *what* they were suggesting, *why, where* they were writing from. All my journalistic instincts and basic skills and sheer curiosity came into play, and it was to me incredible and invaluable feedback and research . . .

I was thrilled people bothered to write in at all, when all they could expect back was, at best, having their tune played and their name mentioned. Was it really a good enough return for their effort?

And there was another element. On past shows, where listeners' correspondence was read out by a presenter, the originals were scrapped, replaced by carefully typed-out, pristine cue cards collated by an office-bound PA. Easy to read, and absolutely devoid and stripped bare of any of the personality communicated by the sender.

So I said, no, I don't want neat, typed-out cards, I want to read *all* the correspondence, in its original form. And take it into the studio, to read from. Live.

That is what made the difference. I'd pick up so much from the handwritten page. Whether it was a PS on the bottom of a postcard, a scrawl on a roll of fake parchment, on a banana, or written painstakingly with each word in a different colour ink. Or with cut-out newsprint 'blackmail' letters, made very fashionable by punks. I would note if the writer could spell — especially if they were studying for an English degree, and pounce mercilessly *in jest* if they made spelling errors.

'Don't fancy your chances much, mate,' I'd say on air to an Oxbridge student who couldn't spell a word like 'cathedral'.

The listeners would go to extraordinary lengths to get attention. Mirror writing, for example. That's everything backwards and only readable, legibly, if you held it up to a mirror. Which I would do, in front of puzzled, bemused fellow passengers on my train home.

This show was organic. It was the listener's show. *Their* choices on air. But strictly policed by myself and the producer. Not out of arrogance, but simply because I've always thought, if *you* don't think this is brilliant, why are you playing it?

Why would you want to subject your audience to something you don't like or approve of yourself? But I didn't know the stats, the listening figures, or whether they were even enough to keep us on air. The show was extended again, and then again. In small increments.

It got weirder. I thought, this is so fun, but it's *so* weird, it's *too* weird, it will get taken off air. Bound to be. This was national radio, the nation's favourite, *the* pop station, and here we were listening to the cruel dig at mall rats, 'Valley Girl' by Frank Zappa. Or Soft Cell's strange, scary, goth marathon 'Martin'. Inspired by George A. Romero's eponymous horror movie. Played annually, ritually, each 31 October.

Sometimes listeners would say to me, 'I would write to you, but I don't know what to say.' So I would suggest themes, if that would help. We had a 'Debbie Day' when you could get a mention if your name was Debbie or a dedication *to* a Debbie. The response was huge!

There was always that element of piss-take. Both ways. The listener to me, and vice versa. But the point of the show was that I wanted people to know that if they came up with the right tune, it would get played.

I don't know where all the weird ones came from. This was post-punk time; as the *NRS* (*Nightingale Request Show* as it became called) got going, there was a lot of humour on records . . . 'Jilted John' by Jilted John, and the 'answer song' 'Gordon Is a Moron'.

The epic that really made you want to hide behind the sofa, a double-headed delight from Barry Andrews, ex of XTC, one side of this now extremely rare 7-inch vinyl . . . is 'Rossmore Road', a song about a real street in the postal area NW1 just off the Marylebone Road in London. I get minicab drivers to detour up that street specially so I can sing the chorus out loud. But the flipside has the real gem . . .

'Win a Night Out with a Well-Known Paranoiac', the ultimate been-up-for-four-days, no-sleep, utterly deranged, ultimate come-down rant. (It's on YouTube — please check it out!)

Another favourite was the sparse minimalist acapella 'It's a Fine Day', credited as performed, sung, just by Jane. This had been a John Peel discovery. Picked up by my listeners, and many of us became fervent converts. The song itself has gleaned an extraordinary legacy. Written by poet and musician Edward Barton who resided in Manchester. And sung by his friend . . . Jane Lancaster. Very lo-fi, simple, but haunting. From the early eighties.

A whole decade later, it was transformed into a — as I thought — *pseudo* rave tune by two of Spiral Tribe, an enormous trance smash hit. I wasn't so taken with that, actually, notwithstanding the credibility of the Spiral Tribe connection. Which I'm not sure I knew about at the time.

Spiral Tribe were, to me, the *real* ravers. Travellers, survivors of police raids and survivors of the Battle of Castlemorton. Even perhaps some veterans of the Battle of the Beanfield, near Stonehenge, in 1985. Originally the Peace Convoy, a group of full-time road dwellers. Part of the anti-Establishment movement, with echoes to me of the bohemians of the fifties and early sixties. Though *they* seemed rather fey, Soho-type city dwellers compared to these eco warriors that were to proliferate from perhaps pagan times . . . druids . . . centuries ago and now being much of the target and the trigger for the 'repetitive beats bill', the 'stop the parties' legislation of 1994 called the Criminal Justice and Public Order Bill.

There appear to be definite parallels with twenty-first-century climate change activists.

These party people had *generators* and *sound systems*, essential prerequisites for putting on raves. Spiral Tribe made techno records. I gained one of their releases, a treasured possession on 12-inch vinyl. I was rather in awe of Spiral Tribe, admired their uncompromising lifestyle, living on the land and roaming around the countryside putting on parties in fields. I felt too much of a bourgeoise cop-out coward to ever have committed myself to that kind of outlaw life.

When an outfit called Opus III emerged with this revamped version of 'It's a Fine Day', it seemed somehow too bewilderingly *commercial* to have been created by two members, or former members, of Spiral Tribe. But who was I to be sitting in judgement? Wasn't this musical snobbery on my part? All that was supposed to have been swept away by joyful, warm, inclusive acid house. Good luck to them. It wasn't supposed to be *them* vs *us* anymore, now it was *us* and *us*, having a group hug.

But it did seem all the more bizarre that the relentless hit maker of the day, the record producer Pete Waterman, was the levering force behind the vast 'big room' hit from the soft, ethereal original 'Fine Day'.

The irresistible hook was sampled for a Kylie Minogue single, and also by Orbital on their track 'Halcyon', and by Norman Cook aka Fatboy Slim in his guise as Pizzaman. Cover versions continue to this day in different languages. There are rumours that part of the tune was used in a Kleenex TV commercial in Japan. Nothing would surprise me. 'It's a Fine Day' is a genie, for ever out of the bottle.

It's a fine night tonight . . . going to be a fine day tomorrow − the lyric of eternal optimism . . .

One of my other perennial favourites was the funk jam of 'Macho City' by the Steve Miller Band, a veiled protest song referencing US military activity in El Salvador and Afghanistan. Sixteen minutes long, it fades right out in the middle . . . totally . . . at *nine* minutes into the track.

For eleven entire seconds there is dead silence. Dead air. That's nearly a lifetime in radio terms.

(I had dread vision of a Radio 1 supremo storming into the studio, saying: 'What do you think you're doing? Playing nothing but silence, no sound at all, on the radio! Who do you think you are? John Cage? Put some harmless pop music back on, immediately.' Fortunately, that never actually happened.)

After this heart-stopping break, the music on 'Macho City' creeps back in, and . . . to continue the allegory, like a platoon of paratroopers stealthily creeping on its belly emerging from undergrowth cover, the insistent bassline booms back into life, KAPOW . . . for the thrilling reward of the finale.

Which is . . . the best-ever recorded extended sharp crackle of live thunder. Followed by the somehow so satisfying sound blast of a deluge, a torrential downpour. (Recorded by Steve Miller hanging a microphone out of his studio window during a storm.) In its wake the menacing *thud thud thud* of military helicopter blades panning across the stereo spectrum.

(This in turn I was acutely reminded of in 2019 when President Donald Trump's helicopter convoy took off from the US ambassador's opulent residence, Winfield House in Regent's Park, London, and rattled and shook *my* windows so ominously, with such sheer force, in my humble abode a couple of miles away. I felt like shouting up to him: It's OK-AAY, we do KNOW you are the most POWERFUL military force in the ENTIRE world, but there's no need to SHOW OFF like this, we GET the POINT.)

The bassline on 'Macho City' is the very one, it is alleged, sampled by David Byrne and Brian Eno on a track from their album *My Life in the Bush Of Ghosts.*

And this type of extended, moody music with looped sound effects and subtle bass beats was, not too far ahead, to have its very own dance genre title . . . ambient house.

I have tweets from people now, in the 2020s, who remember and reminisce over tunes such as 'Macho City'. Some who kept their cassettes taped from the radio broadcasts (illegally at the time) and have now posted them onto Mixcloud.

There's a Spotify playlist of some the most favourite tunes played on the request show, posted there by I know not whom. Under the nom de plume of Annierak. A pun, I presume, on that degrading term music fiends once called themselves . . . anoraks.

Or . . . maybe it isn't?

The Spotify playlist runs to eighty-one tracks and it's gratifying that the music we shared then still resonates now.

There was 'Nelly the Elephant' by the Toy Dolls, and Barnes and Barnes with 'Fishheads'; 'Elstree' by the Buggles; 'Croydon' by Captain Sensible — they *were* popular, but they were also daft.

Most popular were: Joy Division, the Smiths, the Cure, Aztec Camera, the Sex Pistols, the Clash, Prefab Sprout . . . And some of the most loved tunes: 'Looking Through Gary Gilmore's Eyes' . . . 'I'm in Love with a German Film Star' . . . 'Where's Captain Kirk?' . . . 'Tinseltown in the Rain' . . . Patti Smith's 'Dancing Barefoot' . . . 'Is Vic There?' . . . This Mortal Coil's version of 'Song to the Siren' . . . Mark Stack, aka The Merx, one of the The Request Show's most loyal contributors, has now posted on Spotify a compilation of no less than 1700 of the most loved tunes from the show.

But then, hang on, what was *this*? New Order in a bizarre love triangle . . . the Mondays getting stoned in a different way . . . the Roses asking: have you seen her, have you heard? . . . not Britpop, a term I never acknowledged, personally, but *acid house.* Took. The. Fuck. Off. Changed *everything.* Rumbling for a while: Chicago warehouse, rare groove and jacking your body. But now . . . bosh . . . everyone could be havin' it large.

— 19 —

Night Owl of Croydon

The Night Owl of Croydon became a near mythical character on my radio shows. This anonymous being regularly sent me strange artefacts, connected with, well, for instance hand-drawn Wicca calendars, elaborately decorated prayer mats, all kinds of witchy warlock items, poems, cartoons. Even packets of 'magic' seeds.' On which Night Owl had hand-scripted:

'Grown in Croydon'.

I had absolutely, certainly no intention whatsoever to put in any soil, any of these 'magic' seeds, to see what might have grown from them. No doubt some suspicious form of plant life. Poisonous, or rated illegal at the very least.

Halloween, not surprisingly, was his (well it might have been *her*) favourite time of the year. I was always on high alert. Somehow Night Owl found out where I lived. Which was in a densely popu-lated city centre on a main road, with steps leading up to the front door. Opposite was a block of flats set in wooded gardens, where you could hide . . . and watch any goings on, undetected.

So around the time of one particular Halloween, I opened the front door during the day to go out of the house. There was no one else in at the time, and no one had knocked or rung the bell. On the front step was a cardboard box, about a metre square, tied loosely with string. I stepped over it, with alacrity, travelled down the street at speed, to a corner shop, to think what to do about this. Decided it must either be a bomb or . . . some kind of prank.

I detoured and consulted a friend who lived nearby — an explosives expert, fortuitously — and asked his advice. Should I call the police?

'Well,' he said, 'if you do, this is what will happen . . .

'Every neighbour will be evacuated from all the houses and flats and the whole street cleared. Then the police will set a sort of robot to go up the steps of your house and carry out a controlled explosion. This will blow up the box, and whatever is inside it.

'And, as it's you, it will all end up in the newspapers. You will feel really stupid if it's a practical joke.'

With that my friend Chris decided that he would investigate the mystery parcel himself.

'NO, NO, DON'T TOUCH IT, *PLEASE*!' I screamed, visualising him blowing himself to bits in the very next second.

'Look,' he reasoned. (And I had to admit to myself, rationally.) 'It's got to be stable enough for someone to have put it here in the first place.'

Then he ran up the steps, picked up the box and, to my absolute horror, began to *shake* it.

Oh NO!

Well, it didn't explode. My friend opened it, and inside was:

A hollowed-out fresh turnip, a white candle and a drawing of a familiar figure. With a message:

'Happy Halloween — Night Owl of Croydon.'

Whether Night Owl was watching from across the street, I will never know. He has never revealed his identity. He once wrote that he was thinking of moving to Eastbourne, or Bexhill. Both respectable coastal towns, with high levels of retirement residencies. But somehow Night Owl of Eastbourne didn't have the same ring about it. And certainly not Night Owl of Bexhill.

Night Owl even had his own groupies, girls who used to write to me asking for a date with him. It's true! He always replied via the show that he was too busy doing spells at midnight at the top of Glastonbury Tor.

Was he, or she, a harmless prankster, or a more ominous stalker? That's now a criminal offence.

People ask me if I've heard from Night Owl of Croydon lately. No, I haven't.

Wonder what happened to him? they say.

I don't know, I reply . . . hope it's nothing too unearthly.

Or undeadly.

— 20 —

Brighton – Acid House

If the late eighties, early nineties were to be moulded by any one force, for me it was Primal Scream. Glaswegian, originally a rock band, two of them decamped to Brighton. They embraced acid house, so did I, and it changed my life, for the better. The two now honorary Brightonians were their singer Bobby Gillespie and guitarist Robert Young, known as Throb. They enthusiastically championed the new hedonism, and that's putting it mildly.

And bit by bit they were assembling what was latterly recognised as the album that symbolised that period, *Screamadelica*. The other major force in the band was the guitarist Andrew Innes. His base was in London. He shared a flat in Hackney with my son Alex, who was now the band's manager. Often Andrew drove from Hackney to hang out in Brighton.

This was the weekend procedure. I had a Friday residency at the second underground arch at the Zap Club, looking out onto the beach. It was a slightly more chilled area than in the main room, where the weekly club nights happened. At around midnight the Scream contingent arrived and took up residence at their usual table. I was behind the decks, watching their comings and goings.

I had made rather a rash agreement with a proto pop-up radio station to play their Saturday morning slot. After DJ'ing till the late early hours at the Zap. Foolish. But it was fun to do and the nearest I ever got to being a real pirate radio DJ. There was only one studio area, so a lot of climbing in and out each other's way went on when it came to the handover. The slot after mine was celebrated by the presence of . . . Carl Cox.

Saturday afternoons were a ritual of music shopping. The record shops of Brighton were second only to Camden, Covent Garden and Soho in London. This was where the community flourished. Listening and buying cherished, desirable, very, very limited-edition 12-inch vinyl.

These were specialist shops, independents, not branches of national chain stores. And you needed to earn their trust before they would sell you any of their stock. I was inevitably, at the time, often the only female customer.

There was always a crucial rapport to be built between the DJ and the guy behind the counter. When you had established that bond, they might keep a special copy ready for your next visit.

It was a different and necessary experience for me to learn in this new acid house world. I'd been used to having sackfuls of free cassettes, vinyl singles, albums and CDs sent to me every week by record companies, for years.

But the ones you've chased up, sought out, pleaded and cajoled for and bought are always far more precious.

Paper flyers were stacked on the counters and windowsills with info on all the upcoming club nights. But there was also the secret word-of-mouth only communication, to discover where the real underground and secret raves, house and warehouse parties were happening that and each weekend.

This area of Brighton is called the North Laine, a criss-cross of narrow streets of shops which became the hub of raver activity. There were clothes shops and cafés, as well as record emporiums, both for new and specialist music collectors. Mid-Saturday after-noon might mean a stop-off at the Green Dragon pub.

I had lived in Brighton for nearly three decades but had never felt more excited than by the buzz that was going on there in the late eighties, early nineties. And, miraculously, I had been invited into this thriving new young culture.

Saturday night would begin thus:

A visit to Throb's flat in Hove. This had always been the rather stuck-up, nose-in-the-air sister town to Brighton. Residential, respectable, and with none of the wicked gleam in its eye that Brighton had had, always. My attraction to Brighton went all the way back to my childhood. Visits to Brighton meant slot machines, candyfloss and bumper cars. And that seediness captured by Graham Greene's *Brighton Rock*.

But Hove was, extraordinarily, beginning to change, with its main street becoming a strip of quite upmarket neon-lit bars and restaurants.

Throb held court in his first-floor flat, with his girlfriend, later wife, and close friend to me, Anita. Neets. Also residing there was Throb's long-haired and temperamental cat, Bianca. Throb also had long hair, shoulder length, and lived and dressed — black leather trousers, open-top sports car — the full rock star life. He was a generous host.

After a blast of record playing to get us in the mood, a fleet of the black and white liveried local taxis would then whisk our convoy to Brighton. Throb and entourage then engaged in a sort of nineties *Saturday Night Fever passeggiata* along the seafront. Dropping in on favoured bars and clubs. Mine was called the Shark Bar. No trimmings, walls running with sweat, great music, no membership rules and no apparent door policy.

Other bars and clubs would be visited, but we always seemed to end up back at Throb's place in Hove, him now playing tracks long into the night, ranging from his specialised Italo house set, to Dennis Wilson's (Beach Boy Dennis) poignant 'River Song' from *Pacific Ocean Blue*. I never ever seemed to leave before sunrise.

I soon realised after meeting Bobby that he, like the others, had a vast knowledge of music. I'd invited him to be interviewed on a BBC World Service radio programme. That had gone well.

So he seemed a very suitable choice of guest for Radio 1's long-running music review programme *Roundtable* (nowadays migrated to the station BBC 6 Music).

I'd sat in on the *Roundtable* countless times and hosted on many occasions too . . .

When Bobby became willing and available to take part, Mike Read was by now the host. On the particular Friday when the show aired live, the guests were Bobby, me and the singer in a newish outfit called Blue Pearl, Durga McBroom.

They'd had a hit with the fabulous, ravey, Youth- produced '(Take Me Dancing) Naked in the Rain'. So altogether it felt a cool enough line-up.

Unfortunately, and it happens, this was a dire week for new record releases. Unhelpfully too, an 'aide' to Bobby had given him some kind of pick-me-up just before we went on air. Not necessarily anything illegal, but Bobby is not a habitual alcohol drinker, put it that way.

One duff record followed another. Bobby did not hold back with his criticism, and neither Durga nor myself could find much constructive to say either.

Then came the cruncher. A newly digitised dubbed 'duet' between the deceased Nat King Cole and his singer daughter, Natalie. Of his, well, unforgettable classic, 'Unforgettable'.

'So . . . Bobby Gillespie, I'll come to you now,' said Mike Read. 'What do you think Nat King Cole would make of that duet with his daughter?'

'I think,' said Bob, now almost apoplectic, 'I think that he would wish . . . *that she'd never been born.*'

There was no coming back from that. The show was live, he'd said it, and I knew if I tried to tell Bobby to tone his remarks down he would have just . . . got worse.

The response was immediate. In those fax-driven days, the messages were coming in thick and fast, paper layer by layer. From outraged listeners who said they'd no longer be followers of Primal Scream. One, appalled wrote that he'd always been a fan of Bobby and Primal Scream, even *named his own child* after the singer, but was now horrified at his remarks.

Bobby whirlwinded out of Radio 1's building at the end of the show, into the bright night, off to appear at another radio station. For yet a different, no doubt unpremeditated aural adventure.

For me . . . I was absolutely gutted. I was totally convinced over the wretched weekend which followed that this would be the end for me at Radio 1. I felt entirely responsible for inviting Bob G. onto the programme. And that I would have to bear the consequences.

But *somehow*, and to my huge relief, this was not deemed a sackable offence after all. I am a world-class worrier.

After many appeals and searches through archives, no recording of this episode seems to exist. So you'll have to take my word that it happened. Natalie Cole is deceased now also, and probably, mercifully, never heard it either.

21

The City of Angels in Flames

'*Get out of my house . . . This is a gross invasion of my privacy . . .* Get out!
Get out — now!'

The date: 30 April 1992. The location: South Pasadena, Los Angeles.

The previous day in a courtroom in Simi Valley, west of Pasadena, four white police officers had been acquitted of alleged offences of violence. Against an African-American man few outside of LA had ever heard of.

Now his name was now splashed across the world's media. Rodney King.

The acquittal had been the flashpoint building up for months in South Central LA, in the less wealthy enclaves, generally more populated by non-white ethnicities.

The mid-afternoon verdict the previous day from a mostly white jury on the four officers of the LAPD triggered a complete eruption. A civil war. The worst experiences in LA since the Watts riots in the mid-sixties.

The freeing of the four policemen was the boiling-over point. Rodney King had been shockingly beaten up when arrested — filmed, unknowingly to the police, by a passer-by local resident.

The footage from the incident, a year before, had been endlessly looped on local TV news.

Even by their own brutal standards of treatment meted out to African-Americans by the LAPD, this was shocking, extreme violence.

I had arrived a couple of days beforehand, unaware of what was about to happen. I hung out at a small indie label record company office in Downtown, and all the staff could talk about was, expected that day . . . the Verdict.

The entire Los Angeles region was holding its collective breath.

Surely, speculated the LA folks, these cops won't get off scot-free, after so many had seen the damning video footage.

But in quiet Simi Valley, away from simmering South Central, they did.

Trouble, depending on how the jury voted, was seriously on the horizon . . .

It didn't take long.

By what they call in some quarters EOB (end of business) on 29 April, the first liquor store had been looted. The first fires had been set. The first truck drivers dragged out of their cabs at intersections and beaten up. Live cable TV crews were rapidly on the scene. The news spread faster than the flames.

Watts in 1965 did not have the soundtrack of hip-hop.

LA in 1992 certainly did. 'Burn Hollywood Burn', Public Enemy had rapped just two years before. The lyrics were about Hollywood's history of portraying black people as maids, butlers, bag carriers and subservient characters in its movies. But now the rioting had spread northwards to Hollywood Boulevard itself. Public Enemy's album title *Fear of a Black Planet* seemed more, well, prescient.

It wasn't just the LAPD that the black community resented. There were animosities with some Asian neighbours too. Hundreds of thousands of US military were being deployed during the nineties since the first Gulf War began. I took a keen interest, having had a curious and eye-opening visit to Iraq in the late eighties.

So much so that I had called up the White House (anyone can). Not really expecting to get through live to the president, but to say, please don't bomb Iraq. I've met some great people there.

Many African-Americans felt they were being used as cannon fodder for a war they didn't agree with or properly necessarily comprehend (does anyone really, still?).

The seemingly never-ending saga of US intervention in the Middle East was on the rise again.

A rap by the Disposable Heroes of Hiphoprisy, fronted by Michael Franti, had barely left my 'ghetto blaster' as those pre-digital CD players were quaintly known during the time of the first Gulf War. With an eerie but beautiful synth backing, it was entitled 'The Winter of the Long Hot Summer':

The pilots said their bombs lit Baghdad
Like a Christmas tree
It was the Christian thing to do,
You see
They didn't mention any casualties
No distinction between the real
And the proxy.

Meanwhile I had begun to act on my main reason for this latest visit to Los Angeles. To pick up research with Mike Oldfield, about his life story. The quiet musician who had created *Tubular Bells*, the phenomenal album which launched the entire Virgin brand. With the worldwide success of this one-track album piece, Mike had found fame impossible to face head on, and became a recluse.

Now fifteen years later he was recording a follow-up and was preparing, possibly, to come out of his shell. I was to write his life story. That was the plan.

Mike, with his longish, blondish, straight and shiny head of hair atop a tan, did carry the rock star look, however reclusive. Despite being somewhat of a hermit, he certainly wasn't living in a cave.

He was now residing in a plush gated mansion in Beverly Hills. My recent new-found friend Adrian had volunteered to come along for the ride and drive me around LA. Being a musician and a big fan of the Faces, he was ultra-keen to meet my hosts in LA, Ian McLagan, keyboardist of great distinction and a dear friend.

As was, even more so, his wife Kim . . . previously married to Keith Moon.

Now Kim and Mac lived in South Pasadena. Mac and I had been born in close neighbourhoods in south-west London. Me in Osterley, he in Isleworth. Close to Brentford, home of my grand-parents and unlikely setting for the cult comedy TV series about pirate radio, *People Just Do Nothing*, in the twenty-teens.

Mac would sit at his kitchen table listening to *Morning Becomes Eclectic* on KCRW, the indie radio station. Having lived in LA for close on fifteen years he (an ex-art student) was expert at creating beautiful hand-drawn maps of how to circumnavigate the mysteries of the LA freeways.

'Take the Five, the One-Ten, the One-Oh-One south, the Four-Oh-Five' . . .

He would rattle off the directions, still with that south-west London, slightly nasal twang, as the other former members of the Faces also spoke, years after they had found superstar status else-where. Ronnie Wood speaks like that, and Rod Stewart.

Mac was one of the best keyboard players in the world. He'd played in the Small Faces, the Faces, and with The Rolling Stones and Bob Dylan. He was, however, completely uncompromising. If he didn't feel the music 100 per cent, he would not play it. Consequently, Mac played for much of the time with his own band. So he worked a lot in his home city of LA and knew how to travel it.

They were warm and generous hosts, Kim and Mac; I had been their guest many times before, in different areas of LA, from Malibu to North Hollywood.

The first time I ever visited Los Angeles, and stayed with them, had been the madhouse at Trancas, built on stilts and directly on the sandy beach. Despite the so-called exclusiveness of these houses, they were built incredibly close to one another. The film actor Steve McQueen lived next door. He was not overly thrilled about having Keith Moon as a next-door neighbour. The noise, you know. There had been confrontations between McQueen and Moon.

But, still, it had been quite an introduction to Hollywood. And gave me an unrealistic impression that everyone there had a superstar as a next-door neighbour.

Myself and Adrian set off to meet up with Mike Oldfield, me carrying a small tape recorder and microphone to record any relevant conversation with him.

Secluded, palm-tree-lined Beverly Hills seemed remote from the turmoil going on in the city beneath. But that wasn't quite the case; it was getting closer. Even if the residents there felt somewhat safer for the moment.

We were glued to the TV news after Mike had shown us around his house, and we took photographs in his studio.

Then he stepped outside to the wide sloping gardens and looked down at the city spread out below. Were those wisps of *smoke* billowing upwards?

'I suppose I should go and write some riot music,' mused Mike, in his outwardly resigned, laid-back, mild-mannered way, studying the unfolding scene below.

As the civil unrest was spreading, the LA police chief issued a statement. A curfew was to be put in place, from dusk to dawn.

The situation was in no way under control, and the world media was now on full alert.

Smoke from fires was reaching the international airport LAX; only one runway remained open.

Back on Sunset Strip below Beverly Hills, where it meets Doheny Drive, someone looking suspiciously like an unreconstructed hippy waved a homemade flag which read:

'*Honk your horn for peace!*'

You couldn't help saying to yourself:

Only in LA.

With the city-wide curfew about to be imposed that evening, I headed back to South Pasadena.

But on that drive across town it became clear just how out of control the situation really was. Out on the freeways, never mind downtown.

Buildings were ragingly on fire, unchecked. Not a sign of a police car, or a fire truck or a hose or any water — or any firemen.

Just burning, abandoned . . . no one even trying to douse the flames or put out the fire.

How many more were there?

That's when it began to hit home to me just how big the scale of the emergency was.

Nearly three decades later, I met a firefighter who had been on duty in South Central that day, Jason Kramer. Now he's a DJ on the key Los Angeles radio station KCRW. These are his recollections:

JASON KRAMER: We were driving south on the 110 freeway when my partner and I saw these plumes of smoke in a very close distance. Not sure what it was, we called dispatch to find out what was going on and their response was, 'Stand by.' At this time in 1992, there was no smartphones or even internet. We just had AM/FM radio in our rig for any news or entertainment. An occasional CD player or tape cassette. It was not until we got back to the station where we see the riots unfold all over the city. From South Central to Koreatown to downtown to the Westside. Los Angeles is now uprising.

(It was still daylight. The scene of a burning house against the intense blue sky could have been a Pink Floyd album cover. But this was arson, not art. Well, depending on your point of view. It was protest, for sure.

Just how far across LA buildings were being torched became acutely apparent.)

JASON KRAMER: The city was on lockdown. We would turn on the TV and watch things unfold. From local merchants on their rooftops, shooting at looters, to electronics stores being completely gutted. It was a heart-breaking experience to see the city you grew up in with such anguish. This was years of tension and abuse finally coming to the riots. At around 9 p.m. we were asked to 'move up'. That is a term used when an area needs additional support, or a station is out on a call and we need to cover that area. We left our station in Santa Monica and proceeded east down Santa Monica Boulevard.

The streets were empty, and we drove at a moderate pace until we came upon the corner of Westwood Boulevard and Wilshire. As we gazed to our left, we see two police cars and barricades propped up blocking the entrance to the UCLA campus and Westwood.

I hit the siren for a quick tone and waved as we drove by. We then went back to SM Boulevard, and in an eastward direction, entered Beverly Hills. At this point, I felt very uncomfortable with the police blockades. During that time in the nineties, Beverly Hills had a reputation of being unfavourable to minorities. That seemed to show with major police presence at all the major intersections going into their city from all directions. As we went through BH, we ended up in West Hollywood. This is a city and area that is vibrant and full of people hopping from one bar to another. Except today, nothing was open, and the streets were quiet. We proceeded down SM Boulevard until we got to a street called La Brea, one of the larger travelled streets through Los Angeles. As we drove south down La Brea, we started to see broken windows and also clutter in the streets. At this time, I decided to turn on my red lights and hit the siren at every intersection. Since we were on high alert.

*

I returned to Kim and Mac's house, having parked the hire car against a backdrop of the San Gabriel mountain range. Often obliterated by cloud or smog, its white snow peaks were now glistening in the late April sunshine.

I carried my tape recorder inside the house holding the microphone aloft, the red record button in the 'on' position. The events of the day weren't just news; this was history happening. I was recording 'atmos'. Not for any particular end user, just to capture the moment, and to vox-pop Kim and Mac's reaction.

Wrong!

I pointed the microphone at the TV set, to record the latest news of the riots.

Wrong!

'So, Mac, what do you think of the latest developments?' I posed the question in full BBC reporter mode.

Very wrong!

What I didn't know at that point was that Mac had just returned from downtown Pasadena and heard highly alarming word on the street. Word that the riots were spreading here too. Word that his house, mainly made of wood, like most Los Angelenos' homes, could be the next to be set on fire. The hugeness of Los Angeles also made itself so apparent. The cheek-by-jowl-ness of so many communities. Koreatown, Compton, Crenshaw, and then the mostly comfortable Brentwood, Santa Monica, Los Feliz.

South Central maybe was controlled by gangs, where few white people might venture, but the areas were not physically that far apart. Just a short drive away. Suddenly this multimillion conurbation seemed very, very vulnerable.

*

JASON KRAMER: We kept a sharp eye open. Talking with other colleagues after the riots that they were carrying shotguns on the floor of the ambulances and individual medics were armed with handguns. It was standard to wear flak jackets during certain high-danger calls like a shooting or assaults. Occasionally LAPD Metro would be our escorts during certain holidays and neighbourhoods. As we were slowly gliding down La Brea, things started to change drastically. At this point I was not stopping at red lights at the intersections.

*

So my microphone in Mac's face was, in retrospect, an inexcusable intrusion. In his own home where he had welcomed me as a guest.

His explosion at me was therefore completely justified.

'*Get out, go . . .!*'

I felt immediately intensely mortified at my own insensitive behaviour.

Kim, the nearest being to an angel I had ever met, tried to step in and restore peace.

'She didn't mean any harm, Mac,' Kim reasoned.

We were all now in a state of heightened tension, hysteria almost.

The problem was, it was now dusk, the curfew was officially in place.

I couldn't leave or go out of the house, nor could anyone else.

Eventually the sheer ridiculous craziness of the situation dawned on all of us. I unplugged and put away the microphone. It was the only blip in a forty-year friendship.

Meanwhile throughout LA the pandemonium raged on. Lootings from shops, and some carried out not necessarily by angry black protesters against the Rodney King verdict.

There were people I knew from the Brighton rave scene who were quite gleefully joining in the rampaging.

JASON KRAMER: The streets were dark and empty of all souls except for this red and orange glow with embers popping all over our rig. Both sides of the street were completely on fire. Store after store, building after building just spewing flames out the front. The gas station on fire with automobiles in flames. I was scared, filled with anger and fascinated at the same time. I looked at my partner and she looked back and we sat in silence. My concern was that we were in direct line of getting shot. We kept our heads back strongly to the seats and drove through past the freeway. We would see people in the streets walking around with items. Carrying electronics to their cars. When we finally got past Jefferson, we got a call for an elderly woman who needed assistance. At least sixty people were killed, Captain Scott Miller of the Los Angeles Fire Department was shot in the face and countless people were injured. Needless to say, it was my scariest day on the job. The words will always stay in my head, 'Can we all get along?' This is a day I never want to see again!

*

Leaders from local communities were appearing on TV appealing for calm and common sense, requesting that the TV sets and even packets of Pampers were taken back to local stores. Many were.

The next day my escort thought we should tactfully get out of town, leave in the daytime, till the curfew was lifted.

We headed out of Los Angeles eastwards on the old, well-trammelled, much sung about and romanticised Route 66. Oil derricks nodded their heads incessantly in the oilfields beside the highway. Giant black bees sucking liquid money out of the ground. Nirvana's 'Smells Like Teen Spirit' clanged its already classic riffs out on the stereo.

I knew my travelling companion was an ardent music fan, but quite how ardent I didn't yet realise.

He suggested we should head for the Joshua Tree National Park. Its weird cacti formation had given it a far greater profile as a tourist setting since U2's eponymous album of 1987.

I half expected the entire area to be crammed with visiting U2 fans wearing Joshua Tree T-shirts. But it *is* a desert, empty and desolate, apart from a few watering holes. It was to one of these we headed.

The Joshua Tree Inn, in fact. An inn, in the desert, how charming! How sort of . . . English and quaint, I thought. Would it have a stagecoach outside its heavy ancient stone portal?

Would it hell?

It was a shack motel. Just a collection of one-storey huts — with a small swimming pool of pale water centre stage . . . OMG, this really was the Wild West.

But it had another claim to fame that I didn't know about till we'd checked in. My companion advised we should try to reserve room 8. Turns out room 8 had been the last — well, nearly last — resting place of the famed country rock singer formerly with my great discoveries, and friends, The Byrds. He being Gram Parsons.

Just to put some context in here. I had heard The Byrds early on, in the UK, before their first transformational version of Bob Dylan's 'Mr Tambourine Man' became successful.

The Byrds had cast their dancing spell my way very early on. I was captivated by that mournful twelve-string Rickenbacker guitar and the harmonies of Jim McGuinn (later always referred to as Roger), David Crosby and the rest of the band. Which in its first line-up was completed by Gene Clark, Chris Hillman and the drummer Michael Clarke.

I knew about The Byrds because of Derek Taylor. Derek had been a journalist, worked with The Beatles, become my friend, but had now upped sticks and moved to California to become a press agent. He sent me by post a 7-inch record by a band no one had ever heard of in the UK — The Byrds. It was 'Mr Tambourine Man'. It was so exquisite; I wasn't surprised it went to number 1 in the US and the UK.

Derek brought The Byrds to the UK. To tour. It was disastrous. When they arrived in London I was already their biggest fan. Well, The Beatles themselves were immediate supporters too, but not everyone else. Maybe hardly anyone else. The critics massacred The Byrds' live shows in the UK.

It's hard to imagine now, when their stock is if anything far higher than in their supposed heyday, what a bad reception they had in the UK. Those future classics . . . 'So You Want to Be a Rock 'n' Roll Star' and 'Eight Miles High', adored later by the nineties-dominating British bands such as the Smiths and the Stone Roses, weren't even top 10 hits on first release.

The Byrds played the Fairfield Halls in Croydon, they played Blaises Club on a tiny no-stage corner of the dance floor . . . They played at Hove Town Hall; the sister town next to Brighton. I went to all these gigs.

I invited them back to my flat after the gig in Hove. No one was in a very good mood.

I lived on the top two floors of a Georgian building facing the seafront at Black Rock. Derek looked dubious as he shepherded the musicians through the long black and white marble-tiled hallway.

'I didn't know you lived in a slum,' he said darkly, and not entirely jokingly. Well, it wasn't a five-star hotel, for sure; perhaps I had overplayed my hand. But it was bohemian, if a little peeling-paint run-down. Faded aristocratic charm was how I perceived the building. I loved it. The building was owned by the painter Count William de Belleroche. Truly bohemian-living Viscount Peter Churchill, godson of Queen Victoria, resided in a flat at the back of the house.

I'd never been to the US, let alone California, so perhaps it did feel like a let-down.

My naivety with the hippest band in the world, including the Fab Four, was shortly to be revealed.

Jim McGuinn became known for his mantras, his pronouncements.

He who stays cool is he who survives . . .

I trust everything is gonna work out alright (later a Byrds song title).

All politicians should be on LSD.

This last line he came out with having disappeared into my bathroom for a longish while.

I had never heard of lysergic acid diethylamide. At that time in Britain LSD meant currency: pounds (represented by the £ symbol) shillings and pence. This was before decimalisation. Me and Jim really were completely misunderstanding each other.

Trying to fathom what he meant, I ventured, 'Ah do you mean all politicians should be on LSD . . . sponsored, so that they cannot be corrupted?'

A reasonable deduction, I thought.

'No, man,' said McGuinn, aghast . . . 'LSD is a drug!'

After that rather uncertain start, my bonding with The Byrds went on in leaps and bounds. I continued writing positive reviews, and eventually the music world caught up and agreed.

David Crosby was a stocky chap, in contrast to the ultra-thin McGuinn. He wore a distinctive cape, on and off stage. He gave his other clothes away. Gave me a red and white striped belt and wrote something I couldn't understand in biro on the inside.

An after-do back at the Europa hotel near Grosvenor Square was a night of partying where we scooted up and down the corridors, with the Stones' 'Satisfaction' pounding out of someone's room. *All night*. Nobody slept.

The Byrds were just the trippiest. I was enslaved by them. Musically they evolved, they changed, always they seemed to be the leading edge of where music was going. With The Beatles, and the Beach Boys' *Pet Sounds*, this gang really carved out the sound of the second half of the psychedelic sixties: Dylan's lyrics, phasing, the Mamas and the Papas' style epitomising now hip harmonies.

London met LA and the love affair was full on. Many other Anglo-American friendships and collabs continued. Jimi Hendrix was befriended and initially managed by a Geordie, Chas Chandler of the Animals. David Crosby joined Manchester's Graham Nash who defected from the Hollies. And they became half of Crosby, Stills, Nash & Young. A new, later Byrd line-up member Gram Parsons buddied up with Keith Richards. Gram hung out with Keef and the Stones at Nellcôte, in the south of France. The Stones' country-influenced 'Wild Horses' was a result of the collab between Gram and Keith.

It was said Gram was a 'bad influence' on Keith Richards, if that is not a tautology.

Gram played on later Byrd incarnations such as the Flying Burrito Brothers. And he recorded his own now-classic solo album *Grievous Angel*. So it was a lineage of personal interest.

Gram overdosed at the the Joshua Tree Inn. Aged twenty-six in 1973. That wasn't even the end of the story. So fond of the Joshua Tree Monument desert was Gram and his friend and tour manager Phil Kaufman that they made a pact. Both had been at the recent funeral of yet another member of The Byrds' extended line-up, Clarence White. Phil and Gram agreed that if either of them should expire early on in their lives, they would like to be cremated at the Joshua Tree, and their ashes spread across the desert.

Consequently when Gram's stepfather tried to have his body removed from the Joshua Tree Inn to be flown to New Orleans for a traditional funeral, Phil stepped in.

Ever resourceful, he borrowed a hearse, intercepting the coffin containing Gram's remains at a local airport terminal, and tried to set fire to it in the designated desert area.

This did not go altogether to plan and Phil had to do a runner. That's one version.

So now it was nearly thirty years since I'd first become entranced by The Byrds' music, and it was twenty years since Gram had met his unfortunate, and probably accidental, demise in California. It was proposed that we should stay the night in room 8, a kind of shrine to Gram.

Necro tourism, as it's called. You can also stay at Oscar Wilde's last hotel bedroom in Paris, the one with the wallpaper.

Room 8 was a simple affair, framed mirrors on the wall, fresh white bedding. I wasn't scared, I wasn't taking any drugs, I didn't imagine any ghosts.

But oh when the sun went down, and the lights came on. The horror.

Crawling across the ceiling, appearing through cracks in the walls, dropping onto the bed . . . trying to get in through the outside door to the desert, horrible huge black cockroaches.

I don't do camping. Open air, living with nature? No phone signal or Wi-Fi? Not for me. I couldn't get out of there fast enough. You can keep your simple desert charm.

Kaufman already had had an 'interesting' career working alongside such as Charles Manson and had tour managed Frank Zappa.

He continued his unconventional lifestyle and having sustained injuries in a motorcycle accident aged eighty (he had been a Harley Davidson sales demonstration rider and expert) was planning a new version of the PhilGRAMage. This is a much in-demand tour of the relevant parts of the Joshua Tree park. Phil, last heard of by me in 2018, emailed to say the latest PhilGRAMage had been postponed.

The fascination for this extraordinary shrine never seems to fade. I was faintly astonished to discover that two of my colleagues at Radio 1, now executives, made their own film of a Gram pilgrimage to the Joshua Tree Inn.

It's one of these rock 'n' roll stories that no one ever wants to deny.

Such as the tale or urban myth about Bob Dylan and Crouch End. Bob Dylan is said to have rocked up at a house in Crouch End, north London looking to hook up for a recording studio session. With ex-Eurythmic Dave Stewart. He knocked on the unheavenly and decidedly earthly front door of . . . the wrong house.

A woman answered the door. Dylan asked if 'Dave' was in.

The woman replied that he was not, but if Mr Dylan would like to come in and wait, Dave should be back shortly.

Mr Zimmerman soon realised his error and left the house. Later that evening, the Dave (a huge fan of Bob Dylan) who lived in the Crouch End house, returned home. The woman who lived there said casually, 'Oh by the way, Bob Dylan came round earlier, looking for you.'

Back in LA the number of people killed in the riots totalled 63. Injured: 2383. There were 6300 fires and over 1000 buildings destroyed. Two hundred liquor stores were set alight and 12,000 people were arrested. The damage caused by the rioting and fires clocked up to a billion dollars' worth.

Two years later I was as gripped as the rest of the world watching a live police chase on TV, happening along the 405 freeway between a brace of black police vehicles and a white Bronco SUV. It was being shown all over the world. I was watching from my fairly newly acquired deserted ballroom apartment facing the sea in Brighton, on a tiny Sony TV. It was O.J. Simpson. The chase. The story is well known, as are his trial and subsequent escapades. But his acquittal by a jury of predominantly African-Americans, on two murder charges, was considered by students of the trial to be payback time for Rodney King.

For sure the whole world knew about South Central after that. Protest music . . . NWA, 'Fuck tha Police' . . . were the warning shots that had been echoing across gangsta rap. Not permissible in those days for me to play at seven o'clock on a Sunday evening, on Radio 1, but change was coming. I could not know that the BBC would launch a nationally broadcast radio station devoted to music of black origin called 1Xtra. And that one day my own show would be simultaneously broadcast on that network. I am intensely proud of this.

And one could not know then that, twenty-eight years later, not just the US, but the world, would march to protest and chant that #BlackLivesMatter.

The riots in LA were not *the* key change for US rap, I wouldn't dream of suggesting that, but truly from those times, the sounds of hip-hop really began to command interest from the widest international world of music. The beat had changed. From rock to rap. It was an enormous cultural shift. The greatest in the US since the shock of rock 'n' roll and Elvis in the early to mid-1950s. Took about thirty years to happen . . . You just gotta believe.

22

Andrew Innes – Primal Scream

'Not my department,' Andrew Innes, co-founder and guitarist of Primal Scream has usually, steadfastly replied when asked about interviews or promotion. Eventually, in the mid-twenty-teens, he agreed to have a recorded chat for a radio series, in a studio in west London. To reflect on the early years, through to present days. We are family friends, and neighbours now, too.

ANNIE: OK, Andrew Innes from Primal Scream. This is a rare pleasure and it isn't you normally who does the talking on behalf of the band.

ANDREW: No.

ANNIE: So I feel very privileged.

ANDREW: Thank you. It's nice to be here, Annie.

ANNIE: So you changed the world, I think. A lot of people try and do that and not many succeed.

ANDREW: I think we had help, but the change was there. It was coming.

ANNIE: So we're talking about what kind of year — did you feel that change coming?

ANDREW: We were a wee bit reluctant at first . . . we had friends like Jeff Barrett from Heavenly Records and Alan McGee from Creation Records who kept insisting we had to go down to these clubs in London, because it was new music and, you know, they were exciting. An exciting time.

ANNIE: And this was when?

ANDREW: This was 1988. And we were a bit reluctant at first because we were still into our . . . in our rock 'n' roll phase. Still *are* in a rock 'n' roll phase, but then realised . . . if guys like Barrett and McGee were insistent , , , it would be a good idea to at least investigate what was going on.

ANNIE: So at that time you were in Glasgow?

ANDREW: No, this is in London. Robert [Young, aka Throb] and Bobby [Gillespie] were in Brighton.

ANNIE: But let's go back to establish the beginning of the band. I mean you and Bobby Gillespie had known each other . . .

ANDREW: I met Alan and Bobby through Alan.

ANNIE: Where?

ANDREW: In Glasgow. So the three of us used to come round my house and learn punk songs and try to get a punk band together and it never quite happened.

ANNIE: And what was the name of the first band you had?

ANDREW: Oh, me and McGee had a band called the Laughing Apple. Yeah. Then we moved to London in May, I think it was May 1980.

ANNIE: *That* early on?

ANDREW: Yeah, and then McGee through that, he started Creation Records.

ANNIE: So you had *eight years* before you had any kind of recognition?

ANDREW: I guess so.

ANNIE: That's a long time. So were you able to make a living out of it then?

ANDREW: No. The weird thing is, we all ended up in these Enterprise Allowance Schemes. It was some strange thing that Thatcher had invented to get the dole figures down, and you could start your own business and your rent got paid and you were allowed the equivalent of dole money and you said you were an 'entrepreneur'.

And that got you off the figures so they could say 10,000 people had started new businesses and, for a year, that got you off the dole.

Then you went back on the dole for another year and then you went back on the Enterprise Allowance Scheme. So I think McGee was on that when he started Creation and we all . . . I think Noel [Gallagher] was on it as well.

I think for a lot of musicians in the eighties, this was a loophole that you could exploit. To keep rehearsing your band and basically be a layabout (*laughs*), write songs and . . .

ANNIE: But you must have always believed that you had a future as a musician?

ANDREW: Well you *hope* you have. I don't know if anybody believes they're gonna be successful, because you spend the first few years, you know, *not* being successful. So . . . you just have this hope that something will come good . . .

ANNIE: You say you started off as a punk band, was that your first big musical influence? I suspect not . . .

ANDREW: Well, before that I'd learnt to play guitar, so I guess I was into bands like the Who and Dr. Feelgood before punk and sort of the British rock bands, The Beatles, Small Faces. All the classic sort of sixties bands . . . But the first music that was sort of *mine* was definitely punk rock. I was fourteen and it just had such a great positive influence on everybody I know from that generation. Because it gave you the *confidence*, I think.

Everybody sees punk as negative, but I think for the people who lived through it, and were inspired by it, the kids who liked it, it gave us all this confidence that we *could* make music. You didn't have to be like Yes or the Eagles, an incredibly virtuoso guitar player. It was back to — learn three chords and write a song. So it gave us all hope, and I think even people who *now* make art.

If you meet people who are generally from our generation, my age, they were all influenced by punk because it gave them that belief, that they could do it as well. They can make record sleeves, they can make videos, they could create art. You could do it.

ANNIE: And you could be successful enough to make a living from it?

ANDREW: Yeah. Well, that's the weird thing, I don't think you ever think about making a living when you're starting.

All you want to do is be in a band . . . Making a living comes when you have kids. Then you think: how the heck am I gonna make a living out of doing this? Because you've got responsibilities. Up until then you just want to be in a band and have a great time, and you want to be in the Who and drive a Rolls-Royce into a swimming pool and smash up a hotel room.

ANNIE: Have you actually done that?

ANDREW: Well, I've never done it deliberately. It's happened while we've been there.

ANNIE: An actual Rolls-Royce or . . .?

ANDREW: (*laughing*) No, we've never done the hotel room either because, I don't know, we're a bit nice.

ANNIE: It's not the thing any more, it's not done . . . everyone thinks about the cleaners having to clear it up, don't they?

ANDREW: But I guess while we've been in there, you know, things have come off the walls, but not through vandalism.

ANNIE: The original line-up of the band that became successful was Bobby Gillespie, Robert Young and yourself. Is that right?

ANDREW: I was in London and they were having trouble making the first LP. It was proving quite painful. And Alan and Bobby asked me to come down and help, because they knew I could play proper. I could play quite well, so I got invited down to [do] the first LP.

And it still proved quite traumatic, shall we say. It was just hard because nobody knew what they were doing and nobody seemed to . . . just all the basic things like getting the songs in the right key and stuff that you don't realise you have to do until much later. And all the real technical things about making records.

ANNIE: So you came to London . . .?

ANDREW: Yes, I just liked London. I've been there ever since.

ANNIE: But the others stayed in Scotland, did they?

ANDREW: After they made the first LP, I think, Bobby and Robert decided to move to Brighton. That's when McGee was, by that time, living in Brighton, so I think they went, and he went, he must have gone to this art club where they did these acid house nights, and eventually dragged everybody down there.

ANNIE: And that was a big . . . the great moment of awakening about acid house?

ANDREW: Well, it was just fantastic. You went in the club and there were some right hooligans in there. But you'd bump into somebody, and instead of them wanting a fight, they wanted to cuddle you, and tell you they loved you because of certain chemicals they were taking, and it was just a wonderful, wonderful atmosphere in these clubs.

I mean, you know yourself, it reminded me a bit because I'd been in the early eighties in London, I'd been at some place playing all northern records, like the 100 Club, and it was a similar sort of attitude and just people there to hear music and dance and have a good time. No aggression, no violence. You know, it was wonderful. And then with the acid house thing, they had this new music as well, which I think was lucky, at the time, because of the samples. The innovation in technology crossed with the innovation in drugs.

ANNIE: So you'd arrived and found this club life in Brighton, and it was different to what had come before.

ANDREW: Well, again, I sort of saw parallels with that and the people who were playing old soul records, you know, sixties soul nights.

ANNIE: You mean northern soul?

ANDREW: Yeah, like at the 100 Club. That all-nighter's still going. I think it's the longest-running club in London now. And, you know, so I saw the parallels . . . the atmosphere, this good atmosphere. People wanted to talk about music, you know. There was no hint of violence and basically it was alcohol-free, that's pretty fair.

And that's maybe why it seemed so un-British in a way, because it wasn't fuelled by people being drunk and wanting fights. It was fuelled by MDMA, so . . . it was an incredible atmosphere, you know. And then that crossed with . . . I think the technology had moved on. And the invention of . . . well, the sample hadn't *just* been invented, but it had just become democratised, because there were cheap samplers that had just come out.

ANNIE: Can you explain what a sampler does?

ANDREW: Well, basically a sample is the equivalent of a tape recording except it's a digital recording. And back in the eighties they cost about £30,000 for a minute of sampling. Now, every computer, every laptop, can do as much sampling as you want. It can do hours and hours of sampling.

ANNIE: By sampling we mean taking somebody else's . . .

ANDREW: Well no, it's a digital recording that you take a sample, but what it invariably ended up as, you could record a portion, as much as you want, of somebody else's record, loop it up and repeat it.

People would use the James Brown beats, or they could have a funky beat, the hip-hop artists used that and, you know, it brought this new revolution of sort of . . . I guess it cut up music, I would call it. It kind of reminded me of William Burroughs, because they'd have different samples from different bits of funk records, stick them all together and rap on top.

And then, I guess, similarly with the Detroit techno, the drum machine became instead of a thing that cost thousands of dollars, Roland produced drum machines that only cost several hundred dollars. So it became a big part of sort of black . . . I guess you'd call that techno music. Black rhythm 'n' blues.

ANNIE: Where were you getting all that information about this music from? Records or what?

ANDREW: Yeah, you'd go to the clubs and you'd wonder what this record was and it was McGee [who] bought a lot. He'd dived head first in, as he normally does. And it was great because he just bought all these records from Detroit. You'd go round his house and he'd have hundreds and hundreds of these Detroit records.

ANNIE: So that's what influenced you so much.

ANDREW: Yeah, when you went and heard them in the situation in the clubs, you thought: *this music's great.*

ANNIE: So you'd started off by being a guitar band . . .

ANDREW: Yes.

ANNIE: I think influenced by bands like The Byrds, is that right?

ANDREW: Yeah, just sort of . . . Well what happened, I'll explain, at the end of punk, and I guess you get because it was such a euphoria, punk. But by the time we were eighteen we realised that the Ramones *weren't* the biggest band in the world, *The Police* were, and we realised that 'De Do Do Do', you know, this is as far as it got. And it just . . . sort of . . . made you depressed. I guess turned us against early-eighties rock music, which we really didn't like. And so we took solace in, and we started discovering, sixties garage music, sixties soul music, and we sort of turned to that. And so that's where The Byrds and the Love influence came from. From just being, you know . . . because modern eighties music was just in dire straits of a place. Not a high point of our culture.

ANNIE: OK. So punk then got taken over by new wave and that's what you didn't like.

ANDREW: Yeah, and it sort of got watered down.

ANNIE: So you were a punk rock band and influenced by, as you say, sixties garage music and stuff.

ANDREW: Yeah, which we still are.

ANNIE: Kind of jumped backwards from the eighties, not liking the eighties.

ANDREW: Not really liking, but then again when the hip-hop and the acid house came out it was just suddenly: oh, *this* is exciting, it's modern!

ANNIE: You were *part* of that. I mean, the story has to be told. How the sound of most of *Screamadelica* happened was through Andrew Weatherall, who was not a DJ particularly at the time when you met him. Can you tell us that story?

ANDREW: Well, Jeff Barrett, our press agent, was trying to get us some press for our second album, which nobody really liked. About the only person that seemed to like it was Andrew Weatherall, who did this *Boy's Own* magazine, which was quite an important sort of club magazine in London. And Jeff decided to get him down to review us for the *NME*.

We just got on straight away because we shared a love of Thin Lizzy and he had long hair and we all had long hair and we just hit it off. And so we thought, we might as well try and get him to remix one of our records.

ANNIE: Had that ever happened before?

ANDREW: No, because we hadn't really made any records up until then that we thought could be remixed. We had one ballad on the LP *I'm Losing More*, and it had that whole instrumental section at the end, and we thought: *ah, this could be good to deconstruct.*

ANNIE: Right, so you gave him the tapes and what happened?

ANDREW: Gave him the tapes . . . and then he came back and — *we didn't like it!*

ANNIE: Oh! Why didn't you like it?

ANDREW: Because, I think, he liked the song so much that he was a bit scared to mess it up.

ANNIE: Yeah, he told me that he was a virgin in remixing, and he had too much respect . . .

ANDREW: Yes, he had a lot of respect. He really loved the song, so I think he wanted to keep it.

ANNIE: Leave it much more like it was, and you didn't want that?

ANDREW: So he went in again — *and we didn't like that either!* Because it still . . .

ANNIE: It was too reverent?

ANDREW: Yeah, it was too reverent. And then a third time, and somebody said: 'Why don't we sample some of the dialogue from *The Wild Angels*?' So we went armed with an ancient VHS recorder into the studio, and you had to sort of try and press 'go' as the tape was running by, to get in the right area. This is before you could just pick things up with a mouse and a computer.

ANNIE: It's Peter Fonda, isn't it?

ANDREW: It's Peter Fonda, yeah.

ANNIE: He's saying . . .

ANDREW: 'We wanna be *free*! We wanna *do* what we wanna *do*.'

ANNIE: And so that was a single ('Loaded') . . . because as far as I remember, *Screamadelica* came together in bits.

ANDREW: We'd no idea about making an LP. We wanted . . . because we were so into . . . We'd go out Friday, Saturday, Sunday and then maybe by Tuesday you'd feel like going into the studio again. We were just trying to write tracks that we thought would be good at these clubs. We were in no way trying to write an LP.

It was McGee, at one point, after we had about seven songs, went, 'You'd better finish an album,' and we said: 'What album?' We had no idea. We had just thought we'd make singles. Because it was very singles orientated.

Well, not *singles*, it was more *12-inches*. It was very 12-inch orientated and it was brilliant. You were just living for getting a great 12-inch.

ANNIE: There were awful phrases that started being developed like 'indie-dance crossover'.

ANDREW: Ah yeah! I think we were indie-dance traitors at one point.

ANNIE: Traitors? Traitors to what? Indie?

ANDREW: Indie music. Which we never wanted to be indie in the first place. We wanted to be like, you know, The Byrds or as big as Thin Lizzy.

ANNIE: You wanted to be a gigantic rock band, not an indie or a studio-based thing?

ANDREW: A big rock 'n' roll band. Yeah, all our heroes, Thin Lizzy, T-Rex, Stones, you know.

ANNIE: So you didn't care if the indie people said you were traitors?

ANDREW: No, it was actually a badge of honour, to be honest. People forget there was that friction there, 'They've sold out, they've *gone to the dance side.*'

ANNIE: So that was considered being a sell-out, 'going to the dance side'? And presumably you were then playing in dance clubs rather than in rock venues?

ANDREW: We tried to pick the venues so we could have DJs, and people could dance. So it was quite good. We tried to put on gigs involving DJs and maybe do all night . . . we did all-nighters.

ANNIE: Before that, people went to a rock gig, they might see a support band, then [the main attraction], then, that's it, they go home?

ANDREW: Yeah.

ANNIE: And you're saying: 'No, stay, we've got a DJ on afterwards.'

ANDREW: Yeah, we wanted to make it two in the morning or three in the morning.

ANNIE: And that became very successful . . . the Brixton Academy . . . many of those! And did people 'get' that straight away, that idea of all night?

ANDREW: Yeah, I think they were ready for it with us. That first *Screamdelica* tour . . . people stayed. Because maybe the first couple of nights everybody left when the band finished. But it didn't take long for them to realise, 'No, this is going on. This is gonna be an evening of it.'

ANNIE: So you were bringing together DJs and the band. That was the significant point, wasn't it, looking at the, the bigger musical picture, because that's not what anyone had done before. DJs were now becoming superstars in their own right, weren't they?

ANDREW: I think that was more a couple of years later . . . they were earning more than the bands.

ANNIE: And what did you feel about raves and about events in fields and warehouses and all that?

ANDREW: It was good. But I like things when they're about a thousand people. I tend to prefer being in a sweaty nightclub.

ANNIE: But anyway, *Screamadelica* became *the* nineties anthemic album, or one of them, didn't it? And with it a lot of acclaim and success for you.

ANDREW: Yeah, it was brilliant.

ANNIE: Actually, people don't even remember . . . *I* don't remember whether it was a number 1 album? Maybe it wasn't?

ANDREW: No, it wasn't. It was number 8, I think.

ANNIE: So people think that these ground-breaking albums are the number 1 albums, but they're not.

ANDREW: No, they generally aren't, though, because they're too ahead of their time, I guess.

ANNIE: So you were getting criticism from the indie people. What about the dance people? What did they think of you playing guitars and stuff?

ANDREW: I think it was just such a joyous album that it was infectious, that people liked because it just sounds good, you know.

ANNIE: Was it about that time that the broadcasters at football matches would start using your music at the beginning? Tracks that have become classics like 'Come Together'? And what about 'Don't Fight It, Feel It'?

ANDREW: An old blues line, isn't it? Don't fight the feeling. Don't fight it — feel it. It just was a great line for the times as well. I guess it started off it with us trying to be the Temptations, doing a Norman Whitfield sort of thing. Then Weatherall beautifully deconstructed it and sort of pulled all the, shall we say, the chords on it? And just made it glorious . . . I think it was Hugo [Nicolson, co-producer and remixer], got the whistle . . . acid house music was beautiful because *anything* could become the hook. The whistle isn't really *musical*, but everyone loves it. So, it's kind of strange . . . spaced out . . . doesn't really have a chorus . . . Completely hypnotic and . . . I guess it's the most acid house thing on *Screamadelica*.

I think 'Don't Fight It, Feel It' got used quite a lot on *Match of the Day* or something or *Midweek Sports Special* for some reason. But it's a bit hard to remember. It's bit like the sixties, if you were there, in the late eighties, early nineties it's . . .

ANNIE: And then obviously you weren't around in the sixties so all this comparison, I *knew* that the nineties, when it was happening. I thought this is *fantastic*. This is *special*. Now people are beginning to recognise, only now. I get a lot of young people saying, 'I wish I'd been around in the nineties.'

ANDREW: Yeah, that's interesting. I know Kevin Shields had a great quote one night where he said: 'We suffered during the eighties so that the nineties would be better for everyone else.' Basically saying we had to put up with this terrible eighties rock music, but we explored all the sixties music and all the different influences. And we made the nineties a better place. Kevin Shields from My Bloody Valentine. And I kinda liked that quote from him.

ANNIE: And you started to have different people coming joining you in your line-up, like Kevin Shields? Became a guest?

ANDREW: Well, he was actually in [the band] I think it was *five years* in total. He came along for one gig and I think he played for five years! He couldn't have had such a bad time!

ANNIE: So then Primal Scream began to grow and evolved and got bigger as a line-up, you had Denise [Johnson], a fantastic singer. And Martin Duffy [keyboards]?

ANDREW: Well, the funny thing is Martin was on the first LP, *Sonic Flower Groove*. Martin plays piano on that because he was in a Creation band called Felt. Because he was so good, any time anybody needed piano on their LPs in Creation, they got Duffy to do it. So Martin Duffy's actually been . . . even though he didn't officially become a member I think till after *Screamadelica*, I . . . but he's actually been on every record as well.

ANNIE: At what point did you start, do you think, getting this reputation as the sort of hellraisers, if you like? Was that around the time of *Screamadelica*?

ANDREW: Well, I don't know if we ever did . . . We've always had a good time. I think that's why we're still going. Because we've always known how to enjoy ourselves. And you've got to when you're on tour. If you've been in bands and it's all you know, this tension and everything, you can't do that for too long—

ANNIE: You've actually just reminded me . . . of being on your tour bus going across Germany, and pouring out another what would have been Jack Daniel's and Coke many years ago, but isn't now. I can remember being on your tour bus and how it was so the opposite of that film *Almost Famous* where they're on a tour bus all singing Elton John songs. This was grim silence across this flat, grey landscape. Because . . . one of you had put a tape on in the bus that the rest of you didn't like. And therefore nobody was speaking to anyone else.

ANDREW: Were we tired?

ANNIE: The atmosphere was horrendous. I mean, that's what happens on the road, though, isn't it? You can't be all sort of super-happy and jolly all the time by any means.

ANDREW: I don't remember these bits, which is probably just as well! There were sort of dark forces at work at that point, but we'll not get into that.

ANNIE: But you kind of overcame the dark forces and stuck together. I mean, did you always feel, whatever happens, 'we must stick together'? Or did you ever think of breaking up?

ANDREW: I don't know   We've just never broken up. There's always bits, it's like a family, there's always bits of moaning and groaning, but . . .

ANNIE: But you've stuck together.

ANDREW: In the end, what do you do? You write songs and you play music and what else?

ANNIE: Some of your songs have been very kind of . . . rock music, and you can hear the influences, as you say, like Thin Lizzy, Rolling Stones, whatever. Then you've gone off on some really mad electronic, quite scary-sounding music. So there are all these different facets. When you're working together are these things pulling you in different directions or do you start to feel that same focus?

ANDREW: No, I think you get after a few weeks or something of writing, starting something new, you get an idea of where it's gonna go, whether it be out-there electronic stuff or maybe more acoustic. It just depends what you've been doing and listening to. Sometimes you feel a bit more like doing acoustic stuff, yeah.

ANNIE: So the basic line-up stayed pretty much . . . you added guest people, who came in and then maybe went away again, but the basic . . . and the writers were always Bobby Gillespie, yourself and Robert Young, weren't they? And then Robert left the band.

ANDREW: Yes.

ANNIE: And as we know very sadly, he left us all last year.

ANDREW: That was tragic.

ANNIE: Well it was, wasn't it? Is there anything you want to say about Throb, as he was known?

ANDREW: Don't know what you can say . . . just glad I spent the time I did with him, and it should have been more. But I've got, as I said at the time, I've got great memories of him . . .

ANNIE: Here's one story which was or wasn't centred around Throb, in the old, let's just say, more hedonistic days. You as a band were asked to do *Top of the Pops*. This meant coming into Luton Airport as you were in Ireland at the time. Apparently it's attributed to Throb, but it might have been any one of you who said: 'We're not going to do *Top of the Pops* because we're not gonna fly into Luton Airport. Because it's not rock 'n' roll enough.'

ANDREW: Well, we'll attribute it to Robert.

ANNIE: That actually happened?

ANDREW: Think so. We didn't make it to *Top of the Pops*, no.

ANNIE: Kate Moss, she became a great follower of yours quite early on, didn't she?

ANDREW: I think we met her at, there's a place, Kinky Disco in Shaftesbury Avenue.

ANNIE: Ooh yeah, *I remember that* [place]! She came to that?

ANDREW: Yeah, she used to come down. She couldn't have been very old then.

ANNIE: Yeah. And then she stayed very much as a supporter of yours.

ANDREW: Yeah, known her since then.

ANNIE: You did Glastonbury. You went on just before The Rolling Stones. How did that feel?

ANDREW: I was very nervous for the first time in years. Yeah. I was mostly nerves, actually. Running on nerves for that one.

ANNIE: What, nervous that you'd play the wrong notes or something?

ANDREW: Yeah, just in general. It was strange. But it seemed to be good. I didn't realise it was any good until four months later we were in a bar in Osaka and they were showing it on the TV.

ANNIE: In Japan?

ANDREW: In Japan, and it was about three in the morning and I realised, oh, we were actually quite good. Because I hadn't heard any of it or seen any of it.

ANNIE: I mean you are very, very famous all round the world, you've just been in America on tour. And so you play festivals all over the world.

ANDREW: We just played this Austin Psych Fest. It's run by a band called the Black Angels, and they'd three generations of psychedelic bands. The 13th Floor Elevators reformed for it. There was us, Spiritualized and the Jesus and Mary Chain and then they had the modern bands, Tame Impala and the Black Angels as well. So it's great and it's kind of three generations of bands and then a lot of young kids in a field in Texas and it was a brilliant atmosphere. Brilliant. I wish every night could be like this because young kids seem to be taking to psychedelic music.

I think when the modern pop music gets rubbish, kids take to old-school psychedelic music. You know, they want to get away from the mainstream. And I'd probably include acid house as psychedelic music, because it is pretty strange music that maybe hasn't got the normal song format. You know? And it doesn't necessarily have to have a chorus or . . .

ANNIE: So it's not verse, chorus like a pop song.

Andrew: And that was another thing that attracted us to it. It was very deconstructed and, you know, they'd just have one loop and it would go on for six minutes, but you know it was good, you didn't get bored.

ANNIE: Right. So that feeling that you had with acid house has carried you through actually, then.

ANDREW: Yeah, I think so.

ANNIE: How important was it for your record company or the record label for you to have hits? I mean, after *Screamadelica* was acknowledged a great, classic album, but then the pressure starts, in a way, because you've got to repeat it. You've got to have chart positions and all that.

ANDREW: Well, I think it's the same with every band. Because you're just enjoying . . . you've *finally* had a hit record, you're getting paid for the first time, you're getting a wage, and then somebody goes: 'Where's the next record?'

It's much better now. Just do what you want. But we've always tended to do what we wanted anyway, much to the annoyance of record companies and A & R guys.

I think you've just got to be true to yourself.

— 23 —

Karl Hyde Part 2 – Born Slippy

If we all have an annus horribilis, one of mine might well have been 1996. It's going to happen to each one of us, at some point: losing a parent. My mother had died when she was comparatively young, sixty, and I was in my twenties. I was an only child, so from then on, it was just my father and myself left. My dad died, two months from his ninetieth birthday, in June 1996.

Other things went awry that year, perhaps not unconnected to the strange trance-like state induced by grief.

A fragile and unsatisfactory relationship ended later in 1996. To avoid Christmas with too many painful memories, I took a trip to Cuba, with disastrous consequences. A horrifying street attack in Havana, my leg broken in three places, and a long, long period of recovery . . .

Throughout that year though there were better memorable moments. The thrill of feeling so involved in the Euro 96 football championships. The pleasure and convenience of having a London base as well as my home in Brighton.

There was the strange allure and ubiquity of a particular piece of music. I will always associate my sadness of early summer onwards with the rave song 'Born Slippy' by Underworld. It was known as the 'lager, lager, lager song' to many, but it touched some deeper vibe in me. I never understood why, till much more recently. Karl Hyde takes up the story from the end of his 1983-era band Freur.

KARL: We did two albums with Underworld Mk1 for Sire Records and toured America a few times and had a minor hit in Australia. And again it didn't go well for us. Basically because, you know, Annie, every time we were on the dole we were making music that was honest.

We were making music which was at the root of what we loved, which was film music, dub and electronics. It was that German sound of Kraftwerk, NEU!, Amon Düül II, you know, the roots of electronics and the things that Conny Plank was doing, and dub, obviously, that John Peel was playing all the time.

And David Bowie's *Low*, I remember, was a big one with us at that time when we were living in Cardiff. And film music. We all *loved* film music and so we fused this stuff together and every time we got a deal we thought: 'Oh, we'd better make pop records to get in the charts.'

We were rubbish at it! We were really rubbish at it. So finally, I stayed on in America to earn enough money to pay the rent. I went up to Paisley Park and worked up there as a session player for a while.

ANNIE: Did you? What, with Prince?

KARL: No, but actually . . . he was putting the New Power Generation together at the time, so we were recording there while he was rehearsing his new band. We got to know them and I saw Miles up there towards the end of his days and playing.

ANNIE: (*somewhat awestruck*) Miles *Davis*?

KARL: Miles Davis, yeah, yeah.

ANNIE: Ooh.

KARL: And, you know, when you're up there, in a place like, that you meet a lot of people: Jimmy Jam, Terry Lewis and Sheila E. and all those, they were coming and going and it was kinda normal, when you were living up there in the Prairies.

And then I got a call to go and be Debbie Harry's guitarist in 1990/91, something like that, and so I toured with Debbie and Chris and we played the Summer of XS, you may remember, at Wembley Stadium, which was INXS's extravaganza that summer.

ANNIE: So Blondie was not then being Blondie?

KARL: No, it was just Chris [Stein] and Debbie, and there was a British band put together around them. A fantastic band, actually. Really great band of mostly session players and me. And I'd just come from recording at Paisley Park where it was all California and New York session players and me. And I was managing to somehow convince people that I had something to offer.

Debbie and Chris were incredibly kind to me and took me in. I auditioned for them in New York which basically consisted of me going shopping with Debbie! They were amazing. I can't thank them enough.

And really for me that enabled me to *let go* of wanting to be a *rock* guitarist. There I was, playing for one of the greatest *pop* singers of all time, playing some of the greatest pop songs of all time in this iconic woman's band, and playing at Wembley Stadium. With my dad in the audience. You know, I was never gonna get there playing football, so . . . ticked that box.

Rick had already started working with a young guy called Darren Emerson, I just couldn't make the decision. Do I give up this thing that I have always loved [rock/pop], and throw my lot in with this funny electronic genre?

Which all sounds a bit weedy, unless you hear it through a big sound system?

And. I. Just. Did. Debbie enabled me to sign off on something and kind of go: 'Look, I've done it.'

In fact the last show I did, we played at CBGBs. We formed a band and played CBGBs in New York and that's where—

ANNIE: With Debbie Harry?

KARL: With Debbie Harry, yeah, and at that time I was walking The Streets at night, just writing what I saw, and what I saw became the lyrics for the *Dubnobass* album.

ANNIE: So your experiences were coinciding with what was happening here in the UK.

KARL: Yeah.

ANNIE: And this thing called acid house and this revolution that was happening in the early nineties. So your time was syncing up with everything else that was happening?

KARL: What was exciting was the many things that came together. One, there was pirate radio. Our manager had a little studio in Wandsworth, and at the end of Underworld Mk1, I'd meet up with Rick at Embankment, at the tube station there, and we'd sit by the river and buy some food and coffee and drink it and have the car radio on.

(*Curious how many London Underground stations feature in Karl Hyde's story: Notting Hill Gate, Embankment, and later in his biggest, most iconic hit, Tottenham Court Road.*)

We'd just be picking up all these pirate stations and they'd all be playing acid house. And acid house to me sounded like this fusion of Hawkwind and Tangerine Dream, which as a kid I absolutely loved, and *Autobahn* by Kraftwerk. This relentless trance-type music, it just seemed like *home*.

Rick decided there was nothing left but to go back to being honest, and making the music that made sense to us.

Le Rossignol adopts European *nouvelle vague* style vibe avec
le petit chat qui s'appelle Sidi Bou Said de Tunisie.

Me, a war baby. My family, the Nightingales, in forties floral fashion frocks.

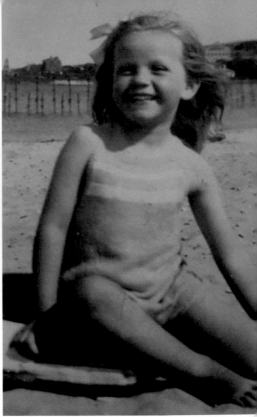

First time on the beach in Dorset. Note the still in place World War Two sea defence stakes stuck in the sand . . . Robust? More *Dad's Army*.

Dennis Wilson of The Beach Boys and me: bringing you good vibrations.

Mick Jagger and me: You can look bored Mick, but so can I.

Wearing Mary Quant, Ginger Group, the 'affordable' line.

Landlord and friend Count William de Belleroche's gift of
his painting to me, above, and me taking the expression
'being top of the pops' rather literally, below.

Kenny Lynch and me at the British
Song Festival. Him with the contested
award, me in that dress.

The posters say it: punk at
The Old Grey Whistle Test.

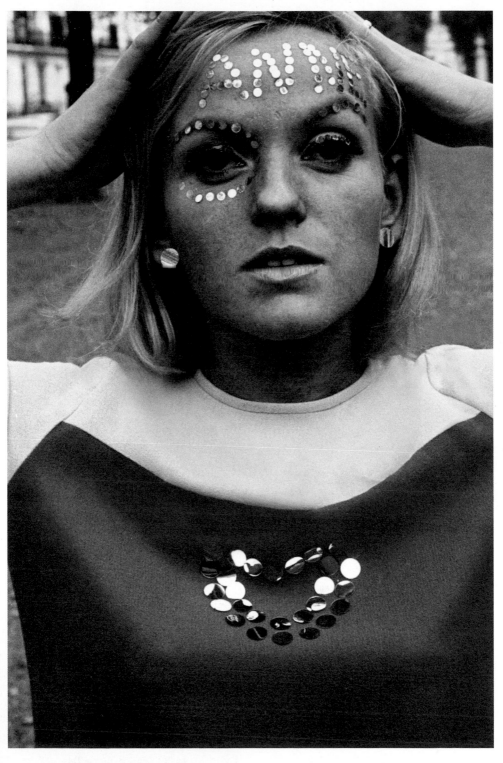

These were stick-on (but never caught on) dotties, avant-garde,
pre glam rock face decoration, in Chelsea.

Jumping Over the Radio 1 DJs.

Gatecrashing Ascot's Royal Enclosure in our irreverent berets: (l-r) me, pop singer Carol Friday and model Nina Jones.

Back in Brighton with the Radio 1 roadshow fans.

Caught in the whirlwind arrival of Billie Eilish at Radio 1.

The elegant Little Simz at Radio 1.

The classic cut and sweep of Alexander McQueen at the Sony Awards.

Ace geezers! *Perestroika* and *Glasnost*: they were the best Russian 'fixers' in Moscow.

Shanghai. At the Oriental Pearl TV tower in China.

Who is this young woman, as John Lennon comes off stage . . . ? What is she thinking: Look at the time, hurry up, you may be The Beatles but the bars close in half an hour?

Come on, she's saying: is that you George Harrison, and that other mop top Paul McCartney behind you?

Oh dear, now she's completely turned her back on the world's most famous drummer and much-loved Ringo Starr. What WAS she thinking?

So that was very, very important. It was pirate radio and it was also the fact that acid house and the rave culture that came out of it seemed to us more punk than punk.

Punk was the first movement I really got, I'd really completely ... that was in a way my generation. I got into it. But what it promised, it didn't deliver, because they all signed record deals. They all were pretending to be outsiders but they became insiders.

And we'd kind of felt outsiders all our lives, and yet we were trying to be insiders too. And then there was this movement that was for outsiders and they didn't care, and they weren't coming inside, and there were like 10,000 people in a warehouse somewhere.

That was really powerful stuff. They didn't need an industry. They were their own tribe. And that was really appealing for somebody who believed in punk for ten minutes. To be offered the opportunity to be part of a tribe which was outside. And was kind of proud of it and making a real success of it. That was too appealing to turn down.

ANNIE: Well it was, I think, such an important time because it was rejecting a lot of stuff that had gone on in the eighties. It was rejecting the sort of what they called 'club culture' there, where you would have the bouncers say: 'Right, it's half past one, everyone go home,' and people were allowed X number of drinks and then, all right kids, that's it, go home. It was so controlled, you felt, by the brewers, the people who were making lager . . .

KARL: (*with a wry smile*) Strangely . . .

ANNIE: That's what it was all about. And so suddenly you had this whole generation saying, well hang on, we don't need this. We'll drink bottled water and we'll have a party in a field. We don't need to have the clubs and the licenses and do it your way.

KARL: And equipment had evolved to a point where people could make music in their bedrooms and they were, and so . . . we were. It's just that they took it on and went, well, you can make music in your bedrooms and for not much money. You can get an acetate made up and play that out, and if people like it, you can sell it.

There is a network of DJ shops which will sell your record. And you could sell a lot of records and you could make good money, selling a lot of records. Maybe never even getting in the charts, but you built up a reputation for yourself that left people wanting more. And the great thing about that time was age *didn't matter*. Nobody cared.

It was about the music. It kinda sounds clichéd now, it almost sounds like a sixties kind of hippy thing, but it kinda was like that era in a way — it was about the music, didn't matter what age you were, there were people *older* than us.

We'd been told 'You're too old now, you've missed your chance.'

ANNIE: What, in the pop world?

KARL: In the pop world. And yet there were people older than us having massive dance-floor hits.

ANNIE: Like? Can you think of a name?

KARL: D'you know, I can't, but I remember seeing pictures of them kind of going . . .

ANNIE: I tell you . . . Who was in System 7 . . .?

KARL: Yeah, Steve Hillage [from Gong].

ANNIE: I was brought into it as well, and I was going to them: 'Look guys, I think this is very exciting what you're doing, but I have actually been round the block. I can't gatecrash your party. I'm not your generation.' They went, 'Yes, come on, join in.'

And I didn't feel like mutton/lamb which is a thing that one might have felt very self-conscious about. They really were very inclusive. Whereas punks had been very, you know, they rejected everybody and . . . didn't *really* hate everybody, but they pretended to.

This was a very inclusive kind of culture and it was more like the sixties. I absolutely agree with you. But you couldn't *say* that because you'd sound like some old hippy!

KARL: Yeah, you would. And yet, look at the projections and the graphics and the acid wheels and it was all very lo-fi. And the dressing up of spaces, that was something that Rick had been talking about for years and years — 'totally immersive spaces'.

And the first rave that we were ever taken to by the guys that were behind the turbo sound systems. They said, 'You've got to come and see this thing.' I remember it was Grooverider who was playing and there were no lights on him. He was up on the stage and no one was looking, and they were all just mingling. The whole space looked like the best Pink Floyd concert you'd never seen. There was some kind of funfair in another room, in another part of the warehouse. The girls weren't being hit on by guys. People were just dancing and having a fantastic time. It was like the audience appeared to be the band. You know?

There appears to be no audience here. It's just all band and the DJ is providing the soundtrack. There was no star culture. There was no superstar culture. It was just about the music, and the challenge was to make a better song than the last one you dropped and to play it . . . I remember going and seeing Jah Shaka, for example, at that time. It had nothing to do with rave, but how he just played with one turntable and you'd think: well, he's just gonna be killing the vibe (having one turntable), and then he'd flip it over, and the other side was *even better* than the last track he'd played. And the place would go *wild*!

And dance parties, they were like that. Each one took you higher and they played with the mood and they knew when to bring it down and take it back up. A good DJ knew when to chill it and when to lift it back up again and how long to do it, and that became really interesting to us.

And going back to what I said about seeing Miles, we'd seen Miles a couple of times, and there was something going on there for me, at that time, watching a great DJ who knew how to read an audience, was basically improvising, like Miles improvised.

ANNIE: (*in case any potential listeners were in any doubt!*) Say Miles Davis . . .

KARL: Oh yeah, Miles Davis. Yeah, yeah. For me, there is only one Miles, sorry. If there's anyone else, it's Miles Davis. There was a comparison there that I felt, watching someone like Miles Davis improvise and watching a great DJ improvise. They were using records and the record decks were instruments. It was all instruments. And we didn't talk about musicians and DJs anymore, we just talked about people playing out with whatever.

In fact, we decided we weren't gonna be a group. We'd given up on that. Rick was doing great. Without him and his vision we wouldn't have had a band. Without him salvaging the studio we'd built and putting it in the back bedroom of his terraced house in Romford, we would never have been able to have made the music that we made in the nineties. So everything was down to him and he tirelessly worked away at learning his craft, at making dance music. With Darren Emerson giving him thoughts and guidance about the things that he was playing out.

ANNIE: And this was sort of early nineties.

KARL: Yeah, it was early nineties. I was backwards and forwards to Los Angeles and then to Minnesota, to Paisley Park, and we were starting to record a bit.

ANNIE: As Underworld?

KARL: As nothing actually. As nothing. And then I think we decided to keep the name. Largely because it was a good name and also because, well, we didn't want to hide the past.

The last thing we wanted was for people to go, 'Well they've got this dirty past, this pop group thing that they're trying to hide.' I thought, no, let's say, 'Of course, and without it, without all those mistakes that we made, we wouldn't be here.'

The early days of Underworld Mk2, they were about putting food on the table and paying the rent, so we did other projects to enable us to do that. We were very fortunate that Rick had friends that gave him little corporate gigs to do, little adverts and things.

I was doing session work. I could make enough money doing session work. And then we formed this collective with a bunch of other fantastic artists that we called Tomato. In the early nineties it became quite an iconic company in terms of graphic design, and TV commercials. The Tomato aesthetic became quite a dominant look in that early to mid-nineties period.

It became a hub for a lot of creativity that was happening right there in Soho. And so with these guys we started making TV commercials and making fantastic money — really, really good money.

ANNIE: Can you say what any of the products were?

KARL: Yeah, we were doing things like Coca-Cola and Levi's. We were doing adverts for major theme parks across America. Though we wouldn't do cigarette adverts and we wouldn't do alcohol adverts. We passed on earning a lot of money by not doing those two products. We decided that even though we both had a bit of a personal problem, addicted to both, it wasn't something that we wanted to sell to people.

That was kind of our problem.

So the money that we made making commercials, it caused quite a few of our contemporaries to put us down and say that we were selling out. But it enabled us to *not* have to sign a record deal and *not* have to compromise our music.

So with the rent getting paid, we could just do whatever we wanted. And it seemed that the more that we did what we wanted — the more people liked it!

The more people it connected with, which was something that hadn't occurred to me before. I'd always thought you *had* to *comply*. Which is stupid. Yeah, that was a real waste of life, that was.

ANNIE: I think you have to take that journey in order to reach that conclusion. You probably couldn't have circuited, shortcut, to arrive at that point.

KARL: Well, there are others that did.

ANNIE: It's probably you had to . . . Were there?

KARL: Yeah, I admired a lot of the others that did.

ANNIE: Like who?

KARL: All the bands that were on Rough Trade. You know, I always admired those guys. And a lot of the guys that John Peel was playing, whether I liked them or not, bands like the Fall. They were cutting their own path. I have a lot of admiration for those people. We didn't do it that way. We made a lot of mistakes.

So eventually, when now we're selling a lot of 12-inches, we've had the great fortune of meeting and being accepted by Junior Boy's Own Records who were such a cool label at that time. Such cool DJs — Andrew Weatherall and Terry Farley, Pete Heller and Steven Hall, who was running the label, who became part of our team and still is. They were amazing, and just guided us so brilliantly, and every 12 sold more and more and more.

And then of course the labels come to your door and they'd put big bags of money on the table and go, 'We're really interested in signing you.'

And we were able to go: 'But we're already making more than that. You know . . . no offence, we're with this great label that's delivering. Thanks ever so much, but these guys, we're really happy with them, and we're gonna stay with them.'

We didn't have a contract. There were no contracts. Because we'd spent years in the business with people saying, 'If we don't get on, this contract isn't worth the paper it's written on.'

Which was never true. So we thought, OK, let's not have a contract, then. And let's just have it as word of honour. And that's what we did. And we stuck with Junior Boy's Own. We just put out a record for Frankie Knuckles on Junior Boy's Own again, they got the label back together and I'm so proud, so proud to have been on that label.

ANNIE: Absolutely. So, to 1996 which was when . . . I guess that was the big, if you like, commercial breakthrough with 'Born Slippy'.

KARL: Mmm.

ANNIE: I know you've probably told this story a lot of times, but to a lot of people it was the 'lager, lager, lager, lager' story. Please, if you could put right or say what it was about *actually*, rather than perhaps it's been misinterpreted or just what your views are.

KARL: OK, yeah.

ANNIE: What was going on at the time? How did it fit into what was happening?

KARL: What was happening was fantastic. It was beyond my wildest dreams. It really was happening for us. And for a period of time Soho was one of the epicentres. There were bands and artists, Goldie and the Metalheadz were just round the corner, the George on D'Arblay Street was where a lot of the new comedy writers gathered, *The Fast Show*, and Vic Reeves and Bob Mortimer were meeting for kind of script madnesses and DJs were in that pub there and other bands and artists. Heavenly Records was just around the corner. There were kind of pop-up clubs happening everywhere. There were mad poetry readings and just random stuff. And I remember for a while thinking, 'We are *where* it's happening.' And it probably lasted for five minutes, but it was a nice feeling.

And what did happen was when we decided that we were gonna make a go of this band and call it Underworld again.

I think it was Rick's wife who very astutely said to me, 'If you're going to be serious about this, you're gonna have to really dig deep this time and pull something special out.' And she was right, because if I'd have carried on the way I was I would have just written generic pap.

So I had to find something special and I remembered when I was at art school I had this kind of pact with myself. I would go out at night, get very drunk down in the docks in Cardiff, but always carry a sheaf of paper and a pen.

And while I was drunk, I would put these ideas on these pieces of paper. I'd wake up the next day and go, 'Wow, these are great ideas!' I'd turn those ideas into artworks and I did really well out of it. I got a very good degree doing that.

So I remembered this and I thought, 'I know, I'll do the same thing again.' So unfortunately, it worked . . .

ANNIE: What, the getting drunk bit?

KARL: Yeah. It worked and I carried a notebook. I mean, it's the same notebook I carry to this day. It's the same make and everything, and I would go out at night on the streets of London.

Particularly the East End, completely drunk off my face, and stuff would happen and I'd write it down and I'd catch the last train back to Romford and I'd write it down. And the next day I would go, 'Wow, this is pretty powerful stuff!' Because this is what I'd seen walking the streets when I was working with Debbie Harry in New York. I'd heard Lou Reed's *New York* album, and I'd thought, I wonder how Lou did that? He sounded to me like he was singing in *conversational American*. I imagined how he did it and did my own version of it.

But to do that, being quite a reserved, shy bloke from the Midlands, I had to get drunk to do it. To go to places that I wouldn't have the guts to go to if I was sober. Do things and be with people and have adventures that resulted in these lyrics. So 'Born Slippy' . . .

There's a few songs on the first album, *Dubnobass*, where I'm asking for help because I'm painting a picture that's so dark, that if you understood that it was autobiographical you'd think, 'This guy, we need to get him out of here!' But of course nobody did.

And at that time everybody thought, 'Yeah, mad, wo-ho!' And the consequence of 'Born Slippy' was that the night that we first played it after it had been released, the lager cans went in the air. I was *horrified* to realise it was a drinking anthem rather than understood as this cry for help — a kind of a rather elaborate and sad, misplaced cry for help on my part.

ANNIE: This happens to people [writers] kind of [saying] . . . Ooh, that's not what I meant.

KARL: Yeah.

ANNIE: A bit like . . . the [Harry Enfield] Loadsamoney comedy character that people started idolising? Thought it was a serious *boast* about having a lot of money . . .

KARL: It was like that. And of course we'd come out of that era of that kind of Comic Strip humour and all of that. That would have gone into our psyche. Yeah, it was interesting.

That night, if we look back afterwards, I was in the Ship on Wardour Street. There was a friend of a friend who was very blonde, and she became the most blonde I ever met, in the lyric.

There was this other guy, and I remember he had this T-shirt on and it had a picture of a bunny and the words Bastard Bunny (*nineties satirical cartoon character*). I always remembered this name and I would tell people: 'Yeah, I was in the Ship with the most blonde and Bastard Bunny,' and people would laugh and I'd go: 'I was, *I was!*'

And I could see this guy's face who wore the T-shirt. And I staggered out the toilet, gave the bloke a tenner and said, 'Get a round in.' Then staggered off up the street, off to Romford and wrote the lyric.

Years later, I think it was only a couple of years ago, I was on Radio 4 and we were in the middle of an interview and it just suddenly became clear who it was wearing the Bastard Bunny T-shirt. It was Bill Bailey. (*For the avoidance of any doubt, the Bill Bailey who went on to become an internationally renowned comedian.*)

And I'm saying: 'Hold it, hold the interview. I remember who it was now. It was Bill Bailey. He was there with me that night.'

The BBC got a phone call from Bill Bailey who'd heard me and he said, 'Yeah, it was me.' So we met up. I asked him, 'What happened then [that night in the pub], Bill?' He couldn't remember either!

ANNIE: So he was there the night of the . . . the creation of 'Born Slippy'?

KARL: Yeah, he was, yeah.

ANNIE: And why was it called 'Born Slippy'?

KARL: Oh 'Born Slippy'? It's the name of a greyhound. We used to go down . . . there's a dog track in Romford and we used to go down the dog track and, d'you know, just to put a few quid on, and it was a good night out. And the racing form books, they have some of the most fantastic names of dogs in them. So the second album's got things like 'Sappy's Curry' in there, 'Pearl's Girl'. They're all racing dogs.

ANNIE: I'm sure lots of people who've done their research would know that, but it's quite nice just to hear it from *you*. So there was your huge nineties success and then that just went . . . that's just carried on.

KARL: But we didn't want to release it ['Born Slippy']. See, we'd released it already as a 12-inch with Junior Boy's Own. It had done incredibly well. And then it was Danny Boyle who picked it up . . . he wanted it on *Trainspotting*. And we turned him down.

ANNIE: Did you?

KARL: Yeah. Because, well, our mates had read Irvine Welsh's book and they told us it was all about caning it and how wicked it was and, 'Oh, it's mad, man. It's all about caning.' And we were like, 'Yeah, right. Our music's not going on *that* film.'

But Danny invited us into the edit suite and said, 'I don't think you quite understand what this film's about.' And he showed us scenes and we were convinced it wasn't glorifying caning it. And we said, 'Yeah, it's fine to use our music.'

But when it took off and the film was such a huge success, the pressure was on us to re-release it. At that time we just thought doing that was cheese, so we fought it. We really fought it. JBO petitioned a hundred DJs around the country and ninety-nine of them came back with: 'You've got to re-release this. The dance floor goes crazy when we play it and people go off their nuts. They're trying to buy it and they can't buy it.'

However, the DJ that was resident at the Top Rank in Cardiff, he *hated* it and to this day we think — good on you, mate!

ANNIE: So the ninety-nine DJs won? They said it's got to be re-released?

KARL: And we did, yeah.

ANNIE: And *Trainspotting* was now out?

KARL: It was, yeah, and it was doing the business. And the two became synonymous. It was *Trainspotting* and 'Born Slippy' that summer really. Nailed it for a lot of people.

*

I am moved to think that every time I heard this song something in me empathised, responded emotionally . . . I had never thought for a moment that 'Born Slippy' was about glorifying lager. Or 'caning it'. It felt altogether much more melancholic.

For me, it became a lament for my father. So it's almost comforting to know that 'Born Slippy' actually was a *cri de coeur*.

— 24 —

Dusty Springfield

Interior. Day. Four-star West End London hotel room. Dusty Springfield has carried out nine interviews already today, to promote her latest album. She is trying unsuccessfully to grab lunch. Bread and salad, which had been laid out in front of her. Some time earlier.

ANNIE: Nice to see you in England, and quite surprisingly, actually . . . you've been living in America for so long.

DUSTY: Eons and eons, far too long.

ANNIE: Welcome back, though don't know what's brought you back (*dubiously*) here?

DUSTY: It was the river. I'd always had this dream of . . . when I was living in LA, for far too long. I would daydream about coming back, finding a place on the Thames. And that's exactly what I've done. I'm ecstatic at the moment; plumbing doesn't work, things fall apart, but it's on the Thames. There are no rivers in LA. Well, an underground one that floods, a canal, that fills up once a year. So I wanted a river. I grew in West Wycombe, not too far away from the river. So I came back . . . for that.

ANNIE: Well, you gotta have a boat, then.

DUSTY: Yes, but, well . . . I can't swim. So perhaps not. It's a bit dodgy, isn't it? People I know have got boats, so . . . Ducks and geese, I just watch them for a while and then I feel (*she exhales*) . . . OK-aay.

ANNIE: Going back to the beginning. I first met you during *Ready Steady Go!* days. And it was *huge fun*. But was it for you, too?

DUSTY: Well, probably less fun for me because I was always trying to stick my eyelashes on, or panic because it was live, and I'd go missing because I was so *nervous*. 'No, I can't go on, till I've got my eyelashes on,' and it was always *late* because the rehearsals had gone on so long, things broke down.

The New Year's Eve ones were the best (*I second that!!*). Totally bonkers because everyone was so smashed, and people did go missing, on the night. I used to do some of the announcing.

(*Curious that the role, the 'job' of being a presenter, had not yet been given a title.*)

The first three *Ready Steady Go!*s were me, before I had a record out. It was so hit or miss. I don't think it was all good. But it always came over fine. There's never been a programme since with that kind of immediacy. The cameras would go so low, they did it on *Top of the Pops* as well. The English TV programmes still do it. They make you look like you've gone eighteen rounds with Mike Tyson. To this day, if I see the camera sink low, I go low as well, I sink, down to my knees if necessary. If you are gonna do it, I'm gonna do it.

ANNIE: Is it true you had big hits with the Springfields in the US *before* The Beatles?

DUSTY: Well yes. Only one. 'Silver Threads and Golden Needles'. One fluke hit. It was made in the downstairs studio at Philips in Marble Arch. It became massive in the States. Everyone thought we were a country act. In those days they wrote a song in half an hour. On the way to Nashville I heard two records that changed my life. One was 'Tell Him' by the Exciters. I heard that and said: '*That's* what I want to do!' Then I heard 'Don't Make Me Over' by Dionne Warwick, and I said: '*THAT'S* what I want to do, too.'

The Springfields had filled a gap. Dropped into a vacuum. We were cheerful. No one else looked like that. Cheerful and loud as we were. We were trying to be the Kingston Trio. We were given a TV series back in the UK before we'd even had a record.

There's one wonderful clip, we'd just done 'Wimoweh', and I back announced it in this very Sylvia Peters [early BBC female TV 'personality'] voice (*adopts patronising posh accent*): 'End thet was a Zooloo twuuune.'

I'd had elocution lessons, had come fourth in England, and all of that, and I thought that was how you were supposed to sound. Very un-pop. I had to unlearn that. It was really easy for me to go solo after that. Because the Springfields never ever intended to stay together. We all wanted to do different things, so it wasn't a struggle.

(*Dusty as a solo singer hit her stride straight away, with continuous hits through the sixties.*)

ANNIE: I remember at the San Remo song festival, for some reason, you ripped up all the lyrics, in front of the audience. Threw them up in the air. There was pandemonium. I can't remember *why* you did that.

DUSTY: Because I didn't know the song. Or the band had played it wrong, or something . . . I was given to doing stuff like that. It wasn't a very good thing to do. That was prior to 'You Don't Have to Say You Love Me', or I wouldn't have been asked back, I'm sure. I was singing something I absolutely hated, and couldn't cope, couldn't do the lyrics without the paper. I'm very near-sighted so couldn't see the lyrics . . . it all seemed like a terrible idea.

But (*sings*): *Io che non vivo senza te* . . . sounds terrific in Italian, was a beautiful song. In Italian. So . . . Italian.

In fact, 'Io che non vivo (senza te)' reached the final of the San Remo song festival in 1965. Dusty heard it there after her own entry, sung in Italian, had been eliminated. She spent the following year trying to engineer a translated version to record in English. Eventually her friend/manager Vicki Wickham, the booker on *Ready Steady Go!* (who had also signed me for my first TV series), and future manager of Wham!, Simon Napier-Bell, famously wrote the English lyrics in the back of a taxi, on their way to a club. Later it was recorded by Elvis Presley, Glen Campbell, Cher, Jackie DeShannon and numerous others.

DUSTY: I'd been sitting on this song for a year, terrified that someone else would do it. I kept it under the bed. The single, the original Italian version. Vicki and Simon found something in the song. But they had no idea what the meaning of the Italian lyrics were.

Nobody knew what it was about, even in English. Especially the second line after 'You don't have to say you love me' — including me. My diction has always been terrible — *just be close at hand*?

(*This song became Dusty's only number 1 hit.*)

ANNIE: You were never a singer-songwriter though?

DUSTY: I wrote the B-sides for my first two singles, for which I was most grateful — for which my bank manager was most grateful. But I'm not a natural writer. Gosh I wish I was! I have *ideas* — and then I can't carry them through. Typical Aries trait. (*I second that, wholeheartedly.*) Not finishing things.

ANNIE: After that initial run of success, what was the next high point?

DUSTY: I think it was moving to the States, really. I'd done as much in England as I could. I'd had the longest run of anyone. The records had started to dip. They were sort of slipping. I'd always had the American Dream. I thought things would be *very* different there. I'd been going there, but it was always a bit flukeish, as though I'd rode in on the coat-tails of the Liverpool invasion. My visits had been intermittent. I'd always have to come back and carry on here [in the UK]. Everything is global now. It was more insular then.

ANNIE: What about having a reputation as a soul singer and going to America in the time of Aretha Franklin?

DUSTY: Well, it was actually very intimidating. What is viewed as soulful here is not necessarily viewed as soulful there, by the real soul people. And I thought it was very sad — in that we used to copy all their material. Most of the time I was kind of 'adopted', certainly by Motown. And could hang out with great people.

ANNIE: Like?

DUSTY: Like? Like Wilson Pickett, and not so well-known people like Sugar Pie DeSanto, who had that great song 'Soulful Dress', and I used to hang out at the Apollo all the time. It was great. I was so protected, there was such affection for me. I had the best time in my life. Terrific. I was treated really well. A lot of partying. I didn't actually move to the States till 1973, but I was in and out of there, liking what I saw and wanting to be there more.

ANNIE: Let's talk about specific songs. 'Going Back'. I read that Carole King burst into tears when she heard your version.

DUSTY: I *worship* Carole King. Nothing could please me more, than have her burst into tears because of me! I know that most everything she writes. I want to sing. And have always wanted to.

We met in the Brill Building in New York, when she was really just a teenager. She sat at the piano and I was *wild* about what she wrote. At the time it was songs like 'It Might As Well Rain Until September'. There just this whole *school* of them: Barry Mann, Cynthia Weill, Ellie Greenwich. Randy Newman later.

ANNIE: Bacharach and David too?

DUSTY: Princes, those people! I couldn't sing everything Bacharach wrote. He wrote truly difficult things. They were too difficult for me. The perfect voice for them was Dionne. That gossamer quality. I didn't have the lightness; it was almost like she was *touching* the notes. Whereas I have a much heavier voice, so it was harder for me to sing them.

So difficult. Songs like, though I never recorded it, 'A House Is Not a Home' . . . such great songs . . .

ANNIE: What about 'Little by Little'? What does that mean to you now? I'm just picking this one now, almost random . . .

DUSTY: Well, it was time to do an uptempo song. It served its purpose, but . . . I'm essentially a ballad singer really. It was never one of my faves.

ANNIE: (*somewhat aghast at this revelation – 'Little by Little' had always been one of* my *favourites among Dusty's songs*) Well, what about 'Son of a Preacher Man', then? (*Was she going to diss this as well?*) What did you think when it turned up in *Pulp Fiction*?

DUSTY: Oh I loved it. It was my first platinum disc. All these years and I'd not got a platinum disc. It showed up at the door. I didn't know it was coming, thought it was something I'd ordered from a catalogue. I was always ordering stuff from catalogues. Like gadgets and things. All lined up under the stairs because I can't use them. Didn't have a label on it. So I took it out of the box; it was enormously heavy, a poster of *Pulp Fiction*, very flashy platinum disc of the soundtrack at the bottom.

I was really touched. That they'd bothered. The film company. I haven't got it up on the wall because it's the wrong colour! So it's just leaning against the wall. I'm renting this old, old house, it's a converted granary. The previous tenants had left lots of holes, where they had banged nails in. All the plaster chipping off.

ANNIE: What did you think of the film?

DUSTY: I haven't seen it.

ANNIE: You haven't? Oh you must! I've seen it twice. (*I had to see it twice – to understand it!*)

DUSTY: Well, it's out on video now . . . but I know it's incredibly violent.

ANNIE: And, well, I was going to ask you what you thought of the social implications of your recording being used that could be seen to romanticise heroin taking? (*The relevant scene is Uma Thurman's character chopping out lines of white powder on a mirror surface as 'Son of a Preacher Man' plays on the soundtrack.*) But if you haven't seen the film yet . . . So just going back in your story, you seem to have then disappeared for ages and ages and I gather not had too fantastic a time?

DUSTY: I got bored with the whole thing. Went into the whole LA bag, the drugs and the drinking. I really did that very badly.

ANNIE: Who does it well?

DUSTY: Well I'm not very talented at it. Some people seem to be able to do it very well. But it starts barking at you. I turned into this really obnoxious person. I am lucky enough to be able to stop. Not everyone can.

ANNIE: Maybe it depends if you have an addictive personality.

DUSTY: Totally. I even took up smoking for a while. A singer! I gave that up twelve years ago. So then I had to take time to put my life back together again. Trail of wreckage everywhere. I'd got very fried. I never did heavy stuff. Coke wasn't a good drug for me. I took it for a very short time, and it finished me off, so I took time to get my life back. I knew I couldn't do music again immediately. Wasn't even sure I wanted to do music . . .

But then, the good things that have happened to me usually come out of the blue.

I was sitting in someone's back garden — back *yard* in LA — under one of the few trees there with branches, and I had a call from Vicki in New York. She said: 'You're not going to believe this idea.'

I'd heard of the Pet Shop Boys. I'd nearly had an accident on the freeway listening to 'West End Girls'. Wow, I thought, who's *that*? And had to pull over. Subsequently rushed out and bought everything they'd done. I just loved them, the sound and the intelligence of the lyrics.

So they sent me a tape of a new song called 'What Have I Done to Deserve This?' And said they needed a fast answer. Like within twenty-four hours. I played the tape *once*, and got back to them within five minutes. I said to Vicki, 'I don't know what they want me to do.' But I knew I wanted to be part of it.

I came to London to record the song with them. But I still didn't know what they wanted from me. Then Neil Tennant said: 'Just your voice, we want the sound of your voice.'

I didn't think that would be enough.

But it was. It was fine.

— 25 —

Paris

It had begun a few years before. An anonymous 12-inch white label vinyl record. Handwritten in biro across it in a scrawl: 'Da Funk'. Not sure it even had Daft Punk written on it.

There was this beeping traffic noise at the beginning, then the yowling synth, and the thudding, insistent beat behind it. The impact was immediate; no soft, mixable, creep fade-in. This was bang, like a maniac speed driving round the utterly bewildering no-lanes-no-system thoroughfare at the Arc de Triomphe. Terrifying, negotiating the craziest Parisian roundabout, especially if you are driving with a right-hand steering wheel.

Never again, I had said, pulling into a nearby side street, body shaking for hours afterwards.

Never again am I driving in Paris with the wrong steering configuration. Or with someone directing me whose nearest grasp of 'straight on' was . . . 'stretch'. Issued in a vague, worried whisper from the back seat.

Maybe that's why I warmed to the opening bars of 'Da Funk'. It felt like the soundtrack to a documentary.

This sensation of a nightmare drive in an endless circle, every other vehicle seemingly gunning for you, ever other vehicle beeping and hooting, and your heart pounding BOMP BOMP BOMP BOMP, four to the floor.

And never forgetting the — to me — always chilling French road rule: *Priorité à droite*.

Anyone, *anyone* coming from the right has right of way.

That was my introduction to Daft Punk and the overpowering music scene they opened up in the mid to late nineties. French music has not adapted well to all areas of pop music culture. Rap, yes, that works a treat in French. Rock songs not so much, punk rather better. But nothing had the impact of those early French balladeers, like Sharrllezz Trennayyyy with 'Laaaar Meeerrrrrrrr' and '*Noooonnn, jeeeeeerrrrrr nerrrrrrr reggggg-gggrrrreettte rrrrriennn*' dragging out the full drama of the French 'g' and 'r' pronunciation as Édith Piaf did so spectacularly. So many native English speakers seem so reluctant, embarrassed even, to have a go at speaking French with a French accent . . . Try rolling out the name of the venue for the annual French Open tennis tournament. Enunciate the words Roland Garros with a gargle deep in your throat in a proper French growl — it's very satisfying. Singing 'No, I regret nothing' in English? Just ain't no comparison.

I believe my entire education was changed for the better over an incident like this. My father had grown up in France. I came home from my convent school aged ten, and repeated to him what the Irish nuns had taught us that day.

'Joan of Arc was burnt at the stake at Roo-enn.'

'Roo-**enn**?' he thundered, normally so mild mannered, my dad. 'It's not Rooo-**enn**, its *Gggrrwwrruuuu-onnnn*.' I was moved schools within a year.

And who couldn't love 'Ça plane pour moi', the Belgian taking-the-piss-out-of-punk hit by Plastic Bertrand who didn't even sing it himself on the record, and which was made in north-west London. In those compliance-free, carefree days, I could play that very readily and frequently on Radio 1, because no one knew what the speeded-up lyric actually meant. There were rumours that it was about masturbation, but people say that about a lot of songs with opaque lyrics.

The UK rave scene, so prevalent in the early nineties, played little creative part in the emerging French dance genre. However, the two Scottish guys out of Slam who gave us the classic 'Positive Education' were running the small but influential label, Soma. They happened on a rave near Disneyland Paris. And met up with Guy-Manuel de Homem-Christo and Thomas Bangalter, who gave them a tape of 'Da Funk'.

A white label fell into my hands. I was entranced, played it over and over, both on Radio 1 and at live gigs and clubs. I included 'Da Funk' by Daft Punk on my compilation *Annie On One* on the so-respected label Heavenly. By then I was discovering that there was a whole raft of French DJs and producers creating this new kind of electronic music. Dimitri from Paris, Laurent Garnier, Étienne de Crécy, the late Philippe Zdar of Motorbass and Cassius . . . and the label Ed Banger Records.

The symbiosis between the rave music scene and football coincided nicely with France being host nation for the 1998 World Cup.

The new French wave of dance music was not about lyrics. It was about very, very funky beats. I hatched a plan to broadcast some of the best French dance music live from Paris on the eve of the *Coupe du Monde*.

This was when Paris really, really came alive as a city again for me. My first experiences there went back more than forty years . . .

*

Through whatever medium we could grab hold of, the newly-baptised teenagers were inhaling influences from all over the USA, the UK and . . . France. Just how devastated the whole of Europe had been by the Second World War was not exactly appreciated by the generally disinterested post-war kids. I found this to be much the same returning to Romania, fifteen years after the spectacular Christmas revolution there in 1989. Spectacular the way the people *really* rose up and showed they'd had enough. The dictator Nicolae Ceausescu was tried one day, and then, no dithering, executed by firing squad the next. I met clubbers while DJ'ing at a Black Sea resort near Constanta, Romania in the mid-noughties; for them the whole issue of the revolution was gone, passé, irrelevant. Dismissed. Whatever. Perhaps tis ever thus, and hence Marty Feldman's classic grumpy old man line to a teenager:

'I *died* in the war for people like you.'

We, they, had been born into the rubble of bombed, burnt out buildings. Now there was an eagerness in the air, an impatience to restart, and move on. If they'd put the lights back on in part, if not all over Europe, we wanted to get out there, celebrate the switch-on and party. The newspapers were full of miserable austerity, rationing, and coverage of government ministers with names to my child's ear, more like ogres from Grimm's fairy tales, or mass murderers . . . Emanuel Shinwell . . . Clement Attlee . . . the even more sinister sounding Sir Stafford Cripps. They appeared only ever to wear black, probably because they were seen never in living colour, only in smudgy newsprint photographs or monochrome film newsreels. All these leaders seemed remote, dark, and really, really gloomy. The age of JFK and the glamour televisual politician was still a way off.

The light, the future, the colour and the rhythm was coming through literature and the movies. From new method actors and directors: Brando and James Dean, Nicolas Ray and Elia Kazan, in Hollywood, and from the beginnings of the *nouvelle vague* in France.

By the mid-fifties, the hippest street in Europe was the Boulevard Saint-Michel on the Left Bank in Paris. Especially around the area of the intersection with the Boulevard Saint-Germain. Here, the new bohemian chic flourished.

To be a scenester here you would hang out at the café Les Deux Magots, and on the streets around the Sorbonne, Saint-Germain-des-Prés, the Pantheon and St Sulpice, or 'up the hill' in the *boîtes* of Montmartre. You smoked American Kent cigarettes, or the far stronger local Gitanes or Gauloises in their loose blue paper wrappers.

You listened to the music of Juliette Gréco, a perfect bohemian icon with long unkempt-looking hair and dark stark clothes, hanging straight off her gaunt frame, a look later adopted by art students everywhere. All of this was happening in the City of Couture, but we might as well been a million miles away from the Rue Cambon, in the always posh 1st arrondissement of Coco Chanel and, not far away, Avenue Montaigne of Christian Dior. Although when Yves Saint Laurent took over Dior and launched 'The Beat Look' in 1960 . . . his Rive Gauche had been inspired by . . . guess what.

This was the street Paris of strong smells (and few of them fragrant as Guerlain's 'L'Heure Bleue', or Balmain's 'Vent Vert'). This was the Paris of pungent garlic fumes being breathed all over you on the Métro, and strong body odour wafting across those languishing in the bars. It was the world of impoverished artists, writers, students and the already cliched notion of the Irma La Douce sex worker with her almost visibly beating heart of gold.

Every apartment block wall on every street corner was adorned and daubed with faded painted aperitif advertisements for Byrrh, Dubonnet, Ricard, Pernod. The first time I went to Paris I lost ten pounds in weight in a week and nearly picked up an STD. But I so wanted to be there. Paris had the zeitgeist. You whistled the theme music to *Rififi*, a cult gangster heist movie (movies like this always featured chain-smoking leading actors wearing trilbys, turned-up collars and tooled up with guns). There were dodgy people everywhere. You would get ripped off at the railway stations, gullibly giving money away in exchange for bogus directions. Well, only once unless you were happy to be treated as a complete *idiot*. It was a steep learning curve.

You would read Jean Paul Sartre and admire the wiry sculpture of Giacometti and the paintings of Kandinsky and Klee. Paris had night clubs and neon and sex, and no one seemed to care if you were underage. New York had its jazz, advertising, and skyscrapers. Paris had ruthless hard-edged judgmental chic. Before rock 'n' roll handed popular culture to the young, literature and cinema were still proving the inspiration. In Paris, at the open-air book stalls along the Seine, were blatantly available copies of controversial and previously censored books such James Joyce's *Ulysses*, Henry Miller's *Tropic Of Cancer* and *Tropic of Capricorn*, published in the 1930s in Paris by Obelisk Press and banned in the United States until the sixties. These were the novels smuggled into the US that were to inspire and influence Jack Kerouac and the entire Beat Generation movement.

Oh, how the Parisiens mocked the Brits and Americans for their prudery and showed stylised aloofness towards anyone who didn't speak their language. Especially if you didn't know what *merde* meant. Or *enculé*. (But I'm with them on that. Go to France — speak French!)

Their writers seemed to be connecting with the young like only J. D. Salinger with *Catcher in the Rye* was doing in the US. And it was a French teenager who led the way, Françoise Sagan, who wrote her first best seller at the age of nineteen. We young girls lapped up *Bonjour Tristesse*. Wow, how cool (even if it was the Hollywood movie version that really made Sagan famous, with very established La La Land stars such as David Niven and Deborah Kerr). Sagan had taken her nom de plume from a Proust character, even more existentially cool, and opened the door to a very glamourous and sophisticated French way of life.

Which is why we flocked to Paris, to hang out and pick up some of that hipness. Sagan's second success was *A Certain Smile*, which made a star of Jean Seberg in the Hollywood version, and short cropped hair on girls was now decreed sexy. Well, on some of them. It was the louche way we were impressed by — bored teenagers having sophisticated sexual affairs with older men. Sagan herself led a fairly colourful life, being caught up in a financial scandal with the French government and arrested for cocaine possession in the nineties. She died in 2004.

Hollywood provided the soundtrack, still all a bit syrupy, now upgraded with a bit of French accordion thrown into the mix for local authenticity. That smooth-as-Armagnac voice of Johnny Mathis made 'A Certain Smile' an international hit. I'm not sure he really caught the 'milieu' or the genuine 'ennui', but I doubt the recording industry was troubled by any of that.

I rode around Paris singing loudly and out of tune my own version of the Michel LeGrand sweeping-strings hit 'Sous Les Ponts De Paris' whilst clinging onto the back of a scooter driven by a German student with green teeth. I let my long hair stream out behind me, there being no crash helmets then, but mainly because I was trying to emulate B.B. in *Et Dieu . . . Créa La Femme* (*And God Created Woman* — the movie directed by B.B.'s then bloke, Roger Vadim).

This launched the Brigitte Bardot phenomenon, the St Tropez lifestyle and gave her the sex kitten image she was to endure for the rest of her life. Welcome or not. She managed, rather in the style of her successor Kate Moss, to be cool, detached and incredibly successful simultaneously. Girls wanted to be her; the boys lusted after her.

This was my fix. But I ran out of money, even saving every franc possible by nearly starving (as French women do generally, voluntarily) and sharing a single camp bed in a partitioned half a room with a girl who had already caught Le Clap after a few weeks of living the Parisian bohemian existence. You had to sing 'nonnn, je-ne- err-rregg-rr-ett-ere err-rr-i-ienn-erre' rolling the 'rrr's, and gutturally ekeing out as many dramatic syllables as possible. Loudly, defiantly and bravely, to live out this existence.

'Wouldnt it be nice to get on with me neighbours
But they've made it very clear, they've got no room for ravers'

Teenagers elsewhere were on the move, even if they hadn't made it to hardcore Paris. Which is why there were raves. Weekend ragged travelling gangs of noisy young people descending usually on tourist haunts. Raves were, and are, like going on holiday without your parents or any other supervision, with your friends and doing anything you want, and listening to wildly unfamiliar music, flirting and dancing.

The original ravers dressed like French bohemians in vintage, smoking Gauloises or the devil's weed, swigging dubious *vin ordinaire* or Pastis, flash mobbing, the word of mouth having spread from metropolitan clubs and coffee bars. Ravers would descend *en masse* by hitch-hiking, or by train, motorcycle or crammed to the hilt in an old banger of a Hillman Minx or a Sunbeam-Talbot. Seaside resorts on the south and east coasts were favourites because you could sleep for free on the beaches or under the piers. No one had money to stay in hotels. It wouldn't have been half the fun, anyway. Free love was catching on, but risky as there was no contraceptive pill yet and abortion was illegal and very dangerous. Naturally events such as these were extremely discouraged by middle-class parents such as mine. I am *still* furious about not being allowed to go to a particularly attractive-sounding rave at the picturesque Brownsea Island in Dorset.

The ravers were reluctantly welcomed in less than lovely chilly resorts, who were struggling in the bleak post-war years and had to be grateful even for the scruffy, skint student types.

These tight wads would buy one half pint of cider between six and clutter up the pub all evening. If the weather was fine, these young itinerants would rather gather outside anyway, spilling out into the streets, safer for drinking for the underage. And the ravers would bring their own generally unwelcome noise with them. A readymade acoustic band, banjo, bass drum and washboard, a harmonica fished from someone's pocket, and voila! they could rustle up a makeshift jazz outfit or jug band. Music was absolutely essential for the ravers, who were — and still are — compulsive dancers. They would jig about and jive on the pavement, in The Streets, along the promenade or around the fairground. And there was always someone ready to take over the vocals for 'Frankie And Johnny',' Down by The Riverside' or the ubiquitous 'When the Saints Go Marching In'. The ravers danced and jived, for fun, to shock, to get attention. To get the locals staring. And the music? To start with a mish mash, a rather flatulent oompah sound, often not very well played.

But star names began to appear. Humphrey Lyttelton with his 'Bad Penny Blues' (his hit recording was produced by pre-Beatles George Martin); the more purist Ken Colyer and his even more purist jazz-snobby fans who would turn up religiously at the 100 Club on Oxford Street in London, but for no one else but Ken. George Melly became the outrageously flamboyant front man with Mick Mulligan's Magnolia Jazz Band; Chris Barber, the uber British purveyor of New Orleans style jazz, and later the even more mainstream near *pop* star Acker Bilk — they were all showing up at student parties and the more organised raves. But ravers weren't just jazzers. They would adopt different kinds of music . . . especially that one number by the prescient Buddy Holly:

'Rave On'. Though it was not the soundtrack to any rave culture in fifties America; there it was rumbles at the drive-in and dare devil chicken-runs as featured in *Rebel without A Cause*. This terrifying ritual of manhood definition involved racing cars towards a cliff top, each driver bailing out as the car reached the cliff edge. First one out, who lost their nerve earliest, was branded chicken — a coward. Last one out was of course the ultimate fool who went over the edge and crashed onto the rocks below. Uh, Hollywood teenagers!

Whilst rave culture was never allowed to take a real hold in the late twentieth and early twenty-first century in the US, it was being ring fenced in parts of Britain from the 1950s onwards. Brighton was always going to be a Number One destination. Especially for Mods.

The word of original raves spread outwards like some invisible ray (an organic Bluetooth) from Soho. From clubs such as Cy Laurie's on Great Windmill Street — exposed for a sex and drugs scandal in a Sunday tabloid, the very week after I'd first discovered it! The unmarked but always known as 'the French' pub on Old Compton Street, The Gargoyle Club on Meard Street, and my favourite, a café called Sam Widges on the corner of Berwick Street and Broadwick Street. Its sassy jukebox blasted out modern jazz all day long and I thought it was heaven.

It was also a trading post for information about what was happening where, and who was getting busted. Cy's was raided for vice and drugs on a regular basis. This was the time of Bennies and Dexys — benzedrine and Dexedrine — the forerunners of ecstasy, cocaine and ketamine among the stay up all night club drugs of the later ravers.

Frank Sinatra's moody portrayal of a heroin addict in the movie adaptation of Nelsen Algren's *The Man With The Golden Arm* directed by Otto Preminger, was first shown in 1955. It gave many teenagers their first view of a strung-out junkie. An example of Hollywood unwittingly glorifying drug culture? Does Hollywood ever do anything unwittingly? The film had a memorable soundtrack by Elmer Bernstein, three Oscar nominations, and an iconic, collectable advertising poster. The beginning of heroin chic? I went miles and miles on the tube to the outer domains of the Bakerloo line, on my own and underage, to see that film.

And so did others who I would later meet during the outcome of the original rave culture. The same images that were being etched into my impressionable imagination where also having their effect on young people who were going to shape the next decade . . . John Lennon, Paul McCartney, the Small Faces, Andrew Loog Oldham and The Rolling Stones. Girls such as Marianne Faithfull and Astrid Kirchherr, the German girlfriend of original Beatle and artist Stuart Sutcliffe, were mimicking the Bardot look and being inspired by French philosophy of personal and sexual freedom. Those famous Beatle haircuts and Pierre Cardin suits came from Paris, not Hamburg, and Chris Barber's biggest hit had a French title, 'Petite Fleur'.

The cosmopolitan French capital's embrace of African-American jazz was copied by few European cities and there were strong past colonial reasons for that. For the British, enraptured by French cool, it was emerging from trad jazz, the sound of rhythm and blues, wafting through the suburban jazz enclaves that unlocked the dazzling future. You could now even rave in a cave, in the catacombs known as the Chislehurst Caves, in Kent. Take the wrong turn, get lost, panic, think this rave will take you to the grave . . . ooh the thrill!

But still the new music needed a more powerful conduit to get its message across to more people than the hip ravers in a scattering of jazz clubs across Greater London.

We found it through a radio station. which was supposedly broadcasting from a country that had never been associated with

any kind of music at all — *LUXEMBOURG?* While parents were glued to their newly installed goggleboxes for *Sunday Night at the London Palladium* and Liberace, the kids retired to our bedrooms, and tuned in small radios. And dialled up 208 metres on the medium wave band. There was no headphone socket — no headphones, so we just muffled the sound with pillows.

We could now listen, late into the night, undetected, this amazing music called rhythm and blues. That ringing guitar intro '*ding itty, ding itty ding itty, ding itty DING*' of Chuck Berry's 'No Particular Place To Go'; his cranked-up 'Sweet Little Sixteen', Little Richard's I-have-to-dance-round-my bedroom-in-ducing 'Rip It Up', Howlin Wolf's big growly 'Smokestack Lightnin'. And Fats Domino's irresistible bass bashing piano chords on 'Blueberry Hill' and 'Ain't That A Shame.' This radio station *rocked*. Finding Luxembourg's programmes was really, really euphoria-inducing.

Unfortunately for us listeners this sensation was quickly replaced by a complete downer when the music abruptly dropped away and faded out. This happened every few minutes and was hair-tearing out desperately infuriating. But perhaps the so-hard-to-tune-in signal made the music even more desirable.

Radio Luxembourg, having discovered the dream demographic target audience of young impressionable teenagers, was anything but desirable to the British authorities. The BBC, of course, disapproved as well. It would. A government committee, no less, had concluded as far back as 1936: 'Foreign commercial broadcasting should be discouraged **BY EVERY POSSIBLE MEANS.**' By jingoism! Perhaps the government had feared an invasion by means of pop music brainwashing. Anyway, now Radio Luxembourg was playing R and B, black music, what American radio termed 'race records'. So now, ravers' music could be heard all over Great Britain. Among them, some even more disreputable young would-be broadcasters than the operators of Radio Luxembourg, who were about to bring about an even greater music revolution.

*

French footballers had become part of the wider pop culture by the 1990s. David Ginola of the movie-star looks, Ooh Aaah Cantonaaaa and Zinedine Zidane. This new love affair between London and Paris burgeoned because of one cool new train ride — Eurostar! A train that went *under the sea*. I am still, all these years later, incredibly excited by the fact that the Channel Tunnel was begun and finished in my lifetime. And that I would get to travel it, many times. On every occasion I want to run up and down the centre aisle when the train descends, submarine, and scream: 'Isn't this exciting? We are now underneath the sea. On a moving train!'

Eurostar is of course so chilled that they hardly even bother to mention it. (Or possibly it's Gallic tact, not to alarm passengers who might feel claustrophobic.) Whatever. It's immensely civilised, sophisticated and European. (OK, I speak as someone who has not yet experienced a severe Eurostar breakdown.)

This new form of transport linking the UK to mainland Europe in the mid-nineties proved a valuable addition and solution to a new trend. The burgeoning numbers of French DJs, who had so few places to play in petrified wedding cake Paris. Now they could jump on Eurostar of a Saturday evening, DJ at a UK club or at a warehouse party and catch the Sunday morning *aller-retour* ride back to France.

We had Kinky Disco, Love Ranch, Turnmills, Trade, Ministry of Sound in central London, to mention a very few. They had the Rex, the Bain Douches, some theatre spaces and former discos, but they didn't have the *vibe*. Eurostar were very close to agreeing to my idea of a rave train special. London to Paris and back, the whole Eurostar train given over to clubbers and DJs. And I would broadcast it live on Radio 1! Well I'm still working on that one, and how you broadcast live from under the sea.

But Eurostar set up the two-way traffic, and the music bond grew exponentially between the two countries. And as the acid house revolution grew, the football references did as well.

One of the most compelling tunes from that whole era was called 'Raise (63 Steps to Heaven)' by Bocca (*sic*) Juniors. A collective name for the Boy's Own gang, the gods of acid house, Andrew Weatherall, Pete Heller, Terry Farley and Hugo Nicolson. It kicks off with a piano sample from 'Jesus on the Payroll' by Thrashing Doves, with added lyrics by Anna always-on-the-money Haigh and inspired by Aleister Crowley!

I had no idea at the time, that Boca Juniors was a century-old football club in Buenos Aires. (Similarly a 12-inch vinyl with just Van Basten stamped on the label, made by, I believe, a trio from Milton Keynes called Van Basten referenced a legendary footballer from Holland. That was a big favourite of mine at the time, too.) Then there were our own creators of exquisite ethereal wistfulness, Saint Etienne — called after the French football team.

During Gazza-mania in the 1990 World Cup, my first season of real football fan-ism, I hailed a London black cab in Regent Street to take me to Victoria, needing to get the train home to Brighton as fast as possible to watch the next appearance on TV of Paul Gascoigne. Which I explained, perching on the jump seat, and talking to the driver through the glass partition.

'You know what?' he said. 'If I went home and found my wife in bed with Paul Gascoigne — I'd tuck him in.'

So by 1998 the music and football cultures were well intertwined, in time for the World Cup of 1998. I persuaded Radio 1 that we should celebrate this, so we set up in a café called the What's Up Bar in Bastille. Our guys even persuaded the owners to let us knock a hole through the wall to the adjacent building to create an ad hoc recording control room.

Apparently, the chance of winning the World Cup on its own territory, as England had done in 1966, would restore French self-esteem. Or so one of its inhabitants told me. Like most capital cities Paris does not reflect the personality and characteristics of the rest of the country. Similarly, New York and London. But it could not be denied that in the past I had found some Parisiennes to be snobby and aloof.

'Ah,' a French friend in 1998 advised me, 'that is because they are insecure.'

Oh, OK, well that makes it all right, then. Anyway, the Paris of the nineties had become, to me anyway, ultra-cosmopolitan. Portuguese, Russians, Sicilians who'd been drawn like metallic fragments to the magnetic allure of fashion, or couture.

The catalyst for me was a British bilingual model-booking agent. She'd begun as a photographer's assistant, now lived in the second arrondissement near the Louvre.

Rue d'Argout is a tiny side street off the rue du Louvre. It had then a small clothes boutique, a shoe shop called Un Dimanche à Venise and a street-level Moroccan bar-restaurant called Le Bien-Venu that seemed to stay open 24/7. There was also, crucially, a record shop, its name Le Marché Noir mirroring the London store Black Market Records. Sam the model agent took me there. These places were at the time bastions of male intransigence.

'You're a DJ, you say?' I could tell by the expression on the faces in the shop that they were thinking: 'She can't be a DJ, she's a woman, and she's not exactly the epitome of BCBG, *bon chic, bon genre*. Or even *bobo*, bohemian bourgeois.' In my British high-street mass-produced, synthetic fabric slip dress.

I didn't fit the required *très cool* demographic. Sam stepped in on my behalf, flipped back her shoulder-length tresses and, with her informed rich Parisienne patois, launched at speed into a highly colourful description of my passion for French dance music, and of my radio show in the UK.

The atmosphere warmed by several degrees Celsius. 'Would you like a glass of wine?' said the sales assistant behind the counter.

Thus began an ongoing friendship with Sam and the record shop. I stayed in her apartment, on the top floor of a *sixième*, a six-floor climb of winding stairs with no lift.

I began regular buying trips via Eurostar to the shop. They began to keep certain records under the counter for me; began to know what I might go for, buying vinyl there without listening to it first, because I trusted the shop's recommendations.

It was an invaluable link to the emerging underground of French electronic music. These limited pressings were precious to me. The mutual friendship with the record shop grew. I began to make friends there, friends I still have. That's what good record shops do. Thereafter there was always a glass of wine on offer. Sam had opened the door to a vital link with French music culture.

Through her I was discovering the heart and soul of the Paris fashion community too . . . They had a certain way of pronouncing Dior — as *Gdjwyor*, for instance. But it wasn't about just the high-profile supermodels and fashion houses, but the worker bees, the seamstresses in ateliers, the artisans making jewellery, the embroiderers, the casting agents, the 'new faces', would-be hopefuls, many of them young girls from quite unsophisticated backgrounds in Eastern Europe, who were being judged and scrutinised by the cruellest of the chic power brokers. Also the struggling designers, the photographers, the drivers, helping the newbie struggling to get a foothold, gain some recognition, put on one little show . . . like Edinburgh Fringe Festival would-be comedians vying for attention at their first stand-up.

Just to find a venue, persuade the strange, towering, bony mannequins to 'walk', to video-stream the show you've spent the last six months, day and night, working on. Then it's all over in twelve minutes and Anna Wintour did not turn up to sit on the 'frow'. Nor were *Vogue*, *Harper's Bazaar* or *WWD* — *Women's Wear Daily*, the most powerful of the fashion judges.

You'd pick up the very real fear among the models, of falling off the stage because the towering heels they've been thrust into to walk the runway were two sizes too big. It's no wonder Parisian models give that glacial stare: they are just plain shit-scared a lot of the time.

Paris, they say, is like a Swiss finishing school; it teaches a newcomer which knife to use, which wine to choose, gives a model girl or boy 'polish'. It's more like boot camp. Yes, for some it's a way out of miserable obscurity. You could end up being married to the president of the United States.

Into this world I was given a minor red carpet entry, because Paris fashion loves celebrity, and if you are not one already, they'll drape some scrap of this year's fabric around your shoulders and create an identity for you.

I holidayed with a gang of the multinationals. There would be faux video shoot tableaux nights, 'Bill Clinton and Monica Lewinsky', or the 'Night of the Red Devils'. My semi-permanent invitation to these ritualistic affairs was to provide the music. I was happy to; I could play the French dance music that I was evangelising about anyway. There was a bigger merger going on. At one party thrown for a Kate Moss birthday in Paris, Donatella Versace weaved her unmistakeable blond veil among the dancers, while Daft Punk DJ'd. Joining up the dots. It became very prestigious for a DJ to spin at a high-end fashion show.

Now it's almost *de rigueur* for a DJ/pop artist to have their own 'clothing line'. Or merch. I have tote bags and T-shirts printed with my own logo: a bird perched on a silver sliver of a crescent moon. Not exactly Kanye West-level marketing, but I thought I should have a go . . .

Meanwhile Daft Punk were getting serious. They were realising that two blokes hunched over a set of decks does not hugely popular entertainment make. Nor was wearing helmets while DJ'ing, thus preserving their anonymity. Though Marshmello wears a white box on his head while performing in the hugely profitable EDM arena.

Until then it was only the Chemical Brothers, Orbital and Basement Jaxx with their dancing troupe that realised a screen projected with gloopy psychedelic images was not going to cut it. Daft Punk upped their game visually — and musically, as I'll come to later.

The regular holiday events ended abruptly and tragically on 26 December 2004.

Sam the booking agent had been the instigator of our travels around Europe in the late nineties and early noughties. Already, at thirty-two, a seasoned traveller to Tahiti and Africa, she'd also been in Manhattan on Fashion Week business during the 9/11 attacks. Sam was energetic, dynamic, caring, unique. A woman of extraordinary charisma. When she heard I was to receive the MBE at Buckingham Palace, she got on the 5 a.m. Eurostar from Paris to London, and waited outside the palace gates for hours, leaning against the railings, with balloons, to greet me.

One August in the late nineties, we had lain in the hot sun, on a pebbly cove in Sicily, reading in turn the novel *The Beach*, the summer blockbuster of that year. (Later there was a film version starring Leonardo DiCaprio and directed by Danny Boyle.) No one was allowed to discuss the ending until the whole group of eight or so had passed around the one Ambre Solaire-stained copy and finished the story.

I believe this is what inspired Sam Archer Fayet to plan the first group holiday to Thailand, for Christmas 2004, where the story of *The Beach* had been set. By now Sam was married and had a six-month-old child, Ruby Rose.

Ruby was scheduled to be part of the group of around seven, including me, to fly from Paris to Thailand arriving on Christmas Day.

I still don't know exactly why I pulled out of the trip. Questions lurked at the back of my mind about whether I'd be able to make the Paris connection and departure or not. Whether I'd be able to find the group if I travelled separately to Thailand. I'd never been there before. Sam, I knew, would have found a communal base as close as possible to the seashore.

On the morning of Boxing Day 2004, having remained in the UK, I received a text from Sam's sister Nathalie, who lived in Barcelona.

'There has been a tidal wave in Khao Lak.'

I will never forget those words.

It was more than a tidal wave, of course. It was the tsunami which killed 230,000 people across Asia. Caused by a 9.2 Richter scale measurement earthquake in Indonesia. The resultant multiple tsunami waves reached fourteen countries.

One of the worst-hit places in Thailand was the beach resort of Khao Lak, on the Andaman Sea.

Three hours after the text, I received a phone call from my son, who had decided to join the group in Thailand but travelled there on his own, via a different route. He'd arrived the night before at Phuket and missed the ferry to Khao Lak. No one at that stage had any idea of the enormity of the disaster. But Sam had not yet been found or heard from . . .

Even now it's very difficult to piece together what happened from the survivors who comprised the whole travelling party, apart from Sam and Ruby Rose.

It was like being hurled about in a giant washing machine was the most coherent answer I could glean. Strong swimmers stood better chances.

It seemed that at least one family had been alerted and saved by their child's knowledge from school geography lessons. He'd been taught that prior to a tsunami, on occasions seawater is sucked out towards the horizon, away from the beach like a deep, fast-ebbing tide. Leaving the still moving and jumping stranded live fish and other normally submarine life now exposed on the shore.

But what if you had only arrived the night before, as Sam's party had done? They had apparently got lost on the way, and were misdirected to another resort, high up in the hills. Away from their intended beach destination. What if they had stayed put there, safe, overnight and into the next morning? What if? What if? If only.

So Sam's party might not have seen the beach view at Khao Lak before the morning of Boxing Day. They might well not have thought it odd or peculiar that the water had receded so far, and that there were fish flapping on the now uncovered sea floor. Would anyone viewing the beach on that first morning have thought that this was an imminent tsunami warning?

Two days later Nathalie was on a plane to Thailand, believing her sister had survived, perhaps having reached, been swept by the force of the tsunami waves into the forests and jungle of the interior.

The world's media had arrived too. Nathalie was interviewed on international TV. Her eyes blazed out of the screen with a fervent green intensity as she told a news reporter how she was so convinced of her sister's survival. And how determined she was to find her alive. It was Nathalie's initial and very understandable coping mechanism.

Sam was not found, among the thousands of other victims of the tsunami, for three months. She was eventually identified by her engagement and wedding rings. Ruby Rose has never been found.

It is for others to tell the full story of the Asian tsunami. But I can't help but want to remember and commemorate an especially vibrant and generous member of the human race who with her small child, was lost on that day.

Piaf's 'La Vie en rose' played at a service to celebrate Sam's life near her childhood home in Marylebone, west London. Afterwards her family untethered clutches of rose-coloured balloons from the cast iron church railings. So very swiftly they sped and floated free up into the azure April sky.

— 26 —

Let's Party Like It's 1999 . . .
Well It Is Now

'Let's party like it's nineteen ninety-nine . . .' I played that tune, hammered it on the radio solidly in the years between 1982, when Prince released the song, 'til the very end of the twentieth century.

Like many tracks now regarded as classics, '1999' was not a hit single. But I latched onto it from the beginning, played it, thrashed it on air, and planned the fantasy party with the radio listeners for New Year's Eve, seventeen years hence. Not that everyone else, or even anyone else, was as enthusiastic about this long-distance, long-term party planning.

'It's *miles* too far away to even *think* about,' the listeners wrote in, one after the other.

'I'll probably be *dead* by then,' so many of them (average age seventeen) wailed.

I was far more likely to be a goner by 1999 . . . And frankly I couldn't possibly imagine that I would still be broadcasting on Radio 1 in another seventeen years. Though extraordinarily my revived request show, relaunched in 1982, lasted for the next twelve years.

It's only now that some perspective can be gained about how valuable that slot at 7 p.m. on a Sunday night was to be. Right through the eighties . . . 'How Soon Is Now?' could have been its own theme tune.

And how soon and how often I was convinced it would be taken off air for being too strange, too weird, too underground.

The very qualities that of course, with hindsight, were to make it such a long-running success . . .

All the way through I would egg on the listeners about planning New Year's Eve 1999, the party to end all parties. Who would play? Where would it be held? Who would the listeners invite as guests?

Who would *your* date be? What would be the all-important midnight tune? There was always that Prince song at the ready to soundtrack it, and keep this thread going, all through the eighties and into the early nineties.

There was not then space to step back and realise that there was a new cultural revolution going on through those years. I've said that you do not find the measure or the personality or significance of a decade in the zero year. Yet for me the signals that the nineties zeitgeist ended on New Year's Eve 1999, really did happen.

By the mid-decade the entrepreneurs had fully realised the money-making opportunities offered by the acid house and rave gener-ation. Superclubs were all over the shop all over the UK. Cream Liverpool, the Zap in Brighton, Godskitchen in Birmingham (what a disastrous night I had *there*), Gatecrasher in Sheffield (my favourite ever residency). Of course, the Haçienda in Manchester . . . every major city, it seemed, was now in on the act. They were brands with sophisticated merchandising. T-shirts, CDs, baseball hats, chrome record boxes, VIP packages . . . DJs became superheroes and super rich. Of a Saturday night they would flit between multiple venues; I say *they* rather that *we*, or *me*, because I had not *quite* matched that DJ superstar status. Again at that stage there were no women.

The tune by the Chemical Brothers 'Hey Boy, Hey Girl' has the line: 'Superstar DJs, here we go'. That stuck, but women were having a tough time even getting a mention in the annual top 100 DJ polls at all. It's not much better now, in that regard.

The Mecca for them all was, of course, Ibiza.

I often wonder how the native Ibicarians view the adoptive pronunciation by the fun-loving Brits of Eye Beefa. I always tried (at the obvious risk of sounding a pretentious pillock) to try to say it the way the locals do: a short 'i' as in hibiscus, then, *tha*. *Ibitha*.

Some years into its reign as host to all the best international dance clubs, Radio 1 decided to give it the full Monty. We would broadcast live from the island. Wow, that would certainly put Ibiza on the map.

Though, of course, it already was. Culturally cool, still a hint of bohemia, sophisticated, Spanish. The British invasion turned parts of its largest resort San Antonio into something like Torremolinos. Radio 1's entry began, with full-on daytime broadcasters included, around 1998. I went along each summer, part of the party, for the next seven years.

And every detail of Radio 1's visits to the White Isle were broadcast and told and retold every single year afterwards. Still are. Like the time when blah-blah-blah partied too hard and missed a show.

Another year I was driven to and dropped at a villa we called Turn Left at the Bins. Out in the countryside, middle of nowhere. I'd brought with me my usual travel kit: a large bottle of vodka and a giant bar of chocolate. While Chris Moyles and Co. frolicked in the pool and splashed each other, I realised that there really was water, water everywhere, but not a drop to drink.

We'd been deposited in a totally empty house, with no GPS co-ordinates. No working mobile phone signal. We had no idea where we had been billeted.

An assistant producer from our station was also later dropped off just beyond the bins and staggered up to the villa, laden with technical equipment. He was starving. I broke open, gladly, my emergency bar of chocolate.

Well, OK, we could have fun around the pool, couldn't we? Someone would rescue us eventually. Wouldn't they?

These hiccups in terms of organisation were not infrequent in Radio 1's first forays there.

The island dances to its own rhythm of time. What's a day here or there? Well it could be crucial with live outside broadcasts, but these broadcasts were not available, could not be heard on the island itself.

You might think you could switch on the radio there and hear our shows, but no. So to the locals, who couldn't hear any of our output . . . what was all the fuss about?

And just getting there was more than a palaver. We would assemble at Gatwick or Heathrow. This was pre no-frills air travel.

The breakfast show host is always Radio 1's biggest star, as it's the flagship programme. So even pre-departure Sara Cox, then the breakfast DJ, was being semi-mobbed in the duty free, being lavishly draped with exotic beach sarongs by opportunist marketing promotions teams. She generously doled out these freebies to the rest of us. Sara is the real deal. I would trust her with my life.

Many flights then went via Barcelona on the Spanish mainland. Which is where the problems seemed to begin. There were not enough seats on the flights to Eivissa airport for the whole Radio 1 contingent.

We waited, looked at the flickering departures board again and again. Waited and waited, checked the board, listening to the regular update announcements in Spanish. The most frequent word of course being . . . *destino* . . .

Listening for *destino* Ibiza, I began composing in my head a sort of rap song:

> Mario Testino
> Had a *sueno destino* . . .
> He can photograph some freesia
> When he gets to Amnesia . . .

I had not so much amnesia trying to reach the club of the same name to broadcast from, as no sleep. As the flight delays dragged into the night, Sara's team was the priority. They needed to get to the island of Ibiza in the next few hours to broadcast the breakfast show live early the next morning. They were running out of hours.

'What about going by ferry? From here, from Barcelona? How long is that journey?

Twelve hours, it turned out. Sara and Co. didn't have even twelve hours left before the live breakfast show. They were chivvied and bumped up the priority passenger list till they got lift-off on the last flight out of mainland Spain that night.

Myself and my producer Dave were diverted to a Mallorca flight for a four-hour airport-hotel-check-in-stopover, and out again at 5 a.m., before yet another flight across the Balearic Islands to our intended *destino*.

Even though she got to hers just in time, Sara faced unforeseeable problems. DJ'ing from an outside sunny location, she and her team had brought their radio music on the new format MiniDiscs, which were like tiny CDs, embedded in plastic. Sara's producer lay them all out for her to play through her live broadcast. Unfortunately, they all melted in the heat.

Surfing those years was of course the biggest technological revolution ever. The internet Myspace, Google, iTunes, webcasting. To its credit, Radio 1 was early into this huge leap into the future.

In the early days of Pete Tong he would be telling listeners how they could now hear his broadcast via the internet: 'You go to aitch-tee-tee-pee, colon, forward slash, forward slash, double-you, double-you, double-you, dot, bee-bee-see, dot co, dot yew-kay.' It seemed so laborious. But not, of course, for long.

Clubland in Ibiza was becoming ever more influential and powerful. The most important place for house music outside America. Each night of the week was allotted, or rather carved out, to a different promoter. That became your patch. As the club-loving holidaymakers arrived on change-over day, so the allotting of club nights evolved. DC10, like most of the open-air clubs, was held in the early hours of the morning . . .

Space was situated near the one airport on the island, and part of its attraction was hanging out on the outside terrace (a car park really), with the holiday jets screaming and pounding low overhead, all in the music mix, all part of the aural excitement package, and each night of the week a major attraction. Manumission was the most daring and featured live sex shows. There was even a special DJ for the toilet area.

But there were clear and strict demarcations made by the club lords of the island. You did not, if you knew what was good for you, step out of line. Or try to put on another attraction of your own on someone else's patch. Hence when Radio 1 launched a beach party as a broadcast event, officialdom mysteriously stepped in and stopped it at the last minute, due to apparent 'objections from neighbours'. Hmm. More likely this event was drawing punters away from another established, pre-staked-out attraction on the island.

And where once Ibiza had created 'the Balearic sound', meshing indie, guitar and house beats together, they did not want you to mess with it. If it ain't broke, etc. The island had created a hugely successful brand. At its height of influence during the noughties, there were during one summer alone, *eighty-four* different compilation album releases with the word 'Ibiza' in the title.

I fell foul Ibiza's ruthlessly strict music policy thus: I was to broadcast my show now playing mostly breakbeat, a variation from the *de rigeur* 4/4 house beats played in the rest of the club called Pacha. I was assigned a special room in the sprawling mansion that makes up this palace of a nightclub. Richly, lavishly, decorated, highly tuned door selection to get the most exclusive crowd. You more or less had to be a bit if a star even to be allowed in. The drink prices? Swift intake of breath. A week's wages for one round, kind of thing.

I was to broadcast live to the UK, at 4 a.m. London time, 5 a.m. local time. Peak hour in Spain's clubland culture.

At a quarter to the hour I climbed into the DJ booth, pulled some vinyl out from my record box, slatted them onto the decks, and began to play some warm-up tunes. Getting ready for the live broadcast in just a few minutes' time. Headphones on, ready.

Then, *bam*, suddenly there was a flurry of action, and the DJ booth was full of big, brawny men. Their big, brawny arms elbowed me out of the way, leaned over the DJ decks, and wrenched the headphones out of their socket.

'Hey what are you *doing*?' I responded to their actions making, I'm sorry to say, no attempt to speak Spanish.

Next a pair of burly shoulders appeared and whipped the arm off the revolving record, grabbed the vinyl and tore it off the turntable.

'What is going *on*?' I demanded to know. 'We are *on air* in *ten minutes*. From *now*. To *London*.'

I've had some DJ'ing experiences but nothing quite as harsh and unexpected as this. The kerfuffle and pandemonium continued. Voices were raised. Horrified Radio 1 execs appeared, moved in, grabbed me and my microphone and bundled me out of the club room. A fight now ensued in the DJ box, and it's true to say there was blood on the dance floor.

The long and the short of it was that there were two related guys among the team that ran Pacha. One had hired out the space we were using as a live broadcast studio. Someone hadn't told someone else. The other didn't like the carefully considered music I was playing; it was not the tightly formatted house style of Pacha. Though I certainly didn't know any of this on the night.

So he came to sling me off the decks.

Far more respected and distinguished DJs than me have been thrown off the decks in Ibiza nightclubs for playing off-message music.

Radio 1 people, anxious for my physical safety, had me bundled downstairs to Pacha's kitchens. Clutching my live microphone in hand. Pacha music policy or no, we still had a broadcast slot to fill. The club replaced me with one of its tame in-house DJs, and it was his selections that were then broadcast for the next two hours on Radio 1.

I was furious, hopping mad and incandescent. But the show had to go on, so it was the Pacha style of safe, uninteresting music that was now playing in my radio slot. This needed explanation to the listeners back home. With gritted teeth and all the expression I could muster into the live links I broadcast from the kitchen, where I was forcibly barricaded, I made a few terse announcements over this dull music.

'You are listening to the *folklorique* music of Ibiza,' I said, hoping the listeners would read between my heavy-on-the-irony words. There was nothing else I could do.

I was gutted.

On schedule, I returned to London the next day. No sleep and still very miffed. At Heathrow passport control the woman in the glass kiosk studied my passport rather too carefully and looked me up and down several times.

Oh no, I thought, am I going to have even more problems now?

Then she spoke. 'I just want to say I really enjoy your shows on the radio. Thank you for the music.'

I could have hugged her.

Had Ibiza cashed in on its success? Of course.

It became, with all that money at stake, less and less musically innovative. No great surprise. As tourists from all over the world landed on this tiny Mediterranean island with their cash, why on earth rock the boat or indeed the sleek white superyacht moored in the harbour below the winding streets of Ibiza town? Ibiza could and still does operate on several levels: commercial music clubs for the masses, and sumptuous villas and super-exclusive parties in secluded enclaves for the billionaires and Trustafarians. The airport now has much, much more traffic from PJs (private jets) than ever.

On a subsequent Radio 1 visit there, it was arranged for me to interview an up-and-coming French DJ who wore a T-shirt decorated with big fat shiny letters on the front saying:

'FUCK ME I'M FAMOUS'.

It was his slogan. It was David Guetta, who in later years became one of Las Vegas's — and the world's — most successful EDM DJs, pulling in an estimated forty million US dollars a year.

So the clock ticked on and the countdown to NYE 99 Y2K began. Gradually excitement about the Big Night did begin to build. And so did fear. Fear that the digital clocks turning from 31.12.1999 at 23.59.59 into 00.00.0000 00.00.00 at midnight would set off Armageddon. The dreaded millennium bug. We were told that anything could happen. Gas leaks could cause explosions in the cities. Water mains would burst causing flooding everywhere. Cash machines at banks would seize up. There might be no money. And resultant fires, riots in the streets.

The BBC made its plans. I was asked to host the breakfast show on the first day of the new century. For the first time in my career. Well, that was fine with me; I wouldn't want to do it all the time, but an early start on that day would be very exciting. Actually, it would be the end of the very long night before. With no disco naps in between.

And even more so if the millennium bug did actually cause chaos. The BBC would then move its live broadcasting onto a footing similar to the outbreak of nuclear war. We would be whisked to a secret bunker and broadcast from there. I was not allowed to know where that would be, or any other details. It was to be 'somewhere in the Home Counties'. I suspected it would be at the BBC's spying centre, sorry, 'listening post' at Caversham Park, which it had operated since mid-Second World War in 1943.

I was really hoping we would get taken off to the bunker.

The person to feel least envious of on NYE 1999 was, of course, the Queen. Who in God's or anyone else's name had had the idea for her to hang at the Millennium Dome holding hands with Tony Blair and singing 'Auld Lang Syne'? Never in her auspiciously long reign had the monarch looked so uncomfortable and frankly miserable. (Apart from maybe the days after Diana's death.)

No doubt it seemed a fantastic idea sitting round a snug table in a focus group. 'Hey guys, let's have the Queen joining in the celebrations.' It's not that she wasn't game, I'm sure, given her appearance with James Bond at the 2012 Olympic Games opening ceremony. It was around this era that someone else had the idea that our prime minister should take part in the annual Radio 1 Christmas photograph; I'll come to that later.

Not only was it to be an auspicious date in the calendar, but NYE '99 was going to be the biggest cash cow for DJs in the entire decade. If not ever. There was a lot of swaggering and bragging about who was going to play at midnight in the most sought-after venue. And how much tickets would go for on this night of nights. Whether you could play on the same night in two different continents.

I was booked to play at the Ministry of Sound at Elephant and Castle, just over the Thames in south London. Perfect. I could then return to Radio 1 and broadcast the breakfast show live. No sleep till well into the new century. No problem — it was an ideal scenario to me. I wanted to be as fully involved in the night I had been banging on about for seventeen years as possible.

A fool-proof plan was put in place. I would be escorted by taxi to the Ministry of Sound, by a producer, to play there till around 3 a.m., and then escorted back to Radio 1, where the breakfast show team would be ready to greet me.

My first inkling that, club-wise, all was not necessarily well was this: the clubbers who had gained entry into the Ministry did just not look all that happy, thrilled, excited, awed, overjoyed to be at the most famous dance nightclub in London, if not on the planet, on the most anticipated club night of the past . . . well at least twenty years.

This was it, New Year's Eve, 1999 — here at last!

It couldn't get much bigger and better than this!

Could it?

Surely they would be ecstatic and rapt by the sheer joy of Being in the Right Place at the Right Time. Having paid a small fortune for the privilege.

Yet the punters didn't seem to be smiling. The trouble seemed to be this. That it was such an exclusive place to be that half, no, most of your mates couldn't be there with you. And when it all comes down, the clubbers, the punters, the people, wanted to see in this New Year of all New Years with their friends and loved ones. Yet most couldn't even dream of gaining entry *that* night to the super-exclusive dance domains.

And so it turned out a lot of other people felt like that. They didn't want to be part of a lottery where only the lucky few were cordoned off behind the velvet rope. They wanted to be with *all* their closest, maybe having a no-entry-fee house party, at home. To an extent it was the night the bubble burst.

I was rather concerned that the clubbers at Ministry didn't seem to be all having the best time (hope it wasn't the music I was playing!), but I had to pack up my record box and make my way back across London to Radio 1.

And once outside again, I was aware it was now . . . raining! I know . . . December, January, midwinter, every likelihood of rain in London.

We had planned and scheduled, in every minute detail. Somehow I had never thought about such a mundane factor as the weather.

I had missed the fireworks on the Thames (a let-down was the general consensus), but here, several hours later, there were massive queues of revellers bunched up and huddled outside Kennington tube station at way past 3 a.m. Waiting to get out of the rain, into the station to get on a train, to make their way home. Tinsel headdresses and fairy wings soggy and sodden. They looked drenched. Bedraggled. Forlorn. I hoped this wasn't going to be a metaphor. An omen for what might overshadow the first years of the new century. As it turned out, we had one year, eight months and eleven days to find out. And less than two decades to experience the effects of a global pandemic.

I got back to Radio 1. No millennium bug. No decamping to a secret bunker. The clocks had not stopped. Oh. Really? Ah well.

Best crack on and broadcast to the many who had stayed up all night to greet this new, special New Year. We had planned the playlist meticulously. Around twenty minutes before I was scheduled it play it anyway, a fax came in:

A request for 'Is That All There Is?', once a hit for torch supersinger Peggy Lee. But it was the nihilistic version as performed by the NYC punk queen Christina (herself an early victim of COVID-19) that had the New Year's Day 2000 vote. Banned by its authors Leiber and Stoller ('Hound Dog', 'Stand by Me', 'Jailhouse Rock') on the day of release. They didn't approve of her sick, dark, altered, punkified lyrics.

I kept going, stayed awake, had my first glass of wine of the twenty-first century in a hotel room watching on TV the edited highlights of the round-the-world fireworks, at around 11 a.m. It was inter-city competitive, and to me Sydney was the winner, followed by Paris a close second. The tune of the night . . .? No contest. William Orbit's version of the modern/classical Barber's *Adagio for Strings* — the Ferry Corsten remix, which was to grace a compilation I put together with Ministry of Sound sixteen years later. It became a classic. Catching the awesomeness and emotion of the occasion, the original quite sad and stately adagio, mixed with the urgent banging party-ness of the imminent New Year, new decade and new century, and the cascade of bursting fireworks across the skies of the world. And the urgency of a then still quite contemporary-sounding trance mix (though trance music had peaked for me around 1994).

That's my memory of the night, and everyone remembers where they were that New Year's Eve. Usually I prefer to be working on NYE than passively celebrating. It can be a too-sentimental, poignant moment, the midnight chimes. Best to be behind the decks ensuring everyone else feels the right vibe.

It is said that Prince, the architect, the inspiration for so much of the so highly anticipated New Year's Eve 1999, had staged and videoed a pay-per-view concert. Taped at his Paisley Park studio two weeks earlier, then broadcast on the night of 31 December.

The amount to pay per view was . . .?
19.99.
Nineteen dollars and ninety-nine cents.
Nice one, Nelson.

— 27 —

The First of May

A special day. In France it's the Fête du Muguet: Lily of the Valley Day; on trend there from 1 May 1561. King Charles IX of France doled out to each lady in his court a sprig of these delicate, white, bell-shaped spring flowers, cloaked in thick, green, enveloping leaves. For good luck. The idea caught on, and the tradition has been going on ever since. Very Instagrammable.

But in France and elsewhere 01.05 is much better known as International Labour Day and is in many countries a public holiday. Celebrating workers' rights. By the year 2000 it had become an unofficial protest day in the UK, especially in central London. And of course, Mayday is the internationally recognised distress call.

In 2001, it was the date I was invited to attend an investiture at Buckingham Palace. To receive the MBE from the Queen.

Oh, I had thought long and hard about accepting this. It was completely unexpected. A cream envelope addressed to me at Radio 1, when letters were still a thing. Because of the insignia on the outside, I along with others given these awards, thought it was a tax demand.

I confided only in John Peel, who'd already got an OBE.

'What do you think? Should I accept it?'

'Look at it like this,' he said. 'If you turn it down, you'll be in the pub one day, and the topic of these "gongs", and whether they're right or wrong will crop up. You can say: "Oh I was offered one of those and I turned it down." And people will go, "Oh really?" and start talking about something else. But if you accept? Well, think of it this way, it's a great day out.'

Quite what a day out, he could not have possibly imagined.

Trouble had been brewing big on May Day the year before, in 2000. A protester had draped a grass-covered strip of turf, carefully positioned, onto the bald head of a Winston Churchill statue in Westminster. Thus, giving him an incredibly pictorially newsworthy bright-green Mohican punk hairstyle. This was on a day of demonstrations and anti-capitalism protests.

A McDonald's in the Strand had had all its windows smashed in. In general, the police were criticised for being too lenient. Well, that was not going to happen again, was it?

For the anticipated May Day protests of 2001, an extra 6000 police officers were drafted in. I had other things on my mind in the days leading up to it.

If I was going to accept the gong, then it was going to be a good excuse for a full-on celebration. With the promotion team at Radio 1 we scoured the capital (well, not exactly *scoured*, licence fee payers, I assure you), looking over some suitably iconic venues. One of the most inspired ideas was to hold an event actually **on**, across the top of, Tower Bridge! You know, the one that opens and closes its road across the Thames to let the traffic cross. Almost as well known a London landmark at Buck House itself.

We went on a very exciting, to me, recce. It appears that there are events held *inside* the long glass-walled fixed structure which spans both towers of the bridge. I had no idea.

Then came the three crunch questions from me.

How much?

How loud?

How late?

The Tower Bridge ents team could not tick any of the right boxes. Fine for a no-expense-spared early evening swish corporate do, but no good for a late-night acid house rave-up. In case you were thinking of it, too.

It's quite difficult to come up with a really never-been-done-before location that's central enough for everyone to get the tube home from afterwards. Sometimes the solution is staring you in the face. It was then. It was called the Social, a friendly, lozenge-shaped bar, ground floor at street level, with a corresponding-shaped DJ and dance area in the windowless basement below. The lighting in the basement is of such softly glowing subtlety and trickery that you can you never tell if it's morning, noon or night. Deceptively seductive for a long, long night of musical merriment.

I already knew it well. Still have the original metal membership tag on a key ring. The Social was an offshoot project of the Heavenly record label. The bar, looking like a small shopfront, was/is situated in a side street just off Great Portland Street. Technically in 'Noho', the north side of Oxford Street. Or more poshly known as Fitzrovia. Or more accurately known as the heart of the rag trade district. A stone's throw from two tube stations.

And as was in those days, but a pebble-chucking (oops, not a good analogy given what was going to happen) distance down the street from Radio 1's base.

It was booked for the night. The invitations were designed by me, printed and sent out.

Rather worryingly, hardly anyone replied. The recipients hadn't 'got' the meaning of the design. Which was three rows of sailors flag-waving the semaphore signals for Mayday! Mayday! Mayday! The international distress call. I had also written inside that the celebrations would be held on May Day 2001.

Then I started getting the calls: 'Yeah but when is it?'

'On May Day,' I replied, 'as it says on the invitation.'

'When's that?'

'The first of May. When it usually is. Look on the front of the invite — the flags spell out Mayday in semaphore.'

'What's semaphore?'

Something, everything, had got lost in the concept. In the manner of *Spinal Tap*'s Stonehenge, the images of the sailors' flags had turned out to be much tinier, more miniscule than I had envisaged.

So no one understood the imagery. Or understood the meaning, or the date. Maybe no one would show up. I began to worry about that. And if you think that it's unreasonable to consider that no one would show when there's a free bar to be had, may I disagree? It had happened to me.

In my younger days of fronting a string of fashion boutiques, I had sent out invitations to the opening of a new branch and a party to which everyone would be transported. From central London to Kent, by drinks-laden double-decker bus.

The only person who turned up to the parked bus on Charing Cross Embankment, was — so, so ironically — the legendary 'fifth Beatle' Harry Nilsson. Him of 'Everybody's Talkin' or more latterly if you've discovered him recently singing his revived 'Gotta Get Up' theme tune on the Netflix series *Russian Doll*.

And Harry had bothered to arrive at the outset, to say that he wouldn't be able to come to the party on the bus. But at least he'd bothered to show up and tell me in person. No one, but no one else did.

So I had form in the calamity no-show party stakes.

Meanwhile a bridgehead and ops centre was set up to direct activities to and from Buckingham Palace, on the actual May Day. A make-up artist and friend, Liberty, showed up at a necessary excruciatingly early hour. The three allowed guests to this investiture were my only close relatives . . . uncle, son and daughter. My uncle Harold, aka Bill, had served in the British army in the Second World War in Italy, and I believe had suffered undiagnosed PTSD ever since.

I'm sure he had been recognised for his service, but this had not included a trip to the Palace. He duly donned a morning suit for this occasion, though I felt there was a slight question hanging in the air. Why was a mere DJ (hardly a life-threatening occupation) receiving this recognition?

Bill was a youthful eighty-six at the time. We were to convene at the former Churchillian favourite the Hyde Park, now the Mandarin Oriental Hotel, whizz round the corner to Buck House, then scoot back there with some mates to launch the daytime celebrations.

Hundreds, thousands of people receive the MBE and above, every year. Hence the Palace courtiers handle the shuffling guests with, well, experienced aplomb.

Without wishing to be iconoclastic, the Palace is decorated as the royals approve, although opulent, not what you might call any modern glitz or bling. The ancient and treasured carpets are worn in some places. Investiture guests are given water to drink, not champagne. Which is fine by me. The interior of the public rooms of Buckingham Palace, St James's Palace, Kensington Palace and Sandringham are presented in a similar way. I can say, having been a guest at these palaces too.

The sumptuously bouquet and multi candle-lit Palace sets of the TV series *The Crown*, by comparison, are much more lavish than the real thing.

Everyone on May Day was very respectfully dressed. Ascot numbers of hats.

I was most gratified to be donated a one-off prototype design white tuxedo coat that had never gone into production (therefore not duplicated) by the young British designer Luella Bartley. With that I wore turquoise ankle boots and no hat. I looked around for anyone else who might have gone for unconventional attire.

Ah, there were a couple of big, youngish-looking blokes hanging out together, one wearing what looked like purple sparkly Doc Martens. Which certainly outdid my vivid blue Parisian heels for unsuitability at the Palace. I introduced myself. The couple turned out to be the Olympic gold medallist oarsmen Matthew Pinsent and James Cracknell.

As I had grown up by the Thames, I'd known quite a few schoolboy rowing crews. Attended a lot of waterside regattas in my early teens, before rave took me over. Once in conversation it was quickly established that James Cracknell had been a pupil at Kingston Grammar, a neighbouring school to mine, the Lady Eleanor Holles School, Hampton.

'We called you lot Lady Eleanor Horrors,' cracked Mr Cracknell.

Cheers, I said. After an extraordinarily competitive career as an athlete, James Cracknell joined the *Strictly Come Dancing* competition for 2019. Those purple sparkly shoes he wore at the Palace that day seem to have turned out to be quite prescient.

Receiving a decoration from the Queen or one of her family is very much the school prize-giving. You politely watch and clap as all the other recipients file past . . . How on earth can the Queen find anything to say to all these hundreds of her subjects? Apart from: 'Have you come far?'

I thought, well I'll make it a bit easier for her when it comes to having my badge pinned onto me. Breaking with Palace protocol (as did apparently my Radio 1 colleague Nick Grimshaw when he was presented) I spoke first. Just to try to be friendly and helpful really. I'd found Prince Charles, when I worked for the Prince's Trust, and even more so Diana, Princess of Wales, extremely approachable. But then, they were not the monarch.

'Radio 1 DJ,' I offered. At that time Prince William had been widely publicised as having a go on the decks during his gap year in Chile. So I ventured further: 'I hear your grandson has been DJ'ing recently too.'

And how did the Queen reply to my carefully selected nugget of topicality?

'Probably.'

That's all she said. Just the one word, 'Probably.'

She could have said, 'To the Tower for impertinence. Off with her head.' In the 2020 New Year's honours list, my MBE was 'upgraded' to CBE. The investiture was postponed due to lock-down. Should I be first to address the monarch again?

Probably not.

It was only on leaving the palace in 2001 that anyone noticed the snipers on the roof.

And heading back to Knightsbridge to raise a glass or two, I still had no idea of the growing confrontation in the West End.

By mid-afternoon, the May Day protesters were gathered along Oxford Street, and in and around Oxford Circus. But the police were creating pincer movements and driving the crowds into closed, contained, circled groups. There was a name for this tactic, but I didn't know it yet.

It was only when I reached my home in north-west London for a regroup that I got the news. Radio 1 had cancelled my party.

'What? *What? Why?*' I hollered, horrified, down the phone to the producer. By now the party invitees and acceptees had swelled in numbers, and there were friends planning to come from Brighton, Paris, Los Angeles, as well as from all over London.

'It's too dangerous,' the producer told me. 'The whole area is sealed off. No one from Radio 1 is allowed to come to the party. It's off.'

We'll see about that, I thought.

I phoned for a minicab and headed to the West End. On this day my driver was a rather dashing grizzled veteran from Montenegro in a Mercedes. He drove the aged, low-slung, left-hand drive, military-green motor like it was a Sherman tank. He growled dismissive contempt at my suggestion that our route might be blocked before we could get to the Social bar.

Ahead, right across the dual carriageway of Portland Place, was a solid line of shield-wielding riot police.

Overdoing it a bit, chaps, I might have thought to myself.

It's hard now to convey that feeling of innocence in the air, the sense of bewilderment at this extraordinary police presence in the centre of London. Since the Good Friday Agreement there were no more IRA bombs threatening Oxford Street shoppers. We didn't really know the term 'lockdown' then. 9/11 was three months into the future. Peaceful protest was tolerated or had been. The riots of the seventies and eighties were in the past; love bombing was more the thing now. Hugging strangers. Giving the peace sign. The acid house influence of the nineties was still going strong in my milieu in 2001.

But now, along Great Portland Street, which runs parallel to Portland Place, the whole area dominated by the BBC's HQ, Broadcasting House, was a shocking sight.

A solid line of police horses ranged right across the now deserted street, swept clean of office and shop workers, garment makers, stray tourists. Middle of the afternoon, eerily empty.

So . . . They certainly meant business, then.

My own situation now loomed into reality. What to do? I had many invited guests who were not employed by Radio 1, who were, to be fair, entitled to stop their own employees wading into a riot and possible arrest. Can't imagine what the Health and Safety lot would say now.

But my own friends, and friends of family, were of, shall we say, a different ilk. There was for instance, Mani of the Stone

Roses and Primal Scream fame. His trademark phrase was: 'I was born to 'ave it, and 'ave it, I surely will.' And often did.

Then there was Irvine Welsh. The now superstar author of the blockbuster and era-defining *Trainspotting*. Irv certainly lived up to the image of some of his fictional anti-heroes.

Basement Jaxx, then and now festival headliners, had agreed to DJ at the Social party. Although we had mobile phones in those quaint old days of the early twenty-first century, coverage was not what it is today. I didn't have their phone numbers anyway, so couldn't cancel their set. I needn't have worried. They gamely crossed town from Brixton and showed up anyway. Others fought their way among panicked tube passengers, as central London was gradually completely closed down to transport.

For anyone who had battled through the police lines and reached Little Portland Street, the Social now became something resembling a Chicago speakeasy in the 1930s. The heavily manned front door was opened a crack. Any proven legit guest would be grabbed by the shoulders, hauled swiftly inside, and the door to the street slammed firmly shut again.

Get in quick, stay in, don't wander outside again if you don't want to get arrested, was the very sound advice.

The contemporary sounds of the Chemical Brothers and Death in Vegas were blaring out of the Social's jukebox. In addition to these, I found some other lyrics of a musical number from *The Pajama Game*, which I'd seen as a teenager in the fifties, running through my head.

Just knock three times and whisper low
That you and I went sent by Joe
Then strike a match and you will know
You're in Hernando's Hideaway
Olé!

I'd had to blag my way through the police cordon to get into my own party

'But officer, this is to celebrate me getting the MBE at Buckingham Palace today.'

''Course it is, love.'

(Well I'd have thought it was a pretty lame line too, tbh.)

Inside, the bar was rammed, a roadblock to use an at that time unironic clubbing term.

The by now already partied-up gang inside saw me make my anxious entrance and began chanting, 'Ann-ie, Ann-ie.'

That was almost too much of an emotional overload.

They always say you shouldn't really enjoy your own party too much if you're hosting it properly. Well, the rest of the day was spent greeting guests, getting them drinks, rushing up and down the concrete staircase to the DJ area. All those behind the decks were appearing without a fee, so needed to be looked after in every other way.

Casual and relaxed it was not. Uproarious and rambunctious it certainly was.

The *aux barricades* attitude was unlike any other party I could remember.

Of course there were some, there always are, who ignored the door advice about staying inside the Social bar. Naturally we all wondered what was going on outside. Not so easy pre-Twitter, WhatsApp and Instagram days.

So a few members of my party (Robin Turner of Heavenly Records, included) *did* venture out.

And did not — could not — return.

The defiant ones had been 'kettled' by the police.

I'd never heard the term before. But it has been widely used by the Met ever since. Enclose a group of protesters, demonstrators, inside a street police cordon, and don't let them leave. For hours if necessary. No excuses heeded about needing the loo, or getting back for a babysitter. The police exercise was to marshal you, contain you, for as long as they deemed necessary.

If you got kettled, you stayed kettled.

Kettling, from the Met's point of view, has proved to be an effective deterrent to protestors not of sufficient stoicism or political conviction. Sinister.

Eventually the party inside the Social wound down. It was deemed safe to leave, the streets were clear. The hard core remained.

We needed an after-party. And there was only one place to go, though we were so near the heart of late-night Soho.

Known to party organisers and club DJs as somewhere to go when everywhere else had closed, it was on Hanway Street, itself a tiny sliver of an alley woven deep in the heart of central London. It crosses diagonally from behind Oxford Street, opening up again into Tottenham Court Road. At one time it had five record shops. It was also known for drug transactions. On one corner, its open though discreet door, the Spanish bar. An enclave for homesick or ex-pat Spaniards.

Live flamenco was played and danced downstairs. It was also a secret home from home for late-night London ravers.

No membership, no door policy, no door fee, no dress code. No questions asked. Heaven (as distinct from the club Heaven, not so far away).

We fell in there in the early hours of 2 May 2001, to unwind finally.

And all you'll see are silhouettes
And all you'll hear are castanets
And no one cares how late it gets
You're in Hernando's Hideaway.
Olé . . .

As to the actual medal, the MBE itself, I have it somewhere, safely stored at home. I keep everything (I'm a hoarder), but just not always sure exactly where....

Mislaying of belongings became a bit of a thing during a further visit to the Palace, some four years later.

Along with, I must say, I thought the most hilariously motley posse of guests imaginable. Among the 500 invited, Jimmy Page, Petula Clark, Eric Clapton, Shirley Bassey, Beth Orton, Dame Vera Lynn, Jeff Beck, Kate Bush, Jamie Cullum, 'Spice Girl' Geri Halliwell, Brian May of Queen, and most unexpectedly, to me, Jeannette Lee, ex of Public Image Ltd, an architect of punk, friend of John Lydon who had written the immortal words:

God Save the Queen
She's not a human being
There's no future
And England's dreaming

It was a reception to celebrate Britain's music 'industry'. This time the drinks were flowing and her Maj and consort looked much happier than pinning badges on total strangers. They were milling through the throng, stopping and chatting, it seemed pretty much willy-nilly.

I buddied up with Beth Orton.

Eric said he hadn't seen me for ages.

Jimmy Page (former Prince of Darkness) chattily remarked, like he was a South Downs commuter: 'Didn't I see you on the train today?'

The gin was flowing (not my usual tipple, but hey, when in Buck House . . .). Proving that four decades do nothing to diminish rivalry, no matter how friendly, Jeff Beck was immensely amused that the Queen had not been cognisant of the extent of Eric Clapton's extended worldwide reputation as god of the guitar.

'Have you been playing long?' she was reported to have asked him.

'About forty-five years,' was his purported reply.

But Jeannette Lee? PiL? at the Palace? Somehow, an unlikely splinter group of herself, myself, Beth, Jeff Beck and the pianist Jamie Cullum split together and retired elsewhere for a further 'round'. After that, Jeannette, who was now co-running the Rough Trade record label, and I shared a taxi back to west London.

Someone had to let me into my flat.

The next day I called Buckingham Palace to say, 'Sorry to bother you guys, but I was at a party at yours last night, did anyone find my keys?'

28

The Prime Minister and the Christmas Party

'Yo, Blair!'

You've got to admit it's an odd way for one head of state to address a counterpart. Half hip-hop, half ex-British public schoolboy surname-only formal.

So President George W. Bush might have wrong-footed Tone, as we quite good naturedly referred to him then. On what was to be such a crucial weekend. At a photo shoot, the US prez in designer windcheater, bathed in spring afternoon sunshine, on his ranch in Crawford, Texas. That had been back in April 2002. We got to know more of the Bush—Blair supposed poodle/puppet relationship over the next four years. It's a pretty safe assumption that George and Co. 'love-bombed' Tony Blair.

I was once stopped on the pavement, er, sidewalk, on Fifth Avenue, NYC in broad daylight by a total stranger with these words: 'Just want to say: you look a million dollars!'

And it felt great. Put a spring in my step. If someone was to do that to you in the UK? You would avoid any further eye contact. Perhaps murmur, 'Oh no, thank you, but not even half that, no . . . I mean a quarter, oh well perhaps five grand max,' pull your hoodie up, keep your head down, apologise to anyone else who'd heard this acutely embarrassing encounter (I still blush if anyone pays me a compliment), and rush away to the nearest darkest corner. But be secretly quite thrilled for the rest of the day.

They do it to you in Hollywood too, spectacularly well. The love bombing. You are flattered beyond belief, made to feel on top of the world, cloud 9999. A billion-, not a million-dollar babe. Enwrapped in the warmest blanket of new-found confidence, and roof-top high levels of self-esteem.

You're a *star*. *Wow*.

You've done it. You've cracked America.

Except, actually though, of course you haven't. You haven't cracked it. At all. But in the moment they (the people you're working with, or trying to) will genuinely really make you believe you have succeeded. In the end, it's only results, box office, that counts. I learnt this from the country that coined the expression 'There's no such thing as a free lunch'.

And my quest had not been screen-acting stardom, just to become a film music supervisor.

It is not to be forgotten that Prime Minister Blair did actually want to be a rock star. And hadn't just idly dreamt about it, either.

He was in a band called Ugly Rumours, with Mark Ellen, one of my successors as presenter of *The Old Grey Whistle Test*, also a successful music journalist and magazine editor. Tone had not only played in the band but organised their gigs . . .

November 2002. After bombarding Afghanistan post 9/11, the US now had its sights on Iraq. There was talk of regime change against its dictator Saddam Hussein. To me (not wishing to simplify the Middle East problems to one paragraph or one chapter, or one book, or anything), a lot of the recent confusion there seems to go back to the 1916 Anglo-French Sykes—Picot Agreement. Between an Englishman and a French bloke.

Which essentially carved up that area of the planet, in the wake of the Ottoman Empire break-up, to what we have broadly, today. *Sans* Israel.

Dividing very ancient tribes, their territories and trade routes.

I'd seen first-hand the mess Iraq was in, post the Iran — Iraq war, in which, so piquantly, both sides claimed to have won. It had not seemed like a country internationally aggressive enough, nor with enough will nor resources to take on the West. And we'd been on Iraq's side then. Saddam had been honoured with a state visit to London, the full trappings Buckingham Palace could lay on.

Dubya had declared his war on terror and nominated his 'axis of evil'. Identified al-Qaeda. It had already been proved Bin Laden's 9/11 gang had been Saudis. All I had learnt was that the Middle East was a vast counterpane of contradictions and customs. Iraq had been a closed country. How would the US and/or the UK have managed to infiltrate, gain enough reliable intelligence to know for sure that it was planning to attack the West with weapons of mass destruction. (And as it turned out, they didn't, and they weren't.)

The war efforts in the Iran — Iraq encounter had been pretty poor. One side would lob a bomb over at the other, and it didn't even make it to the border. There were more Iraqis killed by friendly fire than by the opposing side. Forever gun toting, the Iraqis would fire their weapons in the air, not always considering where their bullets would land. I even visited a military hospital in Baghdad where there were children with 'friendly' bullets lodged in their heads.

An experience like that does tend to frame your terms of reference. But that was just a personal perspective, I couldn't claim to be a world expert on Iraq.

When Iraq invaded neighbouring Kuwait in 1991, that episode lasted four days. It didn't win that one.

And then of course, there's the oil . . .

So in November 2002, we in the West held our breath that the Texas ranger of a president would not seriously persuade his British bud Blair to drag us into a war with Iraq.

That same month Radio 1 held its annual 'school' photo. A group picture of the DJs and each member of the staff. These were never published. But each of us was given a souvenir print copy. Over the years it had become a tradition that we might have a surprise guest celebrity join us. We'd had Paul Daniels, the magician, for instance, in a previous year.

I was in a taxi from the West End when I began to get the 'where are you?' calls from my producer.

'On the way, no worries,' I replied breezily. The destination was a photographer's studio complex in north London.

'Well you really must hurry,' said the producer, sounding anxious.

'I'm doing my best, mate, it's rush hour, the traffic.'

Then he called again, and again. Saying if I didn't arrive by 6 p.m., security would close the gates and I wouldn't be allowed in.

A bit over-*zealous* for a photo shoot . . . And for the usual after-party drinks which also constituted our official Christmas party.

When I finally rolled up, I was hustled in, and the tall gates clanged shut behind me.

'*The Prime Minister*'s coming,' hissed a programme assistant.

Oh. Ah. OK.

The DJs were positioned to stand in a semi-circular receiving line. Prime Minister Tony Blair began at one side, shaking hands. John Peel seemed to shrink back. So did one or two others.

It was such a delicate time, politically. And Radio 1 DJs traditionally did not, should not, show any political bias.

Yet it was still regarded as late-Cool Britannia era, 'Spice Girl' Geri Halliwell's Union Jack outfit, Noel Gallagher joining the party at number 10. We had more of a pop prime minister now than ever before.

The world had changed so drastically in that year since 9/11. There were also still-pressing domestic matters. Even under New Labour, the NHS was struggling. I'd had my fair share of hospital visiting in 2002, two of my relatives having been hospital in-patients. I'd spent time talking to registrars, nurses and junior doctors.

So as Tony Blair made his way around the DJs, getting ever closer to me, a dialogue was going on in my head. He was about halfway to where I stood, having reached Jo Whiley by now.

Right, I said to myself. *What are you made of? You have an opportunity now to speak directly to our elected leader. Are you going to waste this chance, and just simper a hello, or are you going to use this moment more usefully? If I was an NHS junior doctor, for instance, what would I say to the prime minister?*

To my almost horror, having moved round the room faster than I had anticipated, Tony Blair was now making a direct beeline straight for . . . me. I hadn't thought before, but of course, he probably recognised me from *The Old Grey Whistle Test*. After all, his fellow band mate Mark Ellen and I had appeared together.

His entourage pulled up opposite me, and the PM said: 'Oh I know who YOU are!'

So far he was having an easy ride, a pleasant unconfrontational, convivial evening. A clutch of DJs, he could talk about the nice safe subjects of pop music and electric guitars.

What could possibly go . . .

In my head I was thinking: *what are the most important issues of the day? Iraq and the NHS. If I tried to take him on over Iraq, I thought, he'll flatten me with rhetoric in milliseconds.*

And also, crucially, I genuinely believed that he and his cabinet *must* have secret inside information about Iraq to even remotely contemplate going to war. The subsequent Chilcot Inquiry proved that was not the case. And as I was probably going to get sacked for saying anything provocative anyway, I had best be on the strongest ground I could muster. The NHS was/is an issue that affects everyone.

So, I took a deep breath: 'Can I say to you that the NHS junior doctors are very unhappy.'

And he *wobbled.*

That left, very blue, eye, so mercilessly drawn and parodied daily by Steve Bell the cartoonist, bulged so much bigger, bluer, it almost vibrated.

'Er, what do you mean?' said the prime minister. Back foot.

'Well, the junior doctors. They say you keep moving the goalposts.'

Click, *whirr* . . . The big blue Blair eye engaged.

'Do you mean any hospitals in particular?'

'Yes. St Mary's, Paddington, for a start,' I said.

The Blair left eye seemed to expand a bit more. It was like a window opening.

I felt I could almost see into his surely super-huge memory file brain vault, zooming up and down its aisles sifting for any, but *any* relevant piece of information.

'I think . . .' he said, like this was my own PMQ, 'there is, er . . . money being spent on new building there.'

Well, I wasn't going to get a full government inquiry on the basis of one question to him, was I? And he didn't answer the question, about moving goalposts.

But at least I'd raised it. That term virtue signalling wasn't in vogue then. I didn't think that that's what I was doing. I wasn't supposed to do anything to bring the BBC into disrepute. On the other hand, I wasn't working on *Newsnight*, where its reporters are expected to challenge politicians.

Tony glided on around the horseshoe of DJs waiting in line.

Trevor Nelson, next to me, said into my right ear: 'I wish I'd fucking asked him something like that.'

Trevor wasn't to know that that comment boosted my morale somewhat . . . Should I have spoken up? Called out the most distinguished radio guest I had ever hosted? The dichotomy of being broadcaster/DJ/'entertainer' versus journalist was never clearer than on that evening . . .

You just never quite know your ground with politicians. I think it's right to treat them with respect as they are our elected representatives. Representatives being the operative word. No more, no less. They might call each other my Right Honourable friend in parliament, but they are still no more than our equals.

I once was roped in by the dynamic Barbara Castle to help collect coin donations at a rally she was speaking at, and I was covering, in early reporting days in Brighton.

Harold 'the Hatchet Man' Macmillan, PM in the sixties, sometimes travelled into London by train on the Brighton line. First-class compartment, of course. I was not above squeezing into the seat next to him if the train was too crowded to sit anywhere else.

I had ended up in a bar in the House of Commons during the nineties, heatedly debating the future of radio with Michael Fabricant, the flamboyant Conservative MP for Lichfield.

During an interview, the MP for Westminster North, Karen Buck, was asked what she would like to have done, had she not become an MP. She replied that she would like to be — me!

At a Women of the Year lunch, I was plonked on a podium to have my photograph taken with the then Home Secretary Theresa May. By way of playful but friendly introduction I said: 'Has anyone ever asked you before if you're related to Lady Gaga?'

She truly did not know how to react.

But on a subsequent occasion she looked at me with what I took to be: 'Oh no, not her again.'

I was attending the infamous *Spectator* magazine summer party. I knew no one there. I could see Emily Maitlis speaking with a group, in the garden, in a corner. I am really a shy person, but I needed to speak to someone who might join me in a conversation.

'Hello, I'm Annie Nightingale from Radio 1,' I said, as always needing an identity to validate myself.

Emily could not have been more friendly, and immediately introduced me to the nearest in her circle. A man who looked like the entertainer David Frost had done in his prime. High forehead and short cropped hair. I almost expected him to lean towards me and say ingratiatingly:

Hello, good evening, and *welcome*.

'This is Matt Hancock,' said Emily, and added helpfully, 'He's riding in a horse race tomorrow,' so we would have something to talk about. Of course in the ensuing years Matt Hancock has become even more ubiquitous on TV than the comedy host ever was.

But I couldn't cling to Emily's bunch all evening. I tried to mingle and, in vain, to find Michael Heath, the cartoonist, with whom I had been friends in my Brighton days. Everywhere I looked were the likes of Rod Liddle and Piers Morgan.

Perhaps time to bail.

As I made my way down the steps of the *Spectator*'s office, a black limo had drawn up behind my waiting humble minicab.

Out bounded a woman with a familiar cap of iron grey hair — she on her way in, me on my way out. Face to face.

It might have been my imagination, but her expression seemed to say: 'Oh no, what's *she* doing here?'

The next day Theresa May became Prime Minister.

⟶ 29 ⟶

Andy Eakins's Action in the Falklands War

After the Falklands War, I had a chance meeting at Kettner's wine bar in Soho. It was what happened in the eighties — one made training videos and met in wine bars. A good friend, video producer Melloney Roffe, introduced me to Andy, a helicopter pilot, who'd been in the front line of the conflict. When he could have been . . . diving for pearls. This is his story. From being a teenage school leaver and punk fan.

ANDY EAKINS: I was a little lost in 1976. I was in the first year of a hotel management course with no real direction except music, booking bands with the social secretariat of Crawley College [Sussex, south of England]. There were four or five of us poring over the *NME* every week.

I guess music should have been my main focus, but in those days . . . I just didn't see it. At Crawley College we ruled the music world and booked the Stranglers, the Jam as a support band, then later on the Clash, Motörhead, Mott the Hoople, Haircut 100, Sham 69, Black Sabbath, Dr. Feelgood, Chuck Berry, Squeeze and Madness.

They all played Crawley College or the leisure centre. At school

I lived on a diet of Lou Reed, the Who and Genesis, then moved on to a purely punk, new wave diet.

The destination record store in those days was Virgin Records, on the corner of Queens Road and North Street, Brighton. After skipping lectures it's a short hop on the train from Crawley [to Brighton]. I often went there to buy records. I'm pretty sure it was *Horses* by Patti Smith on that day.

On the way back to Brighton station about 100 yards up the road, I stopped outside the Royal Navy careers office. On the spur of the moment I walked in and signed up. With less thought than I had put into buying that record.

So in January 1977, aged seventeen, I joined the navy as a 'mouthy southy' from Crawley with two O levels and a cassette collection . . .

There's a knock one morning and a policeman at the door and he said: 'You've got to go to the base immediately. There's been a war in the Falklands.'

And all I said to him was: *'What sort of clothes should I bring?'*

He said, 'You'd better bring everything, lad.'

None of us knew. I think I'd shot a gun once in basic training, about twenty-five rounds of ammunition, and that was my total war experience. We had absolute faith that it [combat] would never happen.

That day we arrived at the base and there was nothing much for us to do. They were loading all the aircraft up, with all the equipment and weaponry and stuff they would need.

It's amazing that we'd got everything together within three days. We landed at an air base in Portsmouth, then onto the *Hermes*, the flagship aircraft carrier of the task force . . . the Harriers landed on the *Hermes* in Portsmouth and we set sail.

I think it was three days from the Argentinians invading the Falklands and sticking their flag up, to the taskforce setting sail.

It was *that* quick. We all went down and there was the *Canberra* going, the *Invincible* with Prince Andrew on it.

We thought that this show of might would completely put them off, and they would back down.

Most of us didn't know where the Falklands were. We didn't have any idea of its sovereignty, of the people. As we steamed across the Atlantic everything got a lot warmer. We started playing volleyball on the deck and sunbathing.

And, you know, there was a bit of a ceremony as we crossed across the equator.

I remember speaking to some of the crew and saying: 'This is quite a good gig, isn't it? We're gonna go down [to the South Atlantic], get a tan and be back in time for summer.'

Things started to happen by degrees. So the first thing was, they started to say . . . the Argentinians have got three submarines, and they could attack the [our] ship. So everyone who had been sleeping below the waterline had to come above the waterline. Find somewhere to sleep. I ended up sort of sleeping anywhere I could. You'd sleep in the corridors, and sleep deprivation started to come in.

We were either briefing, eating, flying or sleeping for days and days and days on end. This was the beginning of our action. Not a phony war. We had submarines, we had a job to do, we were going out there and doing it.

The first big thing was 'I counted them in and I counted them back', BBC's Brian Hanrahan's commentary, and that was the first big raid of the war. We went into Port Stanley with all the Sea Harriers and we bombed the runway. So they couldn't bring other troops in or other weaponry in.

And then there was that fantastic thing where the Vulcan flew all the way from England and dropped bombs on the runway and we'd heard about that, and that was lifting us up.

They came back that day and there was a bullet hole in one of the tail planes of the Harriers and it was a bit sort of . . . this is all right. We could be winning this one. We've shut the runway down. We've shut everything else down . . .

And then we heard *Belgrano* got sunk. *Sheffield* got hit by an Exocet. I was on the *Hermes* when everything was coming off of the *Sheffield*. The first time we'd seen casualties.

Five years through training I'd ended up with my legs swinging out of the back door of a Sea King helicopter, sat next to a machine gun. Flying over the Falkland Islands to San Carlos Water [Bomb Alley].

Worn out, stressed out, the least gung-ho crewman you would find anywhere. The good news was . . . I had a blue aluminium Walkman and unlimited batteries [stolen from stores] plugged into a hacked intercom system playing 'One of These Days' by the Floyd throughout the aircraft. Technology! . . .

We were moved . . . going into San Carlos Water. For days we were bombed and every morning . . . we'd wake up.

Let me describe San Carlos Water: it's like a Scottish loch. It's the loveliest place you could imagine: short green heather, grey granite rocks, blue sea and now SS *Canberra*, HMS *Fearless*, *Amazon*, *Ardent*, all of the A-class frigates are in there, all the Amazon Class frigates.

If you can imagine a loch, and you're looking down the loch and you hear *boof-boof*, *boof-boof-boof*, and then you see the fighters come over the hill. They're coming down fast, weaving backwards and forwards, and it's starting to get louder and louder and louder as the aircraft are coming closer and closer and closer.

They would go up, and the Harriers would try and pick them off. We had missile batteries on either side of this loch that would fire at them as well.

We called it Bomb Alley, and I think they called it Death Valley. The Argentinians called it Death Valley because it was such a dangerous place to be. If you're on a warship at anchor in a loch, you're just a sitting duck.

A top-brass RAF guy told on the World Service that the reason the Argentinian bombs weren't going off was that they were wrongly fused. Had they changed the fusing they would go off. The following day we lost two ships. Not just one.

And poor *Coventry* . . . when she got hit, I did fly on that mission. We saw this boat upside down in the water. The big bronze propellers were just sort of . . . still turning slowly. We saw a boat upside down. A capsized warship. An unbelievable sight.

The Falklands war lasted seventy-four days. Six hundred and fifty Argentinians, the majority on the *Belgrano*, were killed. There were two hundred and fifty-five British casualties.

The Argentinian land forces surrendered.

Margaret Thatcher won an increased majority at the next general election.

A BBC documentary had posed the question: was it worth it? The Falklands War?

*

ANDY EAKINS: I think it was worth it because of the net result. The ends justified the means. Whether Thatcher was right or wrong. Whether it was right to send people down there. Whether we should have protected the Falklands or not. Whether we should have sunk the *Belgrano*. Argentina became a democracy. Galtieri and his cronies got deposed and democracy came in and Argentina's been a democracy ever since. Will it ever happen again? Of course not.

(Andy Eakins received the South Atlantic Medal for his service during the war.)

ANDY EAKINS: I returned home on the aircraft carrier *Hermes* and bought a little cottage, with a massive mortgage, in Cornwall, music still a huge part of my life. I decided to 'settle down' and do something less dangerous, working on search and rescue helicopters.

(At which point I'm thinking: hang on a minute! . . . Settle down? Working on search and rescue? Less dangerous? Very laudable, and I guess safer than being in a war. Comparatively. It was the next part of Andy's story that stayed in my mind the most. He had, despite all the dangers, survived the Falklands War. But then . . .)

I was flying on search and rescue on 21 June 1984. The aircraft I was in the back of crashed into a hill in Scotland, killing the pilot and changing my life.

(What? After surviving front-line combat in the Falklands war? A peacetime naval helicopter crash?)

The crash landed me in hospital for months with a broken body. And in front of a psychiatrist at the Royal Naval Hospital with a slightly broken mind and PTSD.

I resigned from the navy. Bought a suit. Threw my uniform away.

Headed up to London to stay with an old mate from my college days in Crawley, Jim, and got into Apple Computers and music technology.

From whence Andy Eakins flourished.

Andy was still recovering from the horrifying helicopter crash when I met him. As usual when I was introduced to anyone new, we'd talked music. No doubt about punk and new wave, which by 1986 was considered by some to be a bit . . . well, to continue a naval analogy, that ship had sailed.

Where now for the fans of punk? But the mid to late eighties to me was a great lesson. Hang on in there, don't despair, you don't know what's around the corner. I didn't feel ready to be playing an oldies, greatest hits kind of set. Madonna ruled the mainstream. It was hard to see where hopeful new music might be coming from. I lost touch with Andy for a while.

But had absolutely no reason whatsoever to think he might have discovered the very same pathways, have made the same connection through a love of punk and new wave into . . .

Cut to twenty-one years on: straw bales made up the boundary areas in the dawn light of Glastonbury's Glade stage. Beneath the trees, leaves made brighter by the acid green lights hanging from the branches. I was DJ'ing, broadcasting a breakbeat set live on Radio 1 . . .

Suddenly detaching himself from the surrounding crowd appeared a very blissed-out looking Andy Eakins. He had become a rave convert too, through the Berlin techno label Kompakt and the psychedelic dub of the Orb . . . He even had a copy of my breakbeat compilation *Y4K*.

'There's no doubt,' he said, 'that music really did ease my troubled mind.'

An exemplary touch of British understatement, if ever I heard one . . .

These days Andy Eakins sets sail, in his own vessel. To Ibiza.

30

Shanghai

'I want to see somebody dead!' I shouted out loud, aged four years old, running along the road that skirts the famous botanical gardens at Kew, south-west London.

Early morbid tendencies towards future journalistic leanings maybe . . .

Two possible reasons for this outburst: one, I had just seen a strange large black car with glass sides gliding, well, funereally slowly, along the high brick-walled A307 Kew Road, and inside, a long wooden box covered with flowers.

Or two, just as likely; I had been told that someone had just jumped off the top of the Great Pagoda, the showpiece Chinese-style black and red ornamental tower dominating the vast swan-skimmed waters and lush greenery of Kew Gardens.

The jump had been fatal. The Pagoda was then promptly shut to the public for many years. And consequently became a symbol of curiosity for me, as well as piquing my fascination for scaling iconic tall buildings.

Cut to the late 1990s: Radio 1 had been moved from Egton, the squat, ugly sixties block next to Broadcasting House. We were on the move, to our own premises — hooray, how exciting. Even though it was just down the street, off Great Portland Street, to an edifice named Yalding House (all BBC buildings seem to tack

Shanghai

'House' on the end of their addresses). Brock House is where they do contracts and 'business affairs' (quaint, as the British Broadcasting Corporation is not a business). Similarly, Henry Wood House is called after a concert series, and Radio 2's HQ is now named Wogan House, for much cherished Terry.

Curiously, the last time I ever saw Tel was sharing the view with him, at the launch party, of the then newest highest building in London, the shiny, shiny Shard.

Yalding had been a car showroom, so it had floor-to-ceiling windows around the block, right onto the street. When I was working there late at night, alone, people jumped up from the pavement outside to have a gawp — kinda spooky. Yalding, we were told, was to be a temporary home for Radio 1. Yeah, I'd heard that before. Egton had been temporary too, and we had been there for twenty years.

The lift jammed often. Once I was trapped between floors with Simon Bates, who, once we were freed, rushed off to contact the *Sun* newspaper and let them know he had gallantly shielded me from fear of being trapped in a lift with him. This then led to a long-running on-air phone-in topic: whom would you most/least like to be trapped in a lift with?

At our new temporary home we would have state of the art studios, that was what mattered. In the basement. Often, doing late-night shows live, I would think I had caught sight of a human figure beside me. I would turn round to get a closer look, and the figure vanished. I really don't believe in ghosts but there was definitely an unearthly presence there. In the Second World War the block had been an ARP (as in *Dad's Army*) air raid protection depot. Much earlier in its history that part of Fitzrovia/Marylebone was well known for its brothels. Ah well.

Hosting my late, late show I was definitely a lady of the night. People maybe don't realise how much fun you can have when the bosses aren't listening. *Or you think they're not.*

Though of course everything is logged. During the rave/acid house period, myself and the phone team, the self-styled Pussy Posse, directed listeners to all-night and most often illegal raves. And read out messages like: 'Shout out to Gaz, hurry up and get round to ours, mate, we've run out of Rizlas.'

Most significant for me was the view as you exited the building. Look to the right, and there it was/is, looming into the sky, a beautiful silver rocket ready for lift off. The BT Tower. The communications rig from which all BBC broadcasts were beamed across the world. So when I emerged, elated, from Yalding House soon after 7 a.m. on a Sunday morning in the late nineties, this was what I saw. This shimmering beacon that had been for the past three hours beaming my show all over the world.

The original Hollywood RKO Radio Pictures logo (the studio that released *Citizen Kane*) was a powerful image from my childhood. An Eiffel-like tower, perched atop a revolving planet earth, sending out a circle of lightning bolts (à la Ziggy Stardust) and radiating rings of radio waves beaming out to the world beneath.

And the BBC itself used that same image of radiating circles from the top of a tower in black and white, for its early newsreels.

So I thought: let's do the show right here — from the top of the tower!

I knew that there had been a revolving restaurant. The Beatles threw a launch party for Mary Hopkin there; Jimi Hendrix had shown up. But now, like the Great Pagoda, entering the BT Tower was banned to the public, making it even more alluring for me. Like bad boys, I was also attracted to notorious places such as Eel Pie Island, Soho, New York's Alphabet City, Palermo, Havana . . . Baghdad . . .

An anarchist group called the Angry Brigade had planted a bomb in a loo inside the tower in 1971, so it was never opened to the public ever again.

But I had become obsessed. I envisaged an all-night party live-streamed all over the world from the top of the tower.

No, said the BBC.

Why? said I.

Too expensive.

No, said British Telecom.

Why? I asked.

Too much of a security risk.

So I clicked the 'don't take no for an answer' stratagem into place and began my campaign.

I knew I had a strong case if I persisted. Radio 1, like the rest of terrestrial radio throughout the world, was now facing , . . I was going to say an existential threat . . . but all threats seem to be existential now. Technology was overtaking all the traditional media.

First Amazon came for the bookshops, then the high street . . . Who wanted radio when you had Napster, YouTube, Myspace, iTunes and latterly Spotify? Radio 1 *needed* special events to keep our young listeners, and viewers, locked in.

Well that was my pitch anyway. Live streaming, that was all the go, so could we please live-stream a Radio 1 party from the top of the BT Tower observation area and broadcast it across the world through a Saturday night into a Sunday morning sunrise?

This brought my two loves, of music and astronomy, together. There was one optimum date in a year that it could work. Late in September.

It took nearly three years. Jason Carter, then head of live events at Radio 1, and always a blazing blue-eyed visionary, finally gave the plan his blessing. Now we had to persuade British Telecom, which bristled in its corporateness. They had metal name badges and long job titles.

Meetings ensued.

'We would like,' I would say, smiling brightly, to their head of corporate planning and marketing, 'to throw an all-night party at the top of the tower.'

The face of the head of corporate planning and marketing clouded. Darkly.

'*Party?*' she echoed, like she was Lady Bracknell and I'd just said the handbag word.

'Er no, sorry, sorry, *sorry*,' I hastily corrected, 'I mean . . . a, er . . . a . . . *late-night historic broadcasting event.*' Whew, diplomatic error hopefully avoided there. Just. Note to self: never ever use the word 'party' in the context of this proposal ever again.

The head of corporate marketing and planning said she would have a series of internal meetings with BT. Time ticked away. Nothing happened. I sent chase emails.

It transpired that the head of corporate p. and m. had now been promoted. We would have to start again with her successor. This duly, inexorably slowly, came to pass. Wheels creaked slo-mo into action once more. Then my exec producer at Radio 1 got promoted, too, which meant . . . yes . . . start negotiations from the beginning, yet again. Patience is not my strong point.

I had set my heart on one particular DJ who I wanted to head-line the pa— . . . excuse me, *event* . . . Because musically I felt he would best reflect the emotion and romance of my plan and embrace the technology. His name was Brian Transeau.

Probably what impressed me most was that BT, as he was coincidentally known, had made a dance music classic from the mathematical equation the Fibonacci sequence: 0+1 =1; 1+1=2; 2+1=3; 2+3 =5; 3+5 =8; 8+5 =13, adding the last two numbers together so that the sequence continues 21, 34, 55 ad infinitum.

Sunflowers, tree branches and some fruit and vegetable buds and leaves multiply in the same sequence.

As does the double helix of DNA.

Explain *that*, physicists; I certainly cannot.

Whatever. Brian agreed to fly in from LA to headline my crazy idea. *But*, his girlfriend was pregnant and he wanted to be present when their child was born. We might be able to predict to the millisecond when the sun would rise, but not when a baby would be born.

We put the project back. Again. Heaven, once more, would have to wait. This idea of showing London by night into a Sunday morning sunrise, could only be broadcast during my on-air show time of 4 a.m. – 7 a.m., a very tight window of time in the annual calendar.

Finally – the green light from BT. The show would go live on 26 September 2004. They brought in extra staff to host the event, run the bar, give up their weekend, work all night. At midnight we assembled at the tower base to take the seven-metres-per-second lift to the thirty-fourth floor. It's one hell of a fast journey if you don't mind heights. I'd say it's the second-best lift experience after the Ishtar Sheraton in Baghdad, which takes you from the interior atrium of the hotel, then bursts into the open air and climbs up the outside. All glass, with great views of the Tigris river below. It's the tallest building in Baghdad and has thus been the target of many bomb attacks.

We'd done a recce trip up the BT Tower by day, but never after dark. Would we be able to see London spread out on a Saturday night? Or would we be *too* high up? What would happen at dawn, in daylight, as the sun rose?

BBC engineers and technical crew, DJs, photographers, journalists, managers, producers, the online team from Radio 1, filmmakers and documentarians, this was the tower team. I flashed back to another risky project where I'd persuaded a BBC film crew to climb 8000 feet up in the Andes, to a volcano-ringed lake in Chile, to film a total solar eclipse. One wisp of cloud at the wrong moment there and six months of planning would have rendered the whole project useless. Actually, it was breath-taking and remains one of the most beautiful experiences of my life.

So now another team experience with an unpredictable outcome . . . It was pitch black outside of course, but we could see the lights of London twinkling away far below, as I had hoped. I wondered when the dawn might come, when we would see first light. I thought it would be about 6 a.m.

Sure enough, some faint stripes of indigo began to lighten the sky in the east . . . The night had been crystal clear, the sights spectacular. What would the day bring? Now the view from the top of the tower began to take a different shape. BT took to the laptop and the keyboard. (I had to do a longish stint of hard talking while our engineers re-plugged the DJ desk!) Canary Wharf, eerily backlit in glowing red, became a separate mythical citadel rising steeply from another unseen black landscape. Not looking like part of London at all. Or even of our planet.

We named this special to the worldwide audience 'The Last Summer Sunrise' show.

London emerged from beneath our feet, a perfect miniature city. Out of the shadows grew the streets and parks and crescents and hills and trees and . . . what's that . . . oh, it's the green roof over the British Museum . . . The great white wheel of the London Eye, and wow, there's *the river* sparkling away in the early morning light, lazily looping its way through the city crammed along its banks, tiny black silhouettes of bridges marking its progress.

I took a moment away from the broadcast desk to read the texts and emails coming in from Bucharest . . . Malaysia . . . Portland, Oregon, USA, and to scoot round the circular top of the tower to look at London the way very, very few had ever seen it.

Bang on 6.52 a.m., the sun shot into the sky. No shy peeking out of the trees, not as I thought might occur, mirroring a lazy Ibizan sunset, sinking slowly into the west . . .

No, this was *whoomph*! a *sky-sized* flame torch and a full-on, almost blinding light. The morning sun leapt, sprang up, against the BT Tower observation windows.

Our all-night party had hit all-dayer. We staggered about, shading our eyes from the dazzle. It felt very Starship *Enterprise*, like we were flitting from our space bridgehead across the firmament. BT looked shocked, turning round every few seconds to scan the evolving spectacle as the sun blazed in over his shoulder. He had made a 12,000-mile round trip for this moment. His set built to a crowning crescendo as we hit 00.07.00.00 on the dot.

Time to hand over to garage legend DJ Spoony, thirty-four floors down and back to earth in the Radio 1 studio two streets away.

Then the so unexpected happened. Fast.

A brisk wind must have whipped up from somewhere north of London, and within a minute of the end of the webcast, we were engulfed, all around our glass watchtower, in dense white storm cloud. This was not a light mist, or a bit of fog; this was a thick blanket, blocking every view from the tower, which was now completely obliterated. We could see no sky, no blue, no sun, no London. Gone in a matter of moments . . . I was speechless. Imagine . . . if that had happened just a few moments before . . . we would have had no summer sunrise at all.

It did feel like the Red Sea had parted . . . Extraordinary. We'd had our moment. Now it was gone.

I had experienced only one tall tower trip before, the CN Tower in Toronto. But like eclipse chasing, there was a hunger for more from Radio 1, so I made broadcasts from the TV tower in Berlin, and the brilliant blue-lit Spinnaker Tower overlooking Portsmouth, the Solent and the Isle of Wight.

Then when I heard there was to be a conference of tall tower exhibitors in Shanghai, I *had* to be there.

The centrepiece of the conference was to be a recce trip to the top of the Oriental Pearl TV tower, Shanghai's most recognisable landmark (now dwarfed in height by the Bottle Opener, and the Twizzler . . . another one probably being topped out even as I write).

It's a longish flight, London to Shanghai, via Hong Kong, At the time of this trip I was hosting the in-flight rave dance music shows for Cathay Pacific Airways. The anticipated and requested upgrade didn't happen. I wasn't being met at the international airport. I didn't know that there was a brand-new super-fast revolutionary magnetic driverless train service direct to the city centre. Fortuitously I took a good old-fashioned taxi. And the radio was on.

My first opportunity ever to hear contemporary Chinese pop. This was an interesting prospect. And, boy, it was an ear opener. The saddest, slowest, most melancholic music I'd ever heard. Kind of like the mournful sounds of Portuguese fado meets Take That on downers. I wondered if centuries beforehand the great Portuguese world explorers following after Vasco da Gama might have brought an early version of fado to China. I wanted to hear what Chinese people listened to every day.

Respect to the listeners, but if this was typical of popular radio music, were they going to let me play hip-hop breakbeats in their tourist-magnet tower? Travelling into the inspiring, psychedelic architectural centre of modern Shanghai's Pudong waterfront, the prospect wasn't looking good.

*

However, always hungry to conquer and profit, for better or worse, the West has now infiltrated China's indigenous music culture. EDM has made significant inroads into the Chinese aural landscape.

To this extent: a guest on my Radio 1 show early in 2018 was world rave music expert Matthew Collin, who related that at Shanghai club Linx this ritual happens:

An especially wealthy party of guests would be put at a certain prestigious 'bottle service' table area of the club; the table guests would order a particularly costly large Jeroboam of champagne, amid applause and sparklers.

At which point a mechanised series of pumps would elevate the entire group and its table as a platform, high up above the others. So that their ostentatious spending could be better viewed and appreciated by the poorer clubbers at the other tables. (A twenty-first-century version of John Lennon's caustic: 'Those of you in the cheap seats clap your hands, the rest of you rattle your jewellery.')

Capitalism, eh?

Then there's the just as shameful other side of the coin. Ever wondered what happened to your discarded CDs? Those mirror-bright plastic unrecyclable discs of non-destruction?

They've ended up in rubbish mountains, garbage pits, as landfill — in China. Paid for by the West. And here's the poignant part: Chinese detectorists, hungry for Western music, banned in the People's Republic of China, scavenge the surviving CDs, finding in among the deliberately torn and cracked plastic covers some that are still playable.

But with absolutely no idea of their provenance. Music that just about survived the dumpsters and the compacters, to be activated on a Chinese CD player. The foragers having no idea what they are listening to. Joy Division or jazz. Bowie or Acker Bilk. That makes me really melancholy.

At night the Pudong area's buildings become huge video walls and the Pearl Tower becomes a shimmering, multicoloured light show. The river that divides Pudong from the Bund on the opposite bank teems with small and large boats and craft, all highly illuminated, an endless water pageant, weaving their way through the night like shoals of giant neon tropical fish. That was the view from my hotel room. I switched on the in-room computer and typed in www.bbc.co.uk.

Nothing, but nothing came up. But of course — the BBC is periodically banned in China.

The first reception of the conference began next day. People had flown in from all over the world to represent their tourist attraction, their own tall tower: from Tokyo to Paris, to Seattle and its Space Needle, to Kazakhstan. The Pearl Tower is similar to the Atomium in Brussels, a futuristic structure suggesting connecting molecules in the shape of huge bubbles. In the centre shaft, a glass-sided lift whisks you to different platforms inside different pink bubbles. Inside the biggest, pinkest bubble, a string quartet of female musicians in chic black velvet were playing very beautifully executed Western classical music.

Mm, I thought, heart sinking somewhat. I can't see the Chinese authorities, with that country's revered music culture allowing . . . a bangin' midnight rave in their tower, broadcast by the outlawed BBC. Well, not yet. Time will tell.

I noted that in 2007 there was a 'pop' concert in the Pearl Tower. Featuring, among the Chinese artistes, singing 'Nessun dorma' one Sarah Brightman, the British ex-Mrs Andrew Lloyd Webber. I'd interviewed him once. It was an experience not unlike confronting the glass walls of the Pearl Tower. He was invincibility personified inside an invisible wall that surrounded and protected his entire persona. Never had I felt so unable to 'get through' or connect to any interviewee ever.

I had been to see (in the presence of the Princess of Wales, but not hanging out with her on that occasion) his musical *The Phantom of the Opera*. (Princess Diana saw *Phantom* no fewer than three times!)

It opened in 1986 at Her Majesty's Theatre, Haymarket. The most exciting moment comes when a chandelier comes crashing down almost into the audience. (Hardly a spoiler alert as a hundred million people have seen this production worldwide.)

I had been persuaded in the early nineties to see it again in the most unlikely company. That of the former *enfant terrible* entrepreneur, and The Rolling Stones' notorious first manager, Andrew Loog Oldham, and his erstwhile business partner, Tony Calder. Oldham had dreamt up the phrase 'Would you let your daughter go out with/marry a Rolling Stone?' Singlehandedly he had created their 'bad boy antithesis to the lovable, far less threatening Beatles' image.

He near terrified me in the Stones' early days. As was intended. Part of his ex-public school gangsta image . . . being driven around in flash cars with his infamous chauffeur Reg the Butcher, so named by Keith Richards. With us in this theatre party was Calder's tween daughter. She was the perfect age to see *Phantom*. I would have delighted in its sheer ruched taffeta-ness at her age. Unfortunately for her she was accompanied not only by her sober dad, but distinctly unsober Oldham.

This event took place shortly before he embraced complete sobriety. We'd had an enjoyable catch-up over an afternoon of reminiscences, so I cheerfully joined their theatre party later on.

'I just want to see how Mark is in the show,' said Oldham, referring to the former pop singer Mark Wynter who had been one of teenage Andrew's first and pre-Beatles and Rolling Stones PR clients. Now Mark was an actor in *Phantom*.

We had the best seats in the house, centre dress circle. Tickets were like the proverbial gold dust. Even then, several years after *Phantom* had opened. Idolatrous fans would make multiple trips to see the show. An intensely awesome, quasi-religious experience, rather than a musical.

For some.

Not for Andrew L.O.

Almost as soon as the curtain went up and the music started playing, he began singing along. Not to the Lloyd Webber compositions, but to the originals which Andrew felt had 'inspired' the other Andrew with the double-barrelled name. The now Lord Lloyd Webber. More polar opposites than those two would be very hard to find.

Phantom's central musical motif, that dark, doomy *dar-de-de-de-de – dar* had already been widely compared to the main riff in Pink Floyd's 'Echoes' on their *Meddle* LP.

The loud singalong by Oldham created absolute outrage among the other punters. First there were disgruntled rustlings of programmes. Raising of tense shoulders in front of us and angry shifting in seats all around us. I thought, to start with, that this night at the opera was going to be rather hilarious, if not quite Marx Brothers slapstick. The ex-manager of The Rolling Stones at a Lloyd Webber musical? A fun night out.

But I did feel compassion for young Ms Calder at the other end of our rowdy row, who no doubt was consumed with embarrassment. To say nothing of those who had shovelled out the shekels to sit in the circle.

There was to be no hushing and shushing of Oldham. His singing became more and more raucous. And louder.

The audience around us was getting *seriously* pissed off.

You could feel the remarks rising like bubble captions from the seated audience.

'My wife and I gave been waiting eighteen months to see *Phantom of the Opera*, and now you are ruining it.'

'It's absolutely disgusting you behaving like this, in a *West End* theatre.'

'Can you *please be quiet, I've paid a small fortune* to see this show.'

'How dare you spoil this beautiful performance.'

'How could you possibly behave SO selfishly . . . ?'

'If you don't be quiet, I'm going to call the management.'

'I am going to complain.'

'Can you please get these ruffians out of here. *Now*.'

Well he wasn't going to shut up. We had to get out or get Andrew out before the management called the police to eject us. And, as Tony Calder pointed out later, before the press was alerted.

'I don't really think this is your sort of show,' I tried to intone quietly to Andrew.

'I *just* want to see *Mark Wynter!*' he replied, plaintively, verging on the truculent.

'Yes, I know,' I said. 'Let's go and have a drink, it's the interval soon. Mark must be on later.'

I had to persuade him to get out of his seat . . . bundle him away from the circle, out of the foyer, out of sight of the theatregoers who now clearly wanted to punch Oldham's lights out.

Get him to a bar (well, where else?) and convince him he would be far better off not going back for the second half. Meet Mark Wynter backstage after the show. I remembered that there was an American Express ATM in Haymarket where I could get cash for drinks at Green's, the bar round the corner in St James's. It had got to the point where so many people I knew, whether they were paupers or millionaires, didn't have cash when it was really needed. And more than one needed to be discreetly escorted away from an 'unsuitable' event — me as well, on occasions, no doubt.

We certainly didn't see the end of the show. I didn't care, I'd seen it before. It wasn't really my thing either. Jack Tinker, revered West End theatre critic and fan of *Phantom*, was still a close friend, years after our early days on the *Brighton Argus* together. He said to me in a rather pained way: 'Perhaps you just don't like musical theatre at all.'

Maybe true. I hadn't liked *Cats* either and only went because at that time, I too had a friend in the show. My complaint? The cast just didn't look nearly enough like or convincingly enough, like cats at all.

To which you may comment: Oooh — *miaow.* Unless you are a millennial, in which case it might mean something quite different again.

The point is that Sarah Brightman might be welcomed in China to sing Puccini's 'Nessun dorma' at the Pearl Tower, fair enough. But the acceptance of that kind of opera and 'musical theatre' did not necessarily presage the kind of underground bass beat-heavy stuff I had and still do pioneer.

(Don't ask me what happened when I was booked to play a breakbeat set at the sixtieth birthday party of the chef Rick Stein. Let's just say it wasn't quite what he was expecting — and he wasn't very pleased . . .)

Waaal, you can't always get what you want, to quote Andrew Loog Oldham's former clients. It had taken three years to persuade the BT Tower in London to put on my breakbeat show in the early noughties. Maybe I'll have another go with the Shanghai tower in the 2020s! Time will tell. Strange to reflect that it had all begun with my fascination with the Chinese pagoda in Kew Gardens, nearly three quarters of a century before.

John Peel

My immediate reflections for the Guardian on John Peel's unexpected death in Peru, published on 27 October 2004.

The room where the specialist DJs work at Radio 1 is called G12. Over the past year or so it has become the most creative room Radio 1 has ever enjoyed. This large ground-floor office buzzes with sounds. From one side, the rock music of Zane Lowe's show. From another, the drum 'n' bass of Fabio and Grooverider. From another, vibrant Asian-based rhythms from Bobby and Nihal.

Into this maelstrom of music (listening on headphones is abandoned after 6 p.m.) would come John Peel on weekday evenings, clasping CDs, vinyl, tapes, letters, cards. His entrance would be greeted with a low roar of approval from us all.

'How are you, sister?' he would greet me, across our workstations. Our conversation often followed the same pattern. How were we going to find the time to listen to all the music sent to us? For John it had always been an endless problem. He had the widest taste, and so he would be sent a huge variety of music. With a view, of course, to a precious play on the John Peel show. How many careers has he launched? How many thousands of musicians' hearts have soared at hearing their name mentioned, along with the title of their tune, and the meticulous credit of the tiny label that had released it. 'Nottingham's [or wherever's] finest, I'm told,' he would say, drily.

John did not suffer hypocrites gladly. He was honest, sometimes dangerously so. But the BBC couldn't deny that exotic soul of his, which could so fully appreciate Captain Beefheart, the Fall, the Faces and Extreme Noise Terror. Of the latter he would say: 'I am the only person of my age in my neighbourhood who wears their T-shirts.'

Before his shows he would often take his team out for a curry and a glass or two of red wine, before returning to G12. Then it was down to the basement to broadcast his show live from his favourite studio, Y1.

In another studio, some years previously, John had stuck up a photo of Liverpool footballer Kenny Dalglish, with a handwritten caption: 'God, an informal pose.'

Two weeks ago, in a restaurant in Notting Hill, John was a guest at a Radio 1 dinner for its specialist DJs. He was, as always with his peer group, the centre of attention and originator of many of the laughs we had. His latest discovery, he said, was a band called Steveless. 'They make an LP [John never said album] every week. They're called Steveless because there's no one in the band called Steve.'

I don't know what Steveless or I, or anyone else who loves music, is going to do without John.

David Bowie

I had pleaded for a ticket to the opening of the David Bowie exhi-
bition at the Victoria and Albert Museum, London in March 2013.
At the grand entrance, a red, suspended, neon Ziggy Stardust
lightning installation. Huge expectation hung in the air, too.
Would he be there? Would he come to the opening night? Did
David Bowie ever do what was expected of him? No, of course not.
There had been so many troubling stories about him. His health.
His weight. Because there were no press releases, no facts. Just
rumour.

A year or so before the exhibition opened, I was finishing up a
recording in a basement studio at the BBC. A staffer said to me:

'Oh, just before you go . . . there's been an unconfirmed report
from the newsroom, that David Bowie is dying . . . Not expected
to survive the night . . . Could you just record a short tribute to
him? . . . Your memories . . . What he will be best known for,
that kind of thing . . . your top five Bowie songs . . .'

'*Wha!!!!!!*' I went. 'This is *terrible* news, if it's true.' Really, really
shocked. Hand shaking, I tried to compose something, any kind
of adequate tribute to him. Not being the very professional or
competent journalist at that moment.

And I realised that this was a generational matter. To those
under a certain age, the possible passing of David Bowie would *not*

cause the outpouring of grief, which did occur, when he died. As a piece of art. That was breath-taking.

The Strange World of Gurney Slade. There were only ever six episodes.

Broadcast in that netherworld few ever talk about: 1960. It wasn't the fifties, it wasn't yet the sixties.

Yet there were green shoots if you knew where to look. Or didn't blink, and miss these brief, flashing moments. Possible clues to the future.

Surrealism. On TV. Which had been unadventurous as a medium in comedy, still chained to the proscenium arch, or the domestic backdrop of the sitcom. Mother-in-law jokes, 'nagging' wives and unhappy husbands in belt and braces. The radio genius of *The Goons* had never really translated to TV. The satire boom, the scathing wit of Peter Cook and Co. was budding but had not yet really surfaced. Nor thence Monty Python. But the green shoots had been in the theatre. N. F. Simpson's surreal plays such as *One Way Pendulum* at the Royal Court Theatre in the late fifties. Which I saw while a student.

TV was still too much the terrain of safe light entertainment: *Sunday Night at the London Palladium* and the imported *I Love Lucy*, Liberace type of show.

And then, out of nowhere, *The Strange World of Gurney Slade* appeared . . .

There was the weird theme music, sort of flute-led jazz, an unforgettable hook with weird time signatures, chord changes. So awful, but once you heard it, it stayed.

I was totally transfixed the moment Gurney Slade appeared. And with no catch-up TV, if you missed it — you missed it. I was at one end, the very end of my teens. A young bloke called David Jones was at the beginning of his.

We both 'got' *Gurney Slade*. I didn't know anyone else at the

David Bowie

time who did. Though I wasn't to meet David Bowie for another nine years.

I was wondering if I would have a future as a journalist, stuck on the outer shores of Hove. Writing about local parish council meetings.

The popular arts, particularly music, were not very exciting. Buddy Holly was dead. Elvis had joined the army, killed the magic. We had Adam Faith and Cliff Richard. The Beatles were still thrashing out their apprenticeships in Hamburg . . .

Then along came the actor-singer Anthony Newley. With a surreal TV show. In black and white. Looked like a regular domestic set-up, him playing the harassed husband.

But then, suddenly, fleeing stifling domesticity . . . his 'character' runs off out of the three-sided living-room set, *breaking the fourth wall*, on out of the TV studio . . . past the cameras and the technicians, onto the street — and along numerous anonymous pavements. Pushing a vacuum cleaner.

He never speaks in a conventional manner — it's all free association, stream of consciousness voice-over. And all the time powered along by this strange tick-tock, tick-tock theme music.

Newley's commentary voice, sort of poshed-up slightly wobbly-wavery cockney. Sort of wry, wistful. Smiling at itself.

So when 'The Laughing Gnome' record was released seven years later, at the peak of psychedelia, I understood it. It was supposedly comic, puerile, but I got *where it was coming from*. From the bizarre, ephemeral and so short-lived world of *Gurney Slade*. It's well known that David Jones/Bowie was heavily influenced by Anthony Newley. But that didn't really fit any more. Not by 1967.

Newley's ship had sailed . . . to the land of West End musicals.

We'd gone flower power.

David Bowie's 'The Laughing Gnome' carried that most damning epithet, the 'novelty song'. Reminded people of an even more execrable record called 'The Laughing Policeman'.

How on earth was David Bowie going to dig himself out of *this* death pit?

The answer seemed to be . . . make another novelty record. Which is what he was perceived by some to have done two years on. But this time . . . with the use of the Stylophone, Rick Wakeman playing Mellotron, describing planet earth as blue, some beautifully timed handclaps and the skilled producer Gus Dudgeon, it all came sublimely right.

Kenny Everett's support on radio helped. I was a fan and friend of Everett, who used recording tape and a radio studio like an artist uses colour on a canvas.

Kenny was in between being sacked twice by 'the Beeb' — having been the one who coined it thus. He played great music on the radio, where I'd been barred, on account of being a woman.

But I did have a national newspaper column. Where I could rave about music I'd discovered, such as 'Space Oddity'.

I could, and did, draw attention to this strange, ethereal, beautiful tune.

The world of *Gurney Slade* had evolved into David Bowie's first masterpiece.

When I met him in 1969, I told him so.

I have recently unearthed, on faded newsprint, the first feature I wrote about him. At the time 'Space Oddity' had just jumped from number 20 to number 9 on the UK chart. Some thought 'Space Oddity' had been as a topical comment of the Apollo moon shot. And dismissed it as a gimmick. But Bowie emphasised that he had been inspired by Stanley Kubrick's film *2001: A Space Odyssey*. Hence the pun. And puns ran through Bowie's titles, as we would all discover.

This is what he said:

'Actually, I didn't want it released as a single at all. It was meant to be the tour de force of an LP of space music which I have worked on for a year.'

And he went on to describe his 'arts lab' in Beckenham in Kent called 'Growth'. He said it attracted labourers, bank clerks and art students.

'We are trying to encourage people to brighten up the streets where they live. We think they should pull up their paving stones and put down pink and blue ones instead.

'If I make enough "bread" from this record I am going to try to buy up the whole street. Just to show what can really be done.'

This conversation took place in the Colonnade Bar, next to the Theatre Royal, Brighton. And opposite the circular concert space, the Dome, where Bowie had just played, as support to Humble Pie. No theatrics for Bowie then: he had performed his set, sitting on a wooden stool playing acoustic guitar, wearing a white shirt and dark jeans.

I invited him over for a drink in the Colonnade. His support slot had ended. It was early, still daylight. I didn't even notice that he had one eye a different colour to the other. The charisma was there. His persona was absolutely magnetic. We clicked. Over surrealism.

In the wider pop world, there was a looming vacuum. The Beatles were breaking up. The media all speculated as to which *group* or *band* would take their place.

No, no, no, it's not going to be a *group*, was my belief. Everyone was looking in the wrong place. It was this skinny twenty-two-year-old with frizzy blond hair.

'*You* are the future!' I told him.

It was by no means a certainty to others. David Bowie had made one if not two 'novelty' records. And was not to have a further hit for another three years. But I had absolutely no doubt at all. Bowie was a unique visionary.

Outside the Colonnade after the interview, we walked along New Road together. No manager, no bodyguard, no publicist. He told me more about the arts centre in Beckenham.

'I'm going back there,' he said. 'Please . . . come with me.' It was very, very tempting.

Even more recently than discovering the tattered clipping, something else transpired. A documentary maker and Bowie expert had recently seen a copy of it. He remembered it only because I had used, intended as affectionate then, but a plain *wrong* term to describe Bowie's appearance. It had stood out. Now it would be termed, justifiably, offensive. And absolutely unacceptable.

Which I had not intended *at all.* I had likened him to a certain kind of previously popular doll. In all the miles of media written, recorded, filmed, printed and generated about David Bowie, he had kept that early interview, and now almost excruciating description of him, in his personal archive.

— 33 —

Mike Skinner – The Streets

May 2015. A small, windowless, confessional-size audio recording studio at Wisebuddah, Great Titchfield Street, Fitzrovia, London. Interior. Day. I sit opposite Mike Skinner.

MIKE: I'll just move the mic closer.

PRODUCER: (*v/o on talkback*) We're ready now.

ANNIE: OK.

MIKE: Great.

ANNIE: (*into broadcaster mode*) So . . . thank you, Mike Skinner, for joining me.

MIKE: Is this (*gesturing at my headgear*) this . . . headband of roses? Is this something new? This something that you do?

ANNIE: (*somewhat embarrassed, feeling definitely not the generation to be wearing a 'rose crown' as now adopted by the Coachella millennials*) It's not significant . . . just thought I'd give it a go. (*Moving swiftly on.*) Were you in Brighton last weekend? I was there, but couldn't find you?

MIKE: Yes, at the Great Escape, I was doing a thing in the Spiegeltent, a screening with Vice. I'd made a documentary about rappers in

Israel, called *Hip-Hop in the Holy Land*. Kind of what happened at the turn of the century. Mad.

ANNIE: You are very much a twenty-first century person. Is it fair to say?

MIKE: I always wanted to tell a really *simple* story. Looking back it has stood me in good stead, because I think that stories can be really didactic — like you're preaching to people.

ANNIE: You seem to be able speak in the idiom of young people.

MIKE: When I wrote 'Has It Come to This?' people used to say: 'Who wants to hear about "us"?' I gambled a lot about people wanting to hear about 'us', the young suburbans.

ANNIE: You were called The Streets, which in itself was peculiar. Why weren't you called Mike Skinner?

MIKE: I wanted it to be a group. I didn't want to be a performer, I wanted to be a producer. I was working with a lot of guys in Birmingham. Not long before that, everyone used to rap in an American accent. Until the late nineties.

In Shakespearean times they called it the great vowel shift. Within about thirty years everyone spoke differently. Their accent changed significantly, and a lot of new words were invented. So there was a great vowel shift in rap. About 1997 — 1998. I was never good enough to be part of British rap. I completely sidestepped it. The Streets was, in my head, was like Nas rapping over garage. If Nas was from somewhere between Birmingham and London.

I've always been from 'somewhere between Birmingham and London'. I had to completely invent that place in my head. It made sense intellectually to do that. It was about everything in rap we liked, but with someone from England saying it.

ANNIE: Around the year 2000 you started to see the effect of reality shows in the charts. What did you feel?

MIKE: I think the biggest affecter of music in the noughties was what they call the Great Unbundling — iTunes. And the ability to buy one song off the album . . .

What the dance guys have got their heads around is, that they don't really care about sales. They're just like touring musicians. With Ableton or whatever. They go from club to club. You go up and down the country doing these bass nights and you see the same people. It's a bit like being a variety show.

It's completely separate to what you would call mainstream now. Singles have become a big thing again, like in the sixties, for the record companies. The album is just a big risk now.

In the nineties you had these bands like the Chemical Brothers, and the Mercury Prize bands where you could concentrate on being really good, as a band, and trust that the label had enough money to bankroll it, tour support and stuff. But that's all gone.

So it's back to being like music hall, going round the country peddling your wares.

And when you do studio sessions now . . . I might do a tune with rappers now or MCs. In the old days you would pay them five hundred quid. And then someone would have had to do a publishing sign-off, just so that you could get the song *out there*. Whereas now they'd go: 'Put it on SoundCloud', and just get on with their week. It's more creative.

In terms of writing, being specific is a way to people's hearts. It means you don't have to talk in abstractions like *love* or *hate* or *desire*.

If you say: 'I'm sitting on the kerb with my head in my hands', you haven't stated anything abstract, about emotions. That was always my mantra: Don't say 'love', say [describe] what you're doing.

ANNIE: Well I don't know anyone else who would talk about having bars on their phone in a lyric!

MIKE: I used to struggle with the idea that I was an artist. Because where I grew up, being an artist is not cool. Birmingham, because it's not Manchester and it's not London, at the same time as being drawn to London, is repelled by it.

You begin your career by thinking about what everyone at school would think of you. Till you're probably close to thirty. You're always thinking about what everyone at school would say.

ANNIE: Peer pressure?

MIKE: It completely shapes you. So I had to come up with something that meant I was some sort of . . . *craftsman*.

That what I was doing was a trade. I'm sure, in my head, all my peer group were appreciating Anish Kapoor, and great architects and poets — I haven't been back there for a while so I haven't asked them! — so I imagined that I was making a table that had some use.

It had to be *useful*, so I didn't have a lot of time for talking in emotional ways; that was not something I thought I was there to do.

I guess a great table could make you emotional, but it has to do the job first and foremost. It would have to not fall over and gain your trust . . . that all came out in the language.

ANNIE: So how long did it take to get acceptance from radio stations and the like, about your ability as a craftsman?

MIKE: Once I'd done 'Has It Come to This?' (The Streets' first hit release) everything was easy. Nothing stood in the way. But I'd spent probably ten years before that trying to make something. Sending stuff to American labels — I sent an EP to Loud Records. They put out Wu-Tang material. I spoke to the guy on the phone in America. He was very nice. But he was asking why would they want a load of rappers from England, when there's a line of them outside, round the block, to be signed, in New York? I agreed with him!

They're only just wanting to hear the British rappers now.

I went to New York. I did a lot of interviews with Dizzee Rascal, we were sort of bundled together. I think what Dizzee wanted was to be played on black radio there, and it wasn't happening. Now we have grime 2.0.

ANNIE: It took you *ten years* though? You must have really believed in yourself?

MIKE: Well, in poker they call it pot committed. You've put so much money in, you should probably fold, and walk away. But you've put so much into the middle of the table — you just have to carry on. I think it's true of a lot of musicians . . . you can't do anything else.

I think we punch well above our weight in the UK for inventing new kinds of music. Especially in dance music. America is a vast economy. I've mastered records in America. I've been in those mix rooms. People will kill each other to be a success in America. The work ethic is insane. They are so hungry. So competitive. It's not necessarily a bad thing. We don't want to be like that here, in the UK; we sort of sneer at it.

But what comes with that, is that everyone in the chain is completely committed. To making it happen. So the mix rooms are much better, the mastering rooms are much better. There's just more money. There are stylistic differences as well that we can't get our heads around.

Like where the kick drum is placed in R & B. It's much more forward in America than it is in the UK. That's why, when people like Mike Stent, the mix engineer, moved to LA it took him ages to work that out. He'd mixed the Spice Girls, and then onto mixing American pop. Stylistically it's a different culture there; it comes from black music. But we're so innovative in this country.

Look at dubstep for instance. We might not be able to finish it off as well as someone like Rihanna, but we punch above our weight considering our size. I always look out towards the regions; it's a matter of confidence, so you end up, with, for example trip hop in Bristol. They had confidence, so they could say: yes, we know how to do this!

ANNIE: I'm worried about British music getting left behind.

MIKE: I think we are like an incubator here, a very good one. I never assumed anyone was listening to my songs, listening to the words, on the radio. You have to beat people over the head and assume fifty per cent of what you say won't get heard. You have to keep it super simple. But I think within that, there's room to be . . . interesting.

PRODUCER: (*through talkback*): I think that's it for our studio time. Are you going to say thanks to Mike?

ANNIE: Sure, of course . . . Mike, thank you so much for joining me.

MIKE: Thank you for having me in such . . . (*viewing a temperature-control unit*) . . . an even-temperated room. Twenty-three degrees.

Mike Skinner trained as a sound engineer (figures).

The Streets recorded four ground-breaking albums, from 2002 onwards, the first being *Original Pirate Material*. After a seven-year break, the band resumed world touring in 2019.

Announcing the new dates — although he emphasised this was not a priority for returning to the road with a band — Mike Skinner stated that he'd missed travelling in tour buses. Not so readily available to him during his interim period as a solo DJ. (Amen to that!)

34

The Tortoise and the Politicians

In early summer 2016, I was invited to appear on the late-night live TV programme *This Week*, with Andrew Neil, Alan Johnson and Michael Portillo. In the 'and finally' slot, where a non-politico joined the sofa to plug — sorry, talk — about their latest artistic endeavour.

Mine was about an upcoming festival appearance at Hay-on-Wye. But that was not going to be dwelt upon. I was shown onto the red velour guest sofa by the floor manager. I was wearing, as usual for me, even though it was past 11 p.m., sunglasses. Green frames, grey tinted lenses. Neil, host of the show, Johnson and Portillo all promptly each donned a pair of dense black sunglasses. Taking the piss. Fair enough.

There was a surreal late-night Mad Hatter's tea party vibe about the set, in a studio in Westminster, and I felt like Alice in Millbank-land. Yet also the former eminent politicians, now in shades, strongly evoked the dubious characters from *Reservoir Dogs*. Enhanced by Michael Portillo's penchant for wearing brightly coloured clothes. Mr Blue . . . Mr Pink, Mr Orange.

Before the show went live on air, both Alan Johnson and Michael Portillo introduced themselves. Alan talked music, and Michael Portillo rather surprisingly held out, on a hanger, a bright-blue sequined jacket.

'Want to borrow it?' he said affably. Curiouser and curiouser. I felt even more like Alice. I thanked him for the offer.

There was another element to this eccentric but often barbed political talk show that, on this night, bothered me. Sometimes a dog, a friendly pooch, would be seen roaming around the set, sitting up or lying down as it pleased. Maybe it was there to act as a therapy dog, to calm down any antsy or irate guests. This was Molly, a golden retriever. It was not a Rottweiler, the name given sometimes to Andrew Neil (ex-editor, now chairman of the right-wing weekly magazine the *Spectator*) due to his feared forensic style of interviewing politicians.

But on this night it was not Molly the dog on set, but a *tortoise*. About the same domed size and shape as a large teapot, of the kind imagined at the original Mad Hatter's tea party.

Neither tethered nor caged, just free to scurry among the sofas, chairs, tables and cables strewn across the set.

Scurry? A tortoise? Oh yes. They get a bad press for moving slowly, but in truth rather than in myth, it's another story. I should know. I'd had a very adventurous tortoise as a pet for about three decades. (This one would try to swim in a pond, hibernate in a bonfire, disappear for years at a time.) They can really move, baby, when they see something they desire. Like another tortoise, or a delectable-looking feast.

On the night in question I was wearing open, strappy sandals, revealing bare toes. My toenails were painted a bright shiny yellow gold.

You could say almost *buttercup* or *dandelion* yellow.

In my own experience, a tortoise takes one look at a glowing buttercup, or the dense brightness of a dandelion flower, and is reaction is: yay! Lunch, crunch and *chomp*.

Andrew Neil might be able to subdue a politician in seconds, but he clearly didn't know enough about a tortoise's eating preferences.

'It won't come anywhere near you,' he said airily.

Oh yes it will, I thought. I almost expected Neil to say to me, though I'd had none: 'More wine?' (he was forever making references to Blue Nun) or 'More cake?' or 'Why is a raven like a writing desk?'

And more to the point: why was a tortoise roaming round a live TV studio in the midst of a political discussion programme?

The floor manager cued Andrew Neil into his next live piece to camera. To introduce me.

The tortoise advanced. I could not retreat. 'Hey. Ged off,' I went, by now miced up, and therefore pinned to the spot.

Andrew Neil described me to the *This Week* TV audience . DJ . . . blah-blah . . . Radio 1 . . . blah-blah . . . 1970 . . . Fairly standard and not inaccurate introduction. Then his first question:

'How have you stayed relevant?'

'Because,' I said, 'I am genuinely interested, fascinated where new music is going, and (*shifting in my seat*) I am fascinated by this tortoise that's trying to . . .' I looked down, as the camera stayed focused on me, the cameramen widening the shot to show the tortoise at my feet. I bent over, trying desperately to shoo it away. I didn't want to kick it or do it harm, but . . . Where oh where was its studio wrangler? Did it even have a wrangler? Tortoises can bite. People. Fingers. Toes.

This one, as I'd feared, had espied my shiny yellow toenails as the *plat du jour*.

Alan Johnson, former health secretary and home secretary, in HM government, and former minister of transport, Michael Portillo, just looked on, stock-still, seated opposite me. Wearing their fun black gangster glasses and smiling benignly like Cheshire cats.

There was to be a further, more challenging, episode of *This Week* two years on, featuring in the same guest slot I had occupied, Bobby Gillespie, lead singer with Primal Scream.

Pretty much immediately, whether he had known it before or not, Andrew Neil was now faced with an uncompromising, outspoken, hard-left supporter.

Bob G. had no hesitation in expounding his views, and did so swiftly, on the past forty years of capitalism, Boris Johnson, Michael Gove, the prospect of a hard Brexit, food banks and poverty (it could be noted that his father had been a revered Scottish trade union leader).

So Neil closed him down pronto, with an abrupt: 'That's your lot for tonight, folks.'

His regular team then got out of their seats and began prancing around the studio, performing some 'new' excruciating dad dance.

I, watching, realised that by shutting Bob up so sharpish, the show now appeared to be under-running. So the dad dancing went on and inexorably on.

Bob G., refusing to take part, sat immobile on the guest sofa.

Back in Wonderland again, it occurred to me. What is this, an updated version of the 'Lobster Quadrille'?

'*Will you, won't you, will you join the dance?*'

And Bob's silent rejoinder:

'*Would not, could not, would not join the dance.*'

Though I suspect his internal monologue would have been expressed in rather more robust Scottish terminology.

The studio director and vision mixer cut away and then back to Gillespie, again and again, in what looked like horrified fascination. Neil, Portillo and third studio guest Labour MP Caroline Flint, charged on around the studio furniture, their raised elbows flapping and flailing like giant lobsters' claws.

Gillespie remained motionless on the blood-red sofa, which clashed somewhat with the cerise-lit studio wall behind him. Ever more granite faced, ever more pained. The regular *This Week* team meanwhile galumphed on and on around the set. Till finally, mercifully, the programme's production company logo, a purple juniper berry sprig, swam up onto the screen.

The clip unsurprisingly went viral on social media.

Four months later, after a run of sixteen years, it was announced that the TV programme *This Week* was to be cancelled for good. Makes you wonder.

— 35 —

Malcolm McLaren

Malcolm McLaren and I were appointed as judges at a Live and Unsigned talent contest in Portsmouth. This was at the height of the TV talent show onslaught decade, the noughties. What on earth was I doing there, and what was Malcolm McLaren doing there? A reasonably generous fee, to be honest, and curiosity, a genuine interest to see what original talent might abound, unselected by the TV talent shows. Who better than with the master of chaos pop group creation, McLaren himself?

This contest had been running for a number of years and the organisers had whittled down the appearances of the entrants to an extraordinary level of fast-moving efficiency.

No less than sixty acts could be judged in one day. So these were lengthy sessions, and we judges had to mark our papers extremely swiftly to keep up with the assembly line of would-be stars. As soon as we had put pen to paper, an official would whisk our markings away for calculation and the next hopeful hover into view on stage. With such rapidity that after half a dozen it was very difficult to remember the outstanding talents, if any, of the preceding acts.

Eventually I hit on the idea of making my own retained notes on a separate sheet. Because, at all too regular intervals, the compere would pass a mic to each of the judges to make comments on the previous round of competitors. Without notes there was no way of remembering if the singer in the band we'd witnessed ten minutes ago had any more potential than the balladeer strumming his acoustic just seven minutes before that. Bearing in mind we were in full view of the audience who were comprised of the fan clubs/mums and dads/supporters of each act.

I flashed back to an experience I'd had in the eighties, judging a contest of heavy rock bands, at a covered-over ice rink in Moscow. I'd been asked on mic, in front of a huge contingent of each band's supporters, my honest, unbridled comments.

Which I duly gave willingly . . . In Russia. Really? A good plan? For the (in my opinion) least talented bands had an inverse greater proportion of fans present. My criticisms of them, bearing in mind the limitations in the culture there and then: lack of good quality instruments, limited PA, not-up-to-it amps was really too harsh and unfair.

They booed me so loudly it echoed round the freezing ice rink. *En masse* the crowd lifted their arms in the air and gestured angrily in my direction. I got the full evil eye, devil's horn treatment. Sure, they would have done more if they'd been able to corner me. I could hardly blame them. It was extremely undiplomatic of me, not to say insensitive.

Portsmouth, the British navy's base on the south coast of England, is hardly Moscow but still, for my own safety, as well as cowardice and showing more compassion, I gave my end-of-round verdicts on the Live And Unsigned acts a little more generosity of spirit. I tried to be more positive and encouraging, as well as using a bit more common sense. Almost all were adolescents.

From the man who'd built his career on inventing the Sex Pistols, there was going to be no such nuanced comments. As the mic was handed to Malcolm, he growled into it, loudly, as to what he had seen so far. Not impressed, at all, was the gist of it.

Quite the slag off you would expect, really. I felt he was playing up to the role of villain of the piece.

After the first judging session, we headed out of the back door of the Guildhall, Malcolm looking for a pub lunch. The fans of the bands from the first session were waiting for him. Circled him, shouted, chanted and booed. Quite an ugly, threatening and intimidating scene.

Much, much later, Malcolm, his partner and I found ourselves back at a shared hotel in neighbouring Southsea. It was comfortable, not sumptuous. It had been recently newly partitioned and converted from a private home. Time and space for a nightcap. Malcolm dropped the baddie act now. We talked about how much he regretted what had happened to Sid Vicious, and what we might be missing at Glastonbury that weekend. It was the first I was absent from since 1990.

Later, I found McLaren's own reflections of that day, written in diary form for the *Financial Times*. He was much kinder to the Live and Unsigned entrants in print, than he had been to some of them in Portsmouth. He described his feelings as being 'an icon of twenty-first century unhappiness'.

He was to die of cancer ten months later. From being the ruthless Svengali and major manipulating entrepreneur of the punk era, Malcolm McLaren now turned out to be, for me, the Wizard of Oz. The curtain pulled back.

— 36 —

You Don't Own Me

I wasn't quite done with the tall building as performance platform yet. All the music submitted for my radio shows arrives by email downloads now, no CDs or vinyl or cassettes. When I log on first thing every morning, there are pages of tunes ready to be heard, all brand new and unknown. Early in 2016, among the newbies was a song title I remembered.

'You Don't Own Me'.

I just wonder, I thought to myself. Could this possibly be a new version of the classic song first recorded in the early 1960s by Lesley Gore? And that had ever since become an international feminist anthem. And my personal one, too. In 1963, I was fighting off the constraints of staid society trying to push me conform. That wanted me to settle down and give up a future career. That hangover from the fifties where women were supposed to make happy with a fridge and a new vacuum cleaner. As symbols of some kind of domestic utopian paradise. With no intellectual challenges.

Well as I was discovering for myself, no fucking way.

It seemed very, very wrong as well to divide the population in half, as conforming, heterosexual male breadwinners, and compliant female servants/cooks/babysitters. What if you didn't or couldn't or wouldn't fit that mould?

I'm known as the first female DJ on the BBC, on Radio 1, but my struggles for working independence had begun much earlier. In my teens and early twenties, it was convention for women in many occupations that they should literally retire as soon as they got married. And the pressure on young women to marry early was huge. I just couldn't understand it. Why wouldn't a young woman want to explore a career, explore freedom, travel, possibilities, potential, before 'settling down' as a housewife. Though I didn't oppose anyone who was happy to do that. If as a woman you managed to survive that hurdle of being married, and retain your job, you'd be shooed out smartish if and when you became pregnant.

A 'bun in the oven', as the saying went. Knocked up. Similarly, the male, boastful term for sexual conquests, that they had 'got their end away'. I had married, naively admittedly, very young, against my parents' wishes; but to me that had nothing to do with wanting to pursue any future opportunities as a journalist. Or explore other work opportunities as and when they might come along.

I'd only just begun. And so had the youth revolution. Why on earth would I want to give up work just because of my marital status?

There's a publicity photograph of me taken around that time, to which 'You Don't Own Me' was the soundtrack. I'm standing holding apart some optimistically bright yellow drapes as a backdrop; I'm wearing a movie star's (Natasha Parry) hand-me-down, tight chequered Capri pants and a high-street sweater.

Beyond me is a balcony and a wide vista of sea and sky. It held all the promise of a possibly exciting future. But also conflict with a society of disapproving other, not much older than my parents, mother-in-law types and dull-witted bank managers. Society wanted to close the curtains on me. And on the open sky of my optimism for future adventures.

All right, then — if necessary, I would go it alone. You cannot live your life the way others decide you should.

And I wasn't going to change my maiden/real professional name either. It seemed utterly ridiculous to me that in an equal partnership, a woman should cede control and her identity to a man, because he was regarded as wiser, more intelligent, responsible and superior to a woman. More capable of holding down a bank account, a credit card account, a mortgage. At this time a woman could not obtain these without a male partner. Astonishing.

Just because of a chromosome difference — it makes absolutely no scientific sense at all. I always thought it was possibly unfair to the male half of the partnership, too, expecting him to take on all the financial responsibility. We are not all cut from the same cloth. Equality in a relationship seemed the blindingly obvious answer to me, and fifty years or so on, the present and future seem more optimistic. A little. In some societies. We still have a long way to go.

So would 'You Don't Own Me' resonate with a young audience in the twenty-teens? Were the issues still relevant to young people?

This new release was the same song, by a young Australian singer, Grace Sewell, accompanied by a rap over the top by the much better-known American rapper, G-Eazy. Curiously this version too, like the original, was produced by the man who had become Michael Jackson's main musical mentor, Quincy Jones.

Straight away it sounded like the near perfect remake.

Would the song, could it, fifty-three years later, be a hit again? So many others had tried. Dusty Springfield, Joan Jett, Klaus Nomi (who had been my guest on *The Old Grey Whistle Test*, and then gained great acclaim with David Bowie).

Only one way to find out if it would resonate again.

Play it on the radio.

In Australia the recording had become a number 1 hit. Grace now turned her attention to promoting the song in the UK and the rest of the world. My initial enthusiasm had very little effect. Sales didn't seem to be shifting.

That summer I went on holiday to the sparsely populated area of southern Italy, the heel of the boot, Puglia. They make rich dark red wine there and press excellent olive oil. But there's very little else in terms of employment. The youth, or many of them. desert their home villages looking for work further north. I dropped into a corner shop, on the outskirts of a town called Martina Franca. Weaving among shelves piled high with dry pasta, I could hardly believe my ears. Out of a small radio speaker came the words . . .

You don't own me
Don't try to change me in any way
You don't own me
Don't tie me down, cause I'd never stay . . .

Grace's version, sung in English. Somehow this convinced me. If the song had reached rural Italy, to a small village shop, then it must have worldwide hit potential.

On my return to the UK I decided I should play it on my show every week till YDOM did become a hit. I also ran round the other daytime shows on Radio 1, plugging their DJs, and also played it to Jo Whiley on Radio 2. She and her producer were captivated too — *surely* we were on the right track. The weeks and months went by. 'You Don't Own Me', however, did not seem to be setting the top 10 alight. What I didn't know was that it was now being considered for a huge Christmas TV commercial campaign for a department store chain with a big advertising budget to throw at it.

That tipped the balance. Now on TV, the song was blasted out with max rotation exposure on all the hot slots vital to success. It hit all the playlists, after the best part of a year.

Grace was invited to my radio show. She brought me flowers and said how encouraged she'd been that I had backed the tune for so many months, when no one else had.

I wanted her visit to Broadcasting House, and our new eighth-floor Radio 1 studios, all multicoloured neon and purple sofas, to be memorable . . . Momentous, somehow.

Maybe . . . a *Beatle*-type moment . . .

'Hey, let's go out on the roof like they did at Apple on Savile Row.'

So we climbed out, wrapped in scarves and fake fur, onto a narrow outside ledge, the top floor of the bright, newly renovated 1930s BBC HQ. A video cameraman followed us.

Grace, without prompting or warning, suddenly burst into singing an acapella version of 'You Don't Own Me'. It was Christmas cold, our breath white against the backdrop of Regent Street's webbing of winter sparkling illuminations . . . way, way down below.

It was thrilling but I was in shot and on mic. I didn't want to rain on her unique spontaneous parade by singing along, flat and out of tune. So I just sort of swayed next to her, gesticulating aimlessly, unchoreographed, like Theresa May doing her unfortunate cross-country-skiing impression of a 'dance move' to the children of South Africa.

Grace's version of 'You Don't Own Me' hit the top for the prestigious Christmas period and stayed there, high in the charts for many, many weeks afterwards. Its lyrics are open to so many different interpretations besides the most obvious. 'You Don't Own Me' is a refrain taken up by same-sex couples, children disagreeing with their parents, employees against their bosses — and even the individual vs the state! I hear YDOM now played frequently on daytime radio, TV specials, reality shows and documentaries, as a modern classic.

The lyrics, whichever way you look at them, clearly have not dated.

⟵ 37 ⟶

Little Simz

Interior. Day. Radio 1 studio, eighth floor, New Broadcasting House, London.

The internal windows looking onto adjacent studios are hidden by giant, navy-blue, pull-down blinds. Little Simz and I sit side by side on swivel chairs. Little Simz is twenty-one, of Nigerian origin, one of the most promising females among London grime artistes. Has recently released her first album. She is immaculately dressed in red and grey. Microphones are suspended from the ceiling in front of us. The producer is on the opposite side of the DJ desk, adjusting the mic levels.

This is warm-up time. My 'technique' for making the interviewee feel at home. But as is painfully obvious via this transcript, unfortunately hardly letting the guest get a word in edgeways!

ANNIE: . . . yeah, so you really appreciate people who ask different questions. Even if they're just a bit silly, even.

LITTLE SIMZ: Yeah, exactly.

ANNIE: But just not the same old . . .

LITTLE SIMZ: Exactly.

ANNIE: So — 'Is this album gonna be different from the other one?' Well, no one's ever gonna go, 'Yes, it's gonna be exactly the same as the last one.' I mean, you know . . .

LITTLE SIMZ: Exactly.

ANNIE: And somebody actually said to me, 'Well here's a stock question.' And I thought: 'If it's a stock question maybe just don't ask it, then!' You know?

LITTLE SIMZ: Very true.

ANNIE: So, in a way, I should make . . . I like having a conversation. It's not a . . .

LITTLE SIMZ: Yeah, that's what I like, just conversations anyway.

ANNIE: This is the most difficult bit . . . Don't say anything interesting yet. We're not recording yet! Love your coat, by the way.

LITTLE SIMZ: Thank you, thank you very much.

ANNIE: Little Simz, I'm so delighted you're here. I've been waiting a long time to meet you . . .

LITTLE SIMZ: Thank you.

ANNIE: . . . and have you on our show.

LITTLE SIMZ: Appreciate it. Thanks for having me on.
   (*Even if she's hardly managed to say a complete sentence yet. Finally, we are go.*)

ANNIE: You've said 'I am not an MC rapper', what is different about your music is that . . . most of your contemporaries are writing about *themselves*. They're autobiographical. Yours aren't. You're storytelling.

LITTLE SIMZ: English was my favourite subject. English literature, to be precise. And I just kinda like the idea of telling stories and kind of looking at my music as . . . well my album, let's say, is like an audio novel, like a book.

ANNIE: *That's* the word — novel! While I was listening, I particularly noticed the song 'The Hamptons'. I went to school in the 'Hamptons', ha ha, but this was Hampton *Hill*, Hampton *Wick*, Hampton *Court* near London. *Not the* Hamptons, this very posh area in America. So what's the basis of that song?

LITTLE SIMZ: The Hamptons. I feel like, ooh, growing up for me anyway, that was something that I used to hear often. The Hamptons. I wanna house in the Hamptons.

ANNIE: Yeah. Sounds very glamorous, doesn't it?

LITTLE SIMZ: That wouldn't be a bad goal to have, own something in the Hamptons — it was kind of, a metaphor for anything in life that I want. If I want to, let's just say, buy my mum a house — that's not just gonna *happen*. I have to *work* for it.

ANNIE: Whereabouts did you grow up?

LITTLE SIMZ: In north London. Highbury and Islington.

ANNIE: Who have been your people that you've been inspired by when you've been writing or growing up?

LITTLE SIMZ: Definitely Lauryn Hill. Hundred per cent, just her. Everything to do with, again, the storytelling. Before Lauryn Hill I didn't *know* that you can get goosebumps from listening to music.

I didn't *know* that music can make you cry or laugh.

I didn't know that music can make you feel all these types of emotions, and just feeling like how she inflicted all these emotions upon me was like . . . wow, maybe *I* can do that for someone *else*, make *them* get goosebumps or make them think about someone they miss or love . . .

ANNIE: So what had you grown up listening to, then?

LITTLE SIMZ: A lot of Missy Elliott, Busta Rhymes. I was into reggae at one point, like heavily. I used to go to kids' birthday parties and put on reggae music and all the kids would look at me like: what ten-year-old does that?

ANNIE: Were you *DJ'ing*?

LITTLE SIMZ: Yeah, I would just go to where the music was playing and type in 'Bob Marley' and everyone would just look over: *who put this on?*

ANNIE: What, when you were *ten*?

LITTLE SIMZ: Yeah, yeah, when I was young.

ANNIE: What would they have been listening to otherwise that wasn't Bob Marley?

LITTLE SIMZ: (*singing, little girl voice*) 'I'm a Barbie girl, in a Barbie world . . .', and then I would come in:

One love . . .
One heart . . .

and everyone would just look at me. No one expected *that*.

ANNIE: Were they impressed or were they not impressed?

LITTLE SIMZ: I don't think they was impressed. Because obviously they didn't understand it, but I remember for days on end just having Bob Marley in my headphones on the little portable CD, and just having that song in particular 'One Love', just on repeat, on repeat, on repeat, and then I went to this party, put it on and everyone just looked at me like I was *weird*.

ANNIE: What's the first kind of music you can remember?

LITTLE SIMZ: Oooh, I remember there'd be a lot of garage played in my house, my sisters were very much into garage. And then my brother was a very hip-hop head, like Nas, and Biggie, and Jay-Z, so I got the kind of UK sound and the American sound with the garage and the hip-hop.

ANNIE: Excellent. Where do you come in the family?

LITTLE SIMZ: I'm the youngest. Two sisters and one brother. So I'm the fourth child.

ANNIE: So you've got all that music of theirs to *inherit* . . . if you like.

So many people I've met who had very successful music careers have turned out to be the youngest in a large family. It's really interesting how often that happens. (*The name David Holmes came straight to mind: DJ from Belfast, youngest of ten siblings, now film composer* – Oceans *franchise and TV series* Killing Eve.)

LITTLE SIMZ: I am just being aware that things could have been very different, dreams that people can't pursue due to . . . *life* happening. Like the single parent who's abandoned, or given up her dreams, for the sake of her children; because it becomes about *them* now, and not about what she wants or what *she* wants to fulfil.

And so I'm just being aware of that and just not taking anything for granted.

I found an interview online. It's from I guess *Pop Idol* or one of those competitive shows, and the lady . . . her mentality was: 'I want to get to Hollywood and I want to be a star.' I felt like that is a lot of people's perception of what fame is, or what stardom is and what 'making it' is.

Does that make you delusional or does that make you crazy? Or is this what you've just been *fed*? And that concept just fascinated me . . . because I've been to Hollywood and when I've got there it was nothing like what I thought it would be.

ANNIE: What did you think, then, when you got there?

LITTLE SIMZ: I had thought it was the *whole* of California. I thought it was like, once you get there your life is gonna change. You're gonna see *everyone* from *every* movie . . . When actually it's not that big. There is poverty there. I saw a lot of homeless people and I saw it wasn't what I thought at all. However, I do love LA and I've been a few times now and I have a lot of good friends there.

ANNIE: You must have travelled a lot.

LITTLE SIMZ: I go to South Africa soon, so I'm really intrigued to see what is there for me.

ANNIE: I swam with penguins once there. In Cape Town. We were swimming on the beach and all these penguins joined in.

LITTLE SIMZ: I'm excited to see different parts of the world. Especially because for the longest time all my music was written in my bedroom. Just staring upon the same four walls and knowing my studio is just by my bed.

I can never really get away from music. So to then go and travel the world and see all these different things and then just have these cool new experiences and see things I didn't even know existed.

Like, where was I . . .? I think I was in Sweden, and the sun never sets, and just seeing that, it's like, I would never have imagined that is possible. Or like seeing a double-decker *train* I would have never imagined would have existed.

ANNIE: There's a singer, called Joan Armatrading—

LITTLE SIMZ: Yes, yes! Joan Armatrading — sings and plays guitar.

ANNIE: She wrote a lot of interesting things and she said—

LITTLE SIMZ: I actually made a song about her, sorry to cut in on you.

ANNIE: You did?

LITTLE SIMZ: Yeah, yeah, yeah, yeah. It's actually not out. It's unreleased, but I did make a song called 'Joan Armatrading'.

ANNIE: Well that's weird, then. I remember her saying to me once that she got inspiration for her songs at airports. She said, if you look at people at airports there's so many things happening to people emotionally.

LITTLE SIMZ (*excitedly*): I've actually done that! I've actually done that, I've gone to the airport to just analyse . . .

It's so true, there's so much happening at an airport. People are about to miss their flight and you see them at the desk. And they're *pleading* . . .

And then these *goodbyes* and *welcomes* and . . . people taking their time . . . people on their own and just one bag . . . 'I'm leaving the place I love' . . .

ANNIE: You've got people like Kendrick Lamar and Jay-Z who've been giving you a lot of encouragement, yeah?

LITTLE SIMZ: Yeah, Kendrick, for sure. But Jay-Z, it was just my mixtape was premiered on his website so people often get that misconstrued with him co-signing me.

ANNIE: And what about Kendrick Lamar . . .?

LITTLE SIMZ: I've had quite a few encounters with Kendrick where he's openly expressed how he feels about my music and he just gave me really cool advice . . . and he's just so *chill*, man!

ANNIE: Have you always had great self-belief?

LITTLE SIMZ: Yeah. I've definitely believed a lot in myself and my ability and just what I believe I'm capable of achieving and that's, I think, what's carried me through to this point. If I didn't have that, I don't know what I'd be doing, to be fair.

Talent's one thing, but to believe you're good at what you do and then to be a hard worker at that, I think is another.

And especially being twenty-one . . . young girl from London, doing what I'm doing.

At one point I was in uni, I had to step out because there became a point where I was travelling so much I couldn't physically *be* at university. So it just makes me think, if I *hadn't* gone the uni route, what would have happened . . .?

(*A prescient question. Since making her first album Little Simz has referred to experiences among contemporary young Londoners: one friend of hers imprisoned, and another murdered, in a knife crime.*)

ANNIE: What were you studying?

LITTLE SIMZ: Music technology. So it's kind of . . . the science of music . . . a lot of theory and a lot of science as opposed to the practical side, like learning how to play an instrument or performing or writing music. It's a lot to do with, like, how sound travels and a lot of maths.

ANNIE: Right. And so you've left that behind without finishing it off.

LITTLE SIMZ: Yeah. Essentially university isn't cheap and I didn't want to continue to be there without *being* there and not getting the best out of it.

ANNIE: Different life now?

LITTLE SIMZ: Completely different, yeah.

ANNIE: All these grown-up pressures as well. Being a student, there's a lot of freedom.

Did you find being plunged into this world with having now the amount of all the interviews you have to do and all that pressure, how did you deal with that? Easily?

(Little Simz had been a child actor, through her teens, and as an adult appeared in the much-acclaimed Netflix drama series Top Boy. *Set in Hackney, east London. Revived in 2019 by Canadian rap star Drake, who became executive producer.)*

LITTLE SIMZ: I think I'm still dealing with it. I feel like I had an idea of what I was getting myself into, because I've been doing it for such a long time.

I'm not like an industry 'plant' where I've just been put in the midst of all of this and I don't know what's going on . . .

Little Simz's commitment proved rewarding. Her third album, *Grey Area*, released in 2019, received across-the-board rave reviews. It reached number 1 in the UK R & B Chart, was awarded album of the year by *NME*, and nominated for the Mercury Music Prize.

38

Meet the O'Connells: Maggie, Finneas – and Billie Eilish

To understand the Billie Eilish phenomenon is to look at that vast, now near mythical conurbation where she's from. Eighteen million people try to survive and thrive in the eighty-one cities that make up greater Los Angeles. There are few more awe-inspiring sights than when descending to LAX airport at night — the criss-crossing grid of a trillion twinkling streetlamps marking out this most seductive, shimmering carpet on which to land your dreams.

Hollywood stars are the tiny minority of the vast community which makes up the 'entertainment capital of the USA'. As a cinema-loving child, I was riveted by the credit roll at the end of each film. Who were the people named in the cast list as: 'Woman in diner' or 'Third getaway driver'? What was a key grip, or a gaffer? What is a foley artist? Why are caterers called 'craft services'? . . .

All this has sprung up from the original 'Hollywoodland' of a century ago. And with it the economy: principal cast members, bit part players, extras; carpenters, drivers, costume makers, backing singers, lighting experts, composers, editors. The vast interlocking industry and population that brought about the likes of Meghan Markle. Into this community came a working actor couple: Patrick O'Connell and Maggie Baird. They were also musicians. They had a son, Finneas, and, four years later, a daughter, Billie.

MAGGIE BAIRD: I lived in New York for ten years and, as great as New York is, it's hard to live in a studio apartment in a fourth-floor walk-up, carrying your bicycle up the stairs. I was in a play that went to LA on tour. I liked it there.

So, we moved to LA.

We'd had a terrible school shooting — one of the first in the US — at Columbine in Colorado . . . I was from Colorado, and that really scared me. Finneas, I think, was two. We were older parents and we really didn't want our child to be gone all day. We started to question the education system and decided it was right [home schooling] for them.

In LA there's a big community of home schoolers, so you can go to park days and book clubs. I led all the book clubs for almost all of their lives. There are science fairs and talent shows and dances.

You've got this city [LA] with a world-class science centre and the natural history museum.

Basically, you register your home as a private school and teach in the way you want to . . . for us that it's like going to a college that's all over the city. You take this class here and you go on this trip there.

ANNIE: What about conventional subjects: geography, history or mathematics?

MAGGIE BAIRD: We did what's often referred to as 'world schooling' or 'unschooling' which means you're following *their* lead and you're doing things as they come up. So if Billie mentioned something about the moon — what is this? — it becomes a lesson. Get out the volleyball and the tennis ball and you're explaining, and . . . 'Let's go to the science centre tomorrow.'

So you learn it but not in a very rigid way. Maybe for three months we got obsessed with something — how you learn in normal life when you're an adult.

And then also like, let's say we noticed I . . . they don't really understand geography, we'd find a class, and we'd say, this is a subject that you don't want to be at a party and not know, so you should take this class.

We did a lot of cooking for our math and measuring and building. A lot of people also do it for different reasons, more Christian reasons.

There's plenty of socialising, following the rules of society . . . go to a play and learn to sit down and be quiet.

Finneas became obsessed with music, Billie was obsessed with filmmaking and music. It gave them enough time — extracurricular activities became main activities, because the thing you're going to make your living at is probably the thing that you love and that you're good at.

ANNIE: What about your own career, as an actor?

MAGGIE BAIRD: In LA, the last couple of months, I have had several jobs. I do voice jobs. I do voice-overs; we call it looping or ADR. You know . . . when you do the additional voices and replace people's voices. You dub people's voices. That kind of stuff.

The O'Connells up to now have been part of that working entertainment environment: screenwriters, dubbing artistes, music supervisors, heads of production, directors of photography, post-production supervisors, lawyers, stunt doubles, make-up artists, publicists.

In between home schooling his children, Patrick O'Connell would appear in TV series such as *The West Wing*. At home he made mixtapes for his children, many including The Beatles and Led Zeppelin.

MAGGIE BAIRD: Both Billie and Finneas sang in the Los Angeles Children's Chorus, which is world class. They had financial scholarships, financial aid, to be able to do that.

From a very early age we took them to the LA Symphony; it has a good programme for children on Saturdays, really inexpensive, you can see a concert, you can do art.

The Hollywood Bowl has a programme for kids, so you can immerse yourself in music in LA in a very low-cost way, you know.

Unsurprisingly Finneas O'Connell became an in-demand child actor/singer, his most widely known appearance being in the TV musical drama series *Glee*. He formed his own band, wrote and recorded songs at the family home — a modest-sized house in Highland Park, close to Pasadena. Then he began collaborating with his four-years-younger sister Billie Eilish. (Eilish is a Gaelic form of Elizabeth. She was thirteen years old.)

A song they recorded together at home one evening stood out. It was called 'Ocean Eyes'. They posted it on the SoundCloud website. Went to sleep.

The next day 'Ocean Eyes' had been streamed a thousand times.

Billie and Finneas were perplexed.

They didn't *know* a thousand people. Oh, maybe it was a friend, who had a blog. Danny Rukasin, an artist management specialist, heard it. Everything took off from that point. Four years of careful, protective, meticulous planning followed, along with a dual manager, Brandon Goodman.

Fast-forward to February 2020.

In the previous twelve months the now eighteen-year-old Billie had scored a number 1 album, won five Grammys, headlined Coachella, Glastonbury, Reading Festival, sung at the Oscars, been on the cover of *Rolling Stone* and *Vogue*. Billie Eilish had captivated the world.

There could be no one on the planet remotely aligned with show business who was more in demand. Now she and her brother were in London for the Brit Awards.

It would have been unthinkable to me as a judge (one of 1500 of the Brit Awards) had Billie *not* won for the category Best International Female. There was no other category she was eligible for, or no doubt she and Finneas would have swept the board at the Brits, too. Danny Rukasin had arranged for me to meet Finneas and Billie either side of the Brits event. By now the couple had added another string to their bow. They'd composed and recorded the latest James Bond theme 'No Time to Die'. This too became a number 1 hit. Billie was to sing it at the Brits. The first performance of the song live on international TV.

The previous evening Finneas was to make a solo appearance at his London record company AWAL's HQ.

'I like your hair,' was Finneas' opening remark to me. '*Powerful.*'

Well, never been described thus before. 'Through a hedge backwards,' from Kit Lambert, the Who's manager, was probably, over time, more accurate.

Now with the James Bond brand as part of their cachet, the Hollywood publicity machine had powered into action. Different level. And there's a price to pay for this rocketing success. The junkets, for instance. As Finneas had been experiencing first-hand.

'I've been asked the same question fifteen times today,' he told the audience, good humouredly enough. In the midst of a small, twenty-five minute, invite-only live appearance. He switched easily from playing piano to guitar and back, and seemed supremely confident, utterly at home in front of the young crowd who stood, kneeled, or sat cross-legged on the floor in front of him. But then, Finneas has been doing shows like this since he was eleven years old.

'You start trying to predict what the next question will be,' he said to the rapt gathering . . . 'Or . . . making shit up!'

Hmm. Interesting challenge, then. I was to meet him a few minutes later. It took me back to a similar situation: interviewing the youthful John, Paul, George and Ringo when *they* were first cresting the wave of worldwide scrutiny.

Of course, any young person (or of any age) is going to find it hard going trying to come up with a different answer to feed the hungry monster media machine.

So if you are the interviewer, *ask something different.*

'Have you ever had an MRI scan?', I said.

He had not been asked that question before, no.

I asked if it was true he had sampled dentists' drills and the walk-don't-walk alert bleep sound on a street crossing in Melbourne?

'Yes,' he granted, wondering, possibly, where on earth this line of questioning could possibly be going.

'Well,' I said, 'if you have an MRI scan it makes such loud sounds and beats, and being your prolific self . . . you, Finneas, would probably come out humming the chorus. Bit heavy-metally though.'

He got it. 'Oh, you mean put a microphone in the scan?'

Well, I thought, they probably wouldn't let most people.

But as you have just written the James Bond theme and it's gone to number 1; you can probably do pretty much anything you like.

I told him the introduction I had been *intending* to make to him.

'So, tell me about your obvious Russian background, Finneas O Connell.'

Not surprisingly he replied that it had been Irish — southern Irish and Scottish. And with *en brosse*-cut, bright auburn hair, it was a bit of a giveaway.

Billie Eilish and her brother are of artistic and political stock from Ireland, Scotland, England and Germany.

People stood in a semicircle, hovering, watching, waiting to be introduced. So we were having a chat but we had an audience.

'I've heard all about you,' he said. It felt a bit 'circusy'. I felt I must play up to some role, but as what? Freaky woman DJ, been around for ever? . . . knew The Beatles? . . . bit of an oddity, a curio?

Well, so be it . . .

He knew straight away to say 'Good question' to some that perhaps he didn't have an immediate answer for. Or was maybe genuinely relieved to be asked something less banal.

'Whose idea was it to sing The Beatles' "Yesterday" at the Oscars?' I asked.

'Mine,' said Finneas. Firmly.

'Don't you think John Lennon would have been a bit pissed off you choosing the one Beatles song he wasn't on?'

'So which John Lennon song *should* we have sung?' Finneas shot straight back with. Answer the question with another question. Smart.

I began: 'Well "Imagine" would be a bit . . . '

'"Imagine" is *great*,' he interceded. Politely. Diplomatically almost . . .

'. . . crass', I was going to say.

An ineffably polite young man. If I said something he didn't agree with, or he didn't wish to comment upon, he acknowledged this with the response:

'I hear you.'

It oiled the wheels of conversation nicely.

And yet he had an assertive air about him. A Leo. I didn't know who the circle of hoverers were. Record company people? I didn't want to be the one who would take up all the precious time *they* would have with their cherished young star. Label personnel, marketing, promotion . . . This was clearly a business meet and greet. I was somewhat of an interloper. You've got to know when to back off.

I was to meet Billie at Radio 1, the night after she won her first Brit Award, and sang the new James Bond song.

I'd wondered if she'd been out celebrating at the famed

after-parties which follow the Brit Awards as the music biz annual jamboree.

But no, she was in a meeting after the show — at one thirty in the morning.

About her next tour.

At New Broadcasting House I began the trek to the Radio 1 studio area. I sat for a moment outside the glass-enclosed area to shrug off my raincoat. A glut of people strode purposefully in front of me. One of them had neon-green hair. Billie. Schedule running early. Too soon, the heavy studio door swung open. And there she was.

In a loose cream sweater. She looked like a casually cool college student. For the uninitiated, Billie's vocal style is close to the mic, hushed, but with deceptively provocative lyrics. Eilish's appearance has been defined by her style of wearing loose clothing, baggy shorts, oversized tops. Now often designed by Stella McCartney or Gucci.

It's her statement: refusing to allow her appearance to be sexualised.

Which has created her totemic image and idolatry among young women. Those not wanting to be defined by their body shape. And now she is so much of an influencer that Paris fashion collection styles are being summed up as 'Billie Eilish'.

She wears no discernible make-up. She takes off what appear to be reading glasses, and there are the blue eyes. Ocean eyes. The name of the song that launched her.

Not about *her* eyes, about eyes of an unrequited lover.

Billie is calm, friendly, open, not at all world weary. Or wary. Unfazed, a teenager with fifty-five million Instagram followers. Nick Grimshaw's radio show in the studio next door featured a phone-in with eleven-year-old girls. Billie Eilish co-hosted, and volunteered:

'I *hated* being eleven, that's when the hormones kicked in for me.' Empathising.

So at eighteen she was fully fledged. Yet she has retained an extraordinary rapport with prepubescent followers, as well as the growing number of adults worldwide.

The grouchiest of elder statesmen rock critics had to admit, however grudgingly at first, that this brother and sister have once-in-a-generation musical talent. Young people knew how good they were, straight away.

Hard, if not impossible, to media-train anyone to connect on so many different levels. That's what interested me. And the home schooling.

'I feel London is my second home,' she'd said on TV the night before.

ANNIE: Why is that?

BILLIE EILISH: I did my first headline act here.

ANNIE: Oh, at Shepherd's Bush?

BILLIE EILISH: No, at the Courtyard [small theatre, north London; capacity 250] in 2017. There were like, a hundred people there. I was blown away. I was so excited, I thought that was the biggest show I'd ever play.

ANNIE: What does it feel like when the fans sing your lyrics back to you?

BILLIE EILISH: (*emphatically*) Nothing. Else. In. Life. Feels. Like. That.

The first festival I ever played was in San Diego — I was fourteen, fifteen, and eight or ten people showed up, it was a *huge* field.

And there were just these eight people at the front. I sang 'Ocean Eyes' and two of the girls sang along . . . And I got really choked up. I thought, my God, these two girls *know* my song . . . it was a huge deal for me and I remember saying to my brother, if anyone ever sang along to my lyrics, I don't think I could ever hold it together.

Now . . . *every* single thing I do — they do.

She's had a publicist since she was fourteen, and a stylist. She has two managers, a chief publicist, a day-to-day publicist and attention of the promotion heads of her record label. These two youngsters are the centre of a billion-dollar industry. They can be kept calm, shielded, away from as much as possible of the frantic underwater paddling around them. People's jobs are on the line because of them, perhaps.

You'd go crazy.

This was a girl who said she never wanted to be 'normal' (hurrah!) and that being weird could be fun. (Agreed!)

BILLIE EILISH: I mean, I love it. I think it's like I never even realised I was making a statement at all. I just was wearing what I wanted to wear, you know, and then I realised after a while . . . that people were looking at it as this *ground-breaking* thing. When really I'm just dressing how I want. And I think what's even cooler about it to me is . . . well, not cooler, but how I feel about it is like, if anything, if I'm gonna have any sort of message I want it to be that I'm *not* saying, 'You *have to wear* clothes that don't sexualise yourself.'

I think: '*go ahead* and *do that*'. I *applaud* women that are confident in their bodies and want to show it.

But what I want to say is . . . sometimes when people are complimenting me for how I dress . . . they kind of slut-shame women that wanna dress more sexual — and I don't like that.

Just wear what you want to wear. Not wear what *I* wear. (*The full Life of Brian predicament.*)

If you want to cover up, go ahead! If you want to show everything, you should go ahead, completely! . . . I love girls, I love boys. They should do what they want.

ANNIE: I've seen interviews where you say you don't look at social media. Is that the case? So you just kill it. Don't look at it . . .?

BILLIE EILISH: Three, four days ago I sort of stopped looking at comments, but I still look through my tagged photos. I just wanted to hear what people were saying. I wanted the *feedback* because I like feedback, and the problem is no matter who you are, if you're 'big', people hate you and that's normal. I understand that. As somebody that grew up with the internet and laughing at memes that were at a certain celebrity's expense when I was younger.

Well, now I'm that celebrity. It makes me really see it in a different way. Trolls just don't understand. That's all it is.

ANNIE: Do you have major influences, if you'd like to say who they are.

BILLIE EILISH: Oh, lots of them. I mean it started with The Beatles, clearly. And then (*Billie rattled off the names*) . . . Green Day, My Chemical Romance. Then it was Justin Bieber, Lana Del Rey and Tyler, the Creator and Earl Sweatshirt and Odd Future, and then Childish Gambino changed everything. And since there's so many new artists right now that are just inspiring the hell out of me. New artists! It's like you've just got to let yourself be inspired.

Big Pig is dope. Celeste is sick. There's so many that it blows my mind. Like *Dave* — come *on*!

ANNIE: So all these people who want to meet you now from all different generations . . . (*Thinking of Barbra Streisand, who sent Billie a post-Grammy message saying 'welcome to the club', pointing out that Eilish was only the fourth female solo artist ever to win best album with a debut recording besides Lauryn Hill and Norah Jones. And reminding us of course that Barbra herself won the very first. In 1963.)*

BILLIE EILISH: Yeah. It's crazy. I don't know what's going on! They're coming up to *me*. You know, they're hitting *me* up . . . Your idols, like heroes growing up, and then . . . and then it's they're like, 'You're dope, you're cool.' It's really the most surreal thing I think that's happened so far. The Oscars was like that. The epitome of what I just described.

ANNIE: We could see that. We could see that red carpet thing, I mean *(I make a vomit gesture, alluding to the sycophancy towards Billie by the red carpet interviewers)*, I felt for you with that, I thought, OK, that's another experience you'll have to get used to.

Do you feel that young people have got a bit more power now or, if they haven't, what would you like to see happen for them?

BILLIE EILISH: I think they have so much power. I was just doing this thing with a bunch of teenagers, that are changing the world for good, and one of them said something that I'm gonna steal . . . right now.

She said that she feels like a lot of older generations are thinking in nations and not in *generations*. You have to be thinking ahead of time and about the next generation and the generation after that. I'm looking forward to the future because of the teenager who's right now . . . that are moving the world . . .

ANNIE: Like Greta Thunberg.

BILLIE EILISH: Yeah, yeah, for sure. She's doing so much.

ANNIE: So who did that for you? Did you think, if she can do it, then I can? Did anybody specifically inspire you like that?

BILLIE EILISH: There wasn't really anybody that I specifically remember. I mean, now that I'm actually *in it*, now I see that a lot of the artists I did grow up listening to started then, like [at] fourteen, you know.

I was talking to Alicia [Keys], she was doing stuff at fourteen. I didn't even know that about her, but at the time, no, I didn't have anybody, like at all.

So how had this composed young woman, not an *obviously* stage-crazed, obsessive, attention-seeking young Angeleno created world domination in such a short time? Still the mystery hung in the air.

With such acclaim, there is the almost inevitable backlash. Even in the success-celebrated and driven US, Finneas and Billie have been criticised for being privileged and white, benefitting from growing up in LA and profiting from nepotism, on account of their actor parents.

Which might explain the pains to which the family went to emphasise their modest background. Finneas had pointed put that the family never travelled to countries such as Ireland while he was growing up 'as we didn't have any money'. Though he had by now flown the family home.

His mother says, at the time of writing, that she still lives in the same two-bedroomed house, in the far-from-glitzy area of LA that is Highland Park. She and her husband now chaperone their daughter on tour.

As Billie Eilish left the BBC studio, I caught a fleeting glimpse of her footwear, the only apparent sign of any indulgent lavishness. These were not average teenage kickabouts . . . or trainers, you couldn't call them that. Or loafers. Her shoes looked like exquisite silver jewellery.

Modern-day Judy Garland ruby slippers.

Quite where they will take Eilish, on her particular yellow brick road, I shall be fascinated to find out.

39

So You Want to Be a Rock 'n' Roll Media Star?

First things first. Don't be late. Don't ever, ever be late. Don't even think it's all right to be on time. On time can slip into being *not on time* so easily. There could be too many people queuing for the lift. There could be a delay in checking through security.

Unforeseeable hazards can transform you from being Cinderella arriving via glass coach, in shimmering ball gown, back into the shrivelling pumpkin. This is a job where your very existence depends on you being there.

Factor in possible delays. If I have to get somewhere across London by car, and a satnav predicts eighteen minutes to destination, I allow at least an hour!

No one will ever applaud you for being on time, or pat you on the back for being prompt. It's part of the job, so don't expect praise. In fact don't expect praise from anyone for anything from the moment you arrive till the moment you leave. It's a bonus, a nice surprise when it happens. But you are not at school now. Or college. No gold stars.

I know this sounds eye-rollingly obvious.

It's so obvious that no one will ever bother to tell you.

For my first ever TV commercial voice-over for the then new

and fabulous Cross Your Heart bra, I rolled up nearly half an hour late for a one-hour booked session. Everyone involved was horrified. But no one had ever told me how expensive commercial studio time was. I just looked like a very unprofessional idiot. We now had only half of the studio time left to record takes, and I was just a beginner in the world of voice-overs, which is killingly competitive.

For live transmission, if you are not present, you will dread that there will be dead air. *Dead air*. The worst outcome for any radio station. So don't let it happen to you.

Be so afraid of being late, that if it were to happen . . . the word would go around the *whole* industry that you are . . . *unreliable*.

You will never work in this medium again, OMG, and it's all you've ever wanted to do.

So? Sufficiently frightened?

For stage performances, in broadcasting, conferences, anywhere you have a pivotal role, normal excuses for being late for work just do not cut it. Train strikes, thunderstorms, being hung-over, a row with your mum, not being able to find your phone/keys/ tube card. Not acceptable reasons for not showing up on time.

Adrian Juste, a prominent Radio 1 DJ at the time, drove through Britain's only living-memory hurricane in the autumn of 1987. Zigzagged across Kent, dodging huge, car-crushing oak trees crashing all around him, literally defying death, to get to the studios on time. (Probably a bit overzealous, but bigged up for doing so.)

You hear how big-time movie and TV stars are picked up for work by a chauffeur. Not because they are living in a pampered, luxurious world, necessarily; it's because their production bosses don't *trust* them to be on time. An actor not being ready for a scene costs big, big bucks, can make or break the budget. This actor might be collected from home at the unsociable hour of 3 a.m. Be ready for make-up at 5 a.m. And then not be called to the set all day, only to deliver his or her two lines at 6.47 p.m.

The first time I ever had that experience — 'We'll send a car for you' — I was overawed and apprehensive. Associated-Rediffusion, the leading TV company, was collecting me from home in Brighton for an early-call TV special recording. My first ever. It was 6 a.m. and pitch dark in the subdued silence of a seaside resort in midwinter.

I knew it was a big opportunity. Hence remembering the details many decades later.

I was ushered into the back of what was then called a limo. The tyres gently hissed on the wet black seafront road surface; the procession of high-wire, twin streetlamps cast the only pools of light onto the desolately empty Marine Parade. Smoothly, the long black vehicle made a right as we reached the eerie outline of the unlit Palace Pier, and we turned inland. Towards London.

I was an untried beginner. Would I be able to deliver what the TV programme production was investing in me? Making sure at least I'd be on set on time.

Then and now, the procedure for getting you in situ, prepared, is known as 'hurry up and wait'.

And that discipline is much the same throughout the worlds of film, TV and broadcasting.

If you are hosting the show, especially if you are running an early breakfast show or first show/programme of the day, whoever is on before you will have to carry on till you arrive.

It's not dissimilar in the world of live DJ'ing. You might have spent weeks creating your set for it to build to a world-shattering crescendo, timed to the minute. If the DJ taking over from you is late, the promoter hisses in your ear: 'Can you do another twenty minutes, mate?'

And you more or less have to agree.

The music must never stop.

I've only been late for a broadcast once in forty-nine and a half years, and that was because I'd been in a car smash near the M25 and had to phone the radio station from a stretcher in A & E.

I thought the world would fall in.

It didn't.

There are people who will go for a risky commute. One DJ followed me on an early morning Sunday slot. He commuted from the south of France to central London every week.

What a perfect life, I thought at the time! But he was late, more than once. I didn't mind filling in for him, but the bosses had been up early too. Hearing him not being there. You can't escape! It's a big worry for the producer who carries the can for you, if you are late. Nowadays DJs have been flying around the world week in, week out. The chances of being late for a live radio show are much greater. Just ratchets up the tension for your team.

You don't get training for that as a newcomer. And there's possibly bewilderingly little advice forthcoming from colleagues.

Within the media world, you won't necessarily be welcomed as a new member of the team. You are possibly likely to be seen as a challenge, a threat. Not that of course anyone would be unprofessional enough to say so.

Though, thinking back, I had all kinds of insults and downright criticisms about my lack of ability as a broadcaster from producers and fellow DJs alike. If I hadn't had the experience of tough talking from Fleet Street bullies earlier as a journalist, I might not have had the resilience to survive my early days at the BBC.

'Oh, I see,' I thought to myself. 'Some of the men who run this joint are rude and domineering. I get it.'

So I got it, and got on with setting out to prove that being a broadcaster should not be the exclusive domain of the male.

I discovered quite recently that the Royal Air Force put up huge opposition to women becoming fighter pilots at the start of the Second World War. As most of the production staff brought in to run Radio 1 in 1967 were ex-RAF personnel, perhaps that explained their bewildering patriarchal ban on women becoming DJs.

It took three years of my campaign to make them relent. At least to let me have a go at the job. I was completely resigned to walking away if it didn't work out, if I was really rubbish. I certainly didn't feel any *entitlement*. But was I a box to be ticked? A quota to be filled? A token appointment to shut up the complaining fledgling feminist media? (Some of which was me!) It took *twelve* years before another female DJ, Janice Long, was allowed on the scene at Radio 1 after me.

During those solo years I did feel like a freak. While writing this, a comment has just appeared in the not-exactly-known-for-its-feminism-stance magazine the *Spectator*. Commenting on a recent programme focusing on the year 1972, the writer noted that at that time I was indeed the only female voice on Radio 1. Amid all the men. Kate Chisholm wrote: 'her voice, husky and low, could have been taken for a man's anyway.'

And this is, sadly, true. Aided by the forty fags a day. (That habit abruptly and completely curtailed in 1998, by the way.)

Don't expect anyone to give you advice. They will expect you to know it, and expect you to know not to take last-minute days off with 'a cold'.

If you are 'the talent' you will be nearly certifiably dead before you are so ill that you miss a show. I don't know why on-air broadcasters are called the talent as if everyone else around them isn't — talented. It's not meant as a compliment, so don't get airs above your radio station!

Like in many other places of work, especially in the gig economy, you will not want to take days off.

If your bosses know you're not coming in it gives them time to 'get a dep in'. Now this might sound like you can take a few days off and take it easy. Not.

By 'getting a dep in', you are letting someone else who's desperate for your job have a chance to get their feet under the desk. They will shine, they will do much more than you do on a normal day because they are so keen to impress and to get your job.

And if the boot was on the other foot, wouldn't you do the same? *Of course you would.*

We all need opportunities like that.

You will feel totally paranoid about someone else doing your job better than you do it, and you would be right to be paranoid. Paranoia I say reluctantly, but honestly, it can be your ally. It'll certainly keep you on your toes.

Adrenaline — that's your other best friend; it will get you through many a live situation when you are feeling under the weather. And make you feel higher than the sun on any ordinary day.

The problems around taking on a new job are — and I think this applies to so many — the assumptions.

People will *assume* you will know what to do. It's not your fault you don't know everything . . . anything . . . yet. How the light switches work, where the stationary cupboard is . . . simple-as-that stuff.

So whatever job you work in, I think it's good karma to be genuinely as helpful as you can to a newcomer.

Remember your first day, and how scary it was.

And who helped you out. Of course, you will never forget them. Well, pass it on. Do as you would be done by; be the person you want to work with. And I don't mean you should have any scheming, ulterior motive in mind. However, here's a story. True.

So You Want to Be a Rock 'n' Roll Media Star?

The happy conclusion first. The most prestigious radio awards ever were the Sonys. To win a Sony award meant you had been recognised by your profession. These were the Oscars of audio.

In the early noughties my then boss, Andy Parfitt, invited me to be his guest for the evening at the annual Sony Awards ceremony. I had no idea what was in store and Andy was adamant in not allowing me to know anything in advance.

This was a proper dressed-up night. I invested in an Alexander McQueen full-length, obliquely patterned evening dress, and black jacket over the top. Shoes by Louboutin, the highest stilettos, the soles as always in red, and spikes on the see-through uppers. I could hardly walk in them and clung on to Andy for dear life.

I hadn't been mentioned in any shortlists, so why was I there? I was on tenterhooks all evening in the ultra-glamorous ballroom of the Grosvenor House Hotel, the glitziest award venue in London, on Park Lane.

The platform where the prizes were given out was an elevated square in the centre of the room, with four sets of steps up to the specially built stage. I stared in great trepidation at the steps.

No handrail.

How, if I had won anything, would I get up — and back down those steps in my Louboutins? (Yes, I know, I should have thought of that beforehand . . .)

Andy suddenly turned to me at our table. My name was being called out.

'I think you've won something,' he whispered urgently in my ear.

I made my way to the stage steps, clutching hold of Andy like a toddler crossing a motorway.

A fanfare of music blasted out. My image was flashed up on all the giant screens above the seated diners filling the vast ballroom.

'Don't let go of me!' I hissed/pleaded frantically to my boss.

On the way up the steps, I'd caught my heel in the hem of the long sweeping bias-cut skirt.

Most surprising, to me, the whole room, the entire audience, the great and the would-soon-be greats in broadcasting all rose to their feet and gave me a standing ovation.

Please don't let me fall over is all you think of at a key moment like that. On camera, in front of my heroes and all my peer group.

Somehow, I got to the top of the steps. And to my amazement I was being presented with a one-off shiny gold special award.

It was all down to Andy Parfitt. The point of this is . . . way back when, we had worked together on a magazine series *Pick of the Week* on Radio 4. He was the producer. He switched over to a similar job at Radio 1.

'Hey Andy, how great to see you here. Hope you'll enjoy being at Radio 1,' I had said, and gave him a hug. I really was so pleased to see him and welcomed him as warmly as I could on his first day.

Then over several years he rose to become controller of Radio 1, and did the job exceptionally well, putting Radio 1 in front of the digital media revolution, which was absolutely crucial in ensuring the station's survival at that time . . .

But he told me on the night of the Sonys that he'd never forgotten my friendly welcome on his first day at Radio 1.

Recommending me for this highly prized special award was his way of saying thank you.

So you see . . . mind how you go — you never know who might one day be your boss.

As a naive teenager I thought folk succeeded in their chosen careers because it was easy for them, they had natural talent. The dirty secret is, of course, this: it's the grafters who get on. And usually a lot further than those with raw ability, but little application.

There are aspects that can make life nicer for you and for those around you.

What to wear to work? First advice I was given by a radio producer, a bloke, was dress up as though it's TV. I think that's fair. I mean . . . don't overdo it, but still I always have read it this way: you are the only person who doesn't have to look at you in a work environment. At home you can slob about avoiding mirrors, and all and any other reflective surfaces. I certainly do! But at work, or increasingly now, as lives have changed so drastically, on Zoom. Other people will have to gaze upon you.

I think being deliberately dress-down slobby in front of your work mates is quite insulting. It can be saying, 'You don't matter to me, so I don't have to make an effort . . .'

Nowadays there are cameras everywhere, visitors taking selfies; you need to live up to the voice you are projecting. It doesn't have to be loud or especially the latest fashion. Classic and clean is fine. Just look as though you care about how you look.

And how you smell.

You might not have thought of this, but . . . best not to wear pungent perfume or stinky aftershave. You will probably be using the same headphones as the broadcaster before and after you. Their lingering aftershave can bring you out in a rash, so do as you would be done by. Many have intolerance to strong fragrances, me included.

I once foolishly showed vulnerability to a particularly vicious-minded presenter and said I was feeling very sad as a close friend had died the day before.

'Have a curry last night, did we?' came the reply, with no smile in the voice whatsoever. What do they call it in cricket? Sledging? — trying to put the other person off their stroke.

Try and be strong, put on a good face, even if you are shaking with nervousness. It may not show up nearly as much as you think to your colleagues. Plus, if you can exude at least some sort of composure, it reassures those around you.

Right, so you're there, in time for your programme. If you are able, avoid all possibilities of being upset, annoyed, ruffled, made to feel insecure, unhappy, unsure, unattractive.

Yes. Big ask.

There are enough confrontational issues just getting to work. When I commuted from Brighton, an occasional joy was meeting the other non-conventionals who travelled by train. And yes, sometimes those ensuing conversations were not that quiet. Especially with Simon Fanshawe, the gay lawyer comedian, who made a large contribution towards Brighton being turned from a seaside town into a bona fide city.

People complained about us talking too loudly. He gestured at me and said: 'She has a radio show to do. She's warming up.'

Which was true really.

Try to avoid any situation that's likely to be negative or confrontational before a show. Give a wide berth to anyone you don't trust to stay positive with you before you 'go on'.

This can apply to all sorts of situations, way outside broadcasting or showbiz.

But if things do go somewhat seriously wrong, like you fall down a mine shaft, or a heavy door flies open and you break your leg (as happened to me), or you get fired because suddenly your face doesn't fit, here's your mantra: no problems, only opportunities. No problems, only opportunities.

I've chanted that from a hospital bed, leg in plaster, laptop propped on my knee, more than once.

In normal circumstances, though, give yourself a buffer of time, so that whatever might have happened, you are composed enough to do your best professionally.

I'd say, hide in the restroom, or get into your workspace early; let it be your womb-like centre of calm. That's how I feel about a studio before a show. But they are so squabbled over in terms of time, you'll be lucky to have any pre-show calm time there to yourself.

But if you can find that mini ocean of calm, it helps.

If there's a technical problem that is not yours to solve, wrap yourself in an invisible layer of pristine readiness, protect yourself from any panic spreading, so that when it's time for . . .

'Up to speed . . . and *action!*' — you will be.

That is being professional.

It's a unique situation really. An actor stepping on stage or in front of a camera knows his or her lines. Or should do. A newsreader has the bulletin in front of them, script or autocue.

You, though, if you are a radio presenter, have to make it up as you go along. It's like having a phone conversation with yourself. Probably live, too — that's what makes it so exciting. As a TV news reporter covering a 'breaking' story, you might have to 'fill', keep talking, waiting for the prime minister to appear from behind the door of No 10 Downing Street.

The adrenaline kicks in; you had no idea you could be this alert.

You need to be.

Anything can happen.

Although it all needs to be spontaneous, I've never forgotten the advice given to me by Sir Terry Wogan.

'Always write out the words to your first link,' he said. Meaning, you'll be off to a good smooth start that way.

Sensitivity is not a word that you might hear used about presenters. But you need huge amounts of this. You are talking to strangers, a whole bunch of strangers, who may have had any of the following happen to them. They've broken up with their partner, lost their job. Been diagnosed with a serious illness. Grieving.

And however many people may be listening, I believe in never ever addressing them as 'you all'. In the plural. Your listener (singular) would like to believe you are speaking just to that person (singular). Yes, it's an illusion, but it may be one of the principal reasons that radio has survived the onslaught of television, movies, video, MTV, Spotify, the internet, the Walkman, the iPod, podcasts, . . . we seem to have a need for the company of a human voice to speak to us.

You have to tread that path of talking to someone you've never met, being bright, breezy, interesting, fun, warm, friendly, sincere, professional and authoritative. But balance that against being so bland that you are a complete boring turn-off. It's tricky.

This may be a strange point to make. I was an only child. If I wanted company I had to go out and find it. Make friends with strangers, initiate conversations, and to be honest, to get people to warm to me. So I became, maybe, a naturally friendly person. I had to be, if I wanted companionship of my own age outside of schoolfriends.

I'm rather glad really. A big strong family may be a huge advantage in some areas, but it might mean that for your formative years, your siblings provide the company you need.

You do not have to make the effort to win over strangers. You do not necessarily have to build social skills. As lives are becoming more isolated, it's increasingly the case. So if you are naturally talkative, a person who will reach out to a complete unknown, you'll be on the right track.

I think that's a most important attribute for a broadcaster.

Be sincere and mean it. The microphone has an uncanny way of drawing out of you your truthfulness, your sincerity. Or the lack of it. Unless you are a very clever puller of wool over the eyes as well as the ears!

This is not acting, this is not pretending or hiding behind a role. Quite the opposite. Which is why I think you need to be in the best frame of mind possible when you go on air.

Realistically. Of course you cannot not be tip-top, mentally and physically, every day or for each broadcast. You do your best.

Also, you may be nervous.

If you are, well, it's natural to be so, and it won't sound nearly so bad to the listener as you sound to yourself. Most people get a shock when they first hear their voice through a microphone and headphones.

Spend as much time as you can getting used to the sound of your own voice. Practise at home. Talk into a microphone, pretend you are doing a show. Or a podcast. Play it back. Be supercritical of annoying tendencies, like saying 'erm' too often. Keep the tone low — pitch it down a bit, especially if you have a naturally high voice. You can't change it completely, and it is the worth of your personality that has to come through in your voice.

And it's good to practise 'sight reading'. Grab a written article and record yourself reading it out loud, straight off the page, without even skimming through it first. See if you can read the whole thing without stumbling and find the rhythm of the sentences as you go. Try to lift the meaning of the words off the page. And sound like a newsreader. It's fun to do. See how many times you have to record it till you can read the whole piece without making any mistakes.

It will give you fresh appreciation next time you see an anchor use the term:

This just in . . .

It's foreign names or place names that can trip you up worst with pronunciation. Imagine being a World Cup football commentator who has to memorise the entire group of death squads' names, some completely unfathomable, and the ones on the bench! No wonder they sometimes resort to referring to the full back as 'the languid Bulgarian' instead of taking a risky run at his whole six-syllable surname.

There was a horrible phrase that came into use I really don't know how many years ago. And no doubt there are some that still use it: 'a great face for radio'.

What does it mean? Not good looking enough for TV? Someone who can be bundled away, behind a microphone, unseen?

Well, no one remains that way for long. I admit that as a very young and enthusiastic radio listener, I would mentally build a picture of a face that belonged to the voice. And while I would never meet the radio persona for real, eventually a photograph of them would appear, in a magazine or a newspaper. And without fail I would be appalled.

It was always, but always, a huge let-down. Without you realising, you have built a visual representation for the voice. And in 99.9 per cent of the cases, the true likeness will be a shocking disappointment. You've built a false picture. We all do it all the time, even with casual phone callers.

Fat instead of thin, so much older, or younger, or balder, or blonder, or more bespectacled; more braided, taller, smaller.

You will just not get it right.

So as the broadcaster, the voice, the fantasy, you will be however your listener wants to picture you. But get used to the disappointed comments when listeners find out what you *do* look like. And it won't take long — social media will soon sort that out!

Make yourself look as pleasant as you can. Families and close friends can be quite negative forces in influencing the way you look.

You know, the *you're not going out looking like that, are you?* remark. I say: experiment.

You don't have to be Hollywood glamour rated, but really look as good as you can. It's a starry field. Maybe you are working at a new job away from previous colleagues you were afraid would ridicule you. Use the opportunity to *change* a bit. Become a slightly new you. You're a presenter, you are called the Talent, so live up to it. Others you might have admired or possessed what you thought of as natural super style, have helped themselves along the way.

Katy Perry, epitome of glamour, has said: 'You don't think I actually *look* like this!' Stand out, don't blend in. But . . . no experiments on the day or even the week before the job interview. Unless you wanted that *actual* shade of orange hair.

Up. Your. Game.

In the past, regrettably, I did not take up this advice. Or maybe it's that only recently I have realised the value of certain aspects of visual presentation. Why oh why did I think that I needed to change my hairstyle (bleached blond/pink/natural i.e 'mousey'/ aubergine/long/short/straight/bobbed/crimped/permed) virtually every week? *The Old Grey Whistle Test*, the show I appeared in the most, had long runs. Not your six or seven episodes per annual season, but for month after month, right through the year, with just a summer break when we would go filming in the US.

There was no such thing as a stylist, no designer houses biking me great swathes of their latest collections, to 'borrow' for the show and then Instagram. No marketing at all. I had to provide my own clothes and try not to wear the same outfit too often. On a very limited budget. At the time of punk to post-punk, new wave to no wave, and then on to the ruffles and bows of the new romantics. So it was tricky to reflect the times and still adhere to some unseen BBC hierarchical approval.

I get asked quite often: so who was *your* female role model?

The answer is: I didn't have one.

There were no other females on radio to copy or be inspired by. And no one young and reasonably authoritative raving about music, telling topical jokes and stories on TV. Especially not females.

The nearest for me was inspired by the movie *Roman Holiday*.

I mention this nowadays, and the inevitable response is, 'Oh, so you were inspired by Audrey Hepburn?' Well, yeessssss, but not by her part as the hapless princess. It was Gregory Peck playing opposite her as a reporter that inspired me to want to become a journalist. That one light-hearted Hollywood role, and later on, television appearances by . . . David Frost. I wanted, before being inspired by the pirate DJs, to do what *he* did. Work with talented journalists, comedians, scriptwriters, musicians; challenge authority and the Establishment. I loved his irreverent air. He wasn't old-school, high falutin', and for all that he somewhat leered into the camera, it did seem that he wanted to share the joke, and that you, the viewer, were in on it.

I started sending in sketches, skits I'd written, to the BBC, hoping to become part of this new young satirical world. Every single one came back with a rejection note. But so politely worded.

That was the BBC. Praising you so much while saying no, that you think: well if I'm that good, why are you fucking turning me down?

There is even in a glass presentation case in the BBC's archive centre (the staff proudly showed me), a hand-typed — in brown (ergh) ink — letter from me. Home address in the top right-hand corner — 5 Arundel Terrace, Brighton, East Sussex — asking for a job. To no avail. It was to take years before I got any kind of contract with the BBC. But like I always say, hang in there, hover, and be the person they want when the time and opportunity arises.

One of the BBC's vaults is even named after me. One of the others being named after Sir Michael Palin. I went, as did he, to the opening ceremony. I asked if I could do a live Halloween radio show with invited guests, from inside the vault. Sounded suitably spooky.

Nope — turned down again; to do with keeping the temperature control constant.

So while it's great to have a role model, best not copy. Or pick up too many similar mannerisms of your favourite star.

That's a lesson even The Beatles had to learn, before they conquered America. Paul McCartney told me that they had actually failed to ignite the United States on their first try with their first records released there.

'Other British pop stars like Adam Faith before us had not been successful in America, because they were too similar to already-established stars. Y'know . . . "We got one of those already." We realised we had to be different.'

So people will say, ha, just be yourself.

But that can be a mountain to climb. Because inwardly you will reason: 'Me? I'm a nothing. I'm a nobody, no one knows me, why would anyone want to listen to what I have to say?'

Think of it this way. I am sure you have friends, maybe a best friend. So what is it about that friend you like? Probably this person is not a megastar, a world-famous athlete. A prime minister. You say: 'Oh, I like X or Y because, he/she is herself, himself, sincere, genuine.'

You being you, believe it or not, is . . . enough. You don't need to exaggerate your natural personality. Because then you will sound hammy and false. Just being you is incredibly difficult to do, to start with. Because your inner being is shouting: but I am so *inadequate*, I am *not interesting enough*, I am not *exciting enough*.

I remember being given that advice — just be yourself — when appearing on TV early on, as a panellist on a programme called *Juke Box Jury*. I was petrified. Why would anyone be interested in what I had to say? At the time I was a reporter on a regional newspaper. Not famous or well known or well respected in any way. But 'just be yourself' was everyone's advice.

I needed to have an opinion about hearing a new pop record for the first time. It didn't even matter if I was right or wrong, whether the record was going to become a hit or a miss.

The show had an occasional surprise ingredient, which was to produce from behind the set . . . the performer of the record that you as a panellist had just pronounced a success or a failure.

I breathed a huge sigh of relief when the teenage Marianne Faithfull stepped out, more than glad I'd given her a thumbs up rather than written off what was going to be her very long, if bumpy, ride of a career.

The thing was not to exaggerate anything verbally or visually. The camera does that for you. Stillness and calm in front of camera or microphone is all, unless you are an actor. Actually, especially if you are an actor.

You trying to be someone else, or over-projecting, will not work. It's your individuality that will come across, and that's what an audience recognises.

Name two very successful and popular presenters who are very alike in terms of personality?

You can't?

I'm not surprised.

Because there aren't any.

Because that's the very point.

You being you is different to anyone else, just like a set of fingerprints. Unique.

By all means be inspired, emulate others to start with, and then allow yourself to evolve. The on-air and off-air person should be and sound exactly the same. Maybe a bit more cheerful on air, but only by a smidge. (Check out the cleverest ever impersonation/observation of a radio DJ, by Phil Cornwell in the Alan Partridge film *Alpha Papa* . . . capturing that *teensiest* bit annoying and patronising enforced jollity on the er, 'niche' radio station North Norfolk Digital.)

The genuine *you*. That is all you need to be. If the true essence of a broadcaster is within you.

I knew as soon as I sat in a studio and put on a pair of head-phones and spoke into a microphone. This was what I really wanted to do.

But then I do have a great love of communicating. Every show I do I wonder if it's reaching outer space. If someone in a distant galaxy might be hearing me and the music I'm playing. But mostly I'm there because I want to share.

Share my opinions, my emotions. Do you like this piece of music too?

Oh great, great.

So do I. That makes two of us.

Maybe it's a need to be evaluated, validated, agreed with, accredited, approved of. Given the nod.

Maybe inspired by the words of this Bob Dylan song:

All I really want to do
Is, baby, be friends with you

(From 'All I Really Want to Do' recorded by The Byrds in 1965, among other artistes.)

I've always thought that the most accurate definition of being cool is . . . being well informed. This costs nothing but can be priceless to you. Know what's going on in the world, follow the news, be curious; follow sport though you might not personally enjoy it that much.

Many people initially communicate by discussing football news. It's harmless (well, to most!). It does not necessarily involve mentioning politics, religion or money.

'Did you see the game last night?'

Ice breaker.

And if you are planning to work in a specialist area, then your knowledge is probably the most important aspect of you getting the job in broadcasting. Don't hide your light under a bushel. You have no idea when past experience, in any field, might come in handy. It could give you a lifeline with a difficult interviewee. Or get you really on top of a situation with a meandering phone-in caller.

Or even a murderer, it turns out. Detective Chief Inspector Colin Sutton was questioning the subsequently convicted serial killer Levi Bellfield about the murder of Amélie Delagrange on Twickenham Green (a street away from where I had grown up), and about the death of Milly Dowler in Walton-on-Thames. Sutton's opening remark, to encourage some revealing dialogue with Bellfield, was: 'I hear you're a Spurs fan? So am I . . .'

Subjects not to volunteer: your family, your pets, your house/flat. The gastronomical delights of your most recent holiday (unless specifically asked).

I have found that asking someone about music yields results. I've yet to meet anyone who says: 'I don't like music.'

Most folk will *not* respond with: 'I'm only into north Mexican minimal techno from 1998.'

They are much more likely to say: 'Ooh I like all sorts of music. Bit of everything, really.'

And then, with any luck, you're up and away, and you'll reach a reasonably rapid rapport.

Of course, it doesn't, and can't, always work. You can't win 'em all.

Although I had met her once before, and we both had chatted in a friendly way at Bill Wyman's restaurant Sticky Fingers, I was later reintroduced to the fashion maven Vivienne Westwood. I did not expect her to remember me. In fact, it should be a gold-plated rule — never say, to anyone at all:

'You don't remember me, do you?'

It was at some other party, by a well-wisher. He, quite innocently, believed he was bringing together her, the queen of fashion with, as he introduced me, the queen of radio.

Ms Westwood paused and declaimed: 'I never listen to the radio.'

There really was no answer to that.

I'm not sure if that was worse than the late evening I arrived home to find a party going on in my kitchen. Among the guests, Vivienne's son, Joe, who ran the exotic, erotic underwear empire Agent Provocateur. He was on a chair beside a radiator.

On which I had earlier hung out to dry a long line of no-frills, not very white, not very new, not very skimpy M&S knickers.

Acknowledgements

Thanks to Lee Brackstone, Gordon Wise, Jacquie Drewe, Katie Espiner, Ellie Freedman, Jo Whitford, Sarah Fortune, Lucie Stericker, Emma Finnigan, Tom Noble, Francesca Pearce, Helena Fouracre, Cathy Dunn, Maura Wilding, Paul Stark, Emma Power, Madeleine Newman-Suttle.

Lorna Clarke, Aled Haydn Jones, Rhys Hughes, Chris Price, Rachel Barton Nockall, Rachel MacIlroy, Zoe Marcuzzi, Esmeralda Januzi, Joe Gardner, Andrew Rogers, Jeff Barrett, Robin Turner, Keith Althan, Andy Parfitt, Matthew Bannister, Ben Cooper, Johnny Beerling. Jeff Griffin.

Tony Hall, Tim Davie, Jane Garvey, Fi Glover, Jill Thompson, Jason Carter, Bobby Friction, Paul Thomas, Kat Wong, Millie Riley, Ele Beattie, Martha Paziente Caidan, Becky Abbott Black, Matt Fincham, Ty Powell, Nicola di Tullio, Mimi Miraflor, Jane Beese, Tim Byrne, Jason Kramer, Julian Lennon, Pete Ritzema, Mike McCartney, Paul McCartney, Scott Rodger, Mary, Stella and James McCartney, Andy Neill; Jessica Greedus, Pip Hockey, Sacha Taylor-Cox, Ed Bigland.

Danny Rukasin, Maggie O'Connell, Finneas O'Connell, Billie Eilish, Little Simz, Elvis Costello, Elizabeth Clark, Alan Carr, Andrew, Alison, Ava, Syd and Dee Dee Innes, Bobby Gillespie, Martin Duffy, Denise Johnson, Mike Skinner, Karl Hyde, Mike Gillespie, Emily Eavis, Michael Eavis, Nick Dewey, Ronnie Wood,

Acknowledgements

Vicki Wickham, John Lydon, Nick Grimshaw, Jan Younghusband, Nick Carpenter, The Who, Andy Eakins, Fran O'Donnell, Shhh and Zak Starkey, Melvin Benn, Mike Oldfield, Moira Bellas, Clive Banks, Simon Brook, Nina Soufy, Lynn McCarthy, Mani n Melds, Mark Sayfritz, Marietta Pelayo, Mark Simpson, Christopher McLean, Beatrice Welles, Lim-la Richards-Sterling, Jagz Kooner, Sarah Lowe, Sherry Daly, Harvey Goldsmith, Chris York, Chris Smith, Hugh Parker, Sarah Murray, Melanie Lewin, Jess Hallett, Nick Moss, Kate Moss, Kate Mosse, Fiona Young, Jen Ramey, David Morley, Harry Barter, Sven Bayerbach, Emma Saxby, Olivier De Frahan, Karen Buck MP, Cat Farrell, Sahra Jalali, Richard Thomas, Louise Kattenhorn, Hermeet Chadha, Mark Cousins, Robert Glazer, Pratima Glazer, Graeme Wood, Wilberr Wilberforce, Sue Clark, Liam Gallagher, Ringo Starr, Lee Starkey, all the Radio 1 crew past and present, BBC Radio 2 crew past and present, BBC1Xtra crew past and present, BBC 6 Music crew, BBC Asian Network crew, BBC Radio 4, BBC TV Music and BBC Sounds.

Alex Nightingale, Lucy Swanson, William Wilkes and Olie Wilkes.

Credits list

Image credits

Images p.1 © John Davidson; p.2 below right © BBC/Radio 1, Round Table; p.3, p.4 below left © Shutterstock/Dezo Hoffman; p.4 above © Getty Images/John Pratt; p.4 below right © Getty Images/BBC Motion Library; p.5 © Getty Images/Roger Viollet Collection; p.6 above left © Getty Images/Hulton-Deutsch Collection/Corbis; p.6 above right © Getty Images/National Portrait Gallery; p.7 above © Shutterstock/David Fisher; p.8 © The Beatles Book Photo Library. All other photographs are from the author's private collection.

Lyric credits

'Happiness Is a Warm Gun' by The Beatles (Sony/ATV Music Publishing (UK) Limited)

'The Continuing Story of Bungalow Bill' by The Beatles (Sony/ATV Music Publishing (UK) Limited)

'Glass Onion' by The Beatles (Sony/ATV Music Publishing (UK) Limited)

'Revolution 9' by The Beatles (Sony/ATV Music Publishing (UK) Limited)

'Hard Day's Night' by The Beatles (Sony/ATV Music Publishing (UK) Limited)

'Yesterday' by The Beatles (Sony/ATV Music Publishing (UK) Limited)

'Waiting in Vain' by Bob Marley & the Wailers (Blackwell Fuller Music Publishing LLC and Fifty-Six Hope Road Music Limited)

'Three Little Birds' by Bob Marley & the Wailers (Blackwell Fuller Music Publishing LLC and Fifty-Six Hope Road Music Limited)

'Lucy in the Sky with Diamonds' by The Beatles (Sony/ATV Music Publishing (UK) Limited)

'Let There Be More Light' by Pink Floyd (BMG Rights Management (UK) Limited)

'The Winter of the Long Hot Summer' by Disposable Heroes of Hiphoprisy (Frantic Soulutions and Universal Polygram International Publishing Inc.)

'You Don't Have to Say You Love Me' by Dusty Springfield (Curci USA Music Publishing)

'Hernando's Hideaway' by Jerry Ross and Richard Adler, from the musical *The Pajama Game* (J & J Ross Co., Lakshmi Puja Music Limited)

'God Save the Queen' by Sex Pistols (Universal Music Publishing Group)

'You Don't Own Me' by SayGrace (Warner/Chappell Music, Inc.)

'One Love/People Get Ready' by Bob Marley & the Wailers (Blackwell Fuller Music Publishing LLC and Fifty-Six Hope Road Music Limited)

'All I Really Want to Do' by Bob Dylan (Bob Dylan, Sony/ATV Music Publishing (UK) Limited)

Every effort has been made to trace or contact all copyright holders. The publishers would be pleased to rectify any errors or omissions brought to their attention at the earliest opportunity.

Index

Index

Index

Index

Harrison, George, 2, 24, 36 – 7, 39 – 40
Harry, Debbie, 78, 103, 199 – 200
Hatfield and the North (band), 78
Heath, Michael, 276
Heath House school, 133
Heavenly Records, 179, 208, 223, 258
Heller, Pete, 206, 234
Hendrix, Jimi, 174, 286
Henry Wood House, 285
Hepburn, Audrey, 364
Hermes, HMS (ship), 278, 280
'Hey Jude' (song), 131
Hill, Lauryn, 329
Hillage, Steve, 202
Hillman, Chris, 171
Hockney, David, 24
Holly, Buddy, 229
Hollywood, 336
Holmes, David, 331
Hopkin, Mary, 28, 37, 286
Hove, East Sussex, 158, 172
Hudson, Rock, 35
Human League (band), 125
Humble Pie (band), 75, 305
Hurricane Hugo (1989), 117 – 18
Hussein, Saddam, 270, 271
Hyde, Karl, 120 – 7, 198 – 212
Hynde, Chrissie, 130

Ibiza, 244 – 50
Idle, Eric, 24
Incredible String Band (band), 19
Innes, Andrew, 156, 178 – 96

Innes, Neil, 24
International Labour Day, 256
internet, 246 – 7
INXS (band), 199
Iran-Iraq war, 271
Iraq, invasion of (2003), 270
Island Records, 62
Isle of Wight Festival (1970), 15
'It's a Fine Day' (song), 148 – 50

Jackson, Michael, 116
Jagger, Mick, 24, 40, 78
Jah Shaka, 203
Jam, The (band), 277
James Bond movies, 14, 24, 93, 340
Jankel, Chaz, 84
Jerry, Mungo, 17
Jesus and Mary Chain (band), 195
Jett, Joan, 323
'Jilted John' (song), 148
John, Elton, 40, 59, 115, 133
John Peel show, 299 – 300
Johnson, Alan, 313, 315
Johnson, Denise, 192
Johnson, Wilko, 86
Jones, Grace, 113
Jones, Paul, 51
Jones, Quincy, 323
Joshua Tree Inn, California, 171, 174 – 6
Journey into Space (radio programme), 14
Joy Division (band), 123, 152
Joyce, James, 226
Juke Box Jury (TV programme), 97,

Index

Index

Index

Rex (club), 233

Richards, Keith, 174, 295

Ridley, Greg, 75

Roffe, Melloney, 277

Rolling Stones, The, 8, 26, 116, 164, 174, 231, 295

Roman Holiday (film, 1953), 364

Romania, 223–4

Romero, George A., 148

Rosko, Emperor (Mike Pasternak), 78

Rough Trade Records, 108, 206, 268

Roundtable (radio programme), 78, 159

Route 66, 170

Rowling, J. K., 136

Roxy Music (band), 19, 49, 130

Royal Air Force, 353

Royal Albert Hall, 118, 128–30, 136

Rukasin, Danny, 339, 340

Russian Doll (Netflix series), 259

Rutles, The (parody documentary), 24

Sadkin, Alex, 117

Sagan, Françoise, 226–7

Salinger, J. D., 226

Sam Widges (café), 230

Screamadelica (album), 156, 186–91, 196

Seberg, Jean, 227

Selassie, Haile, 63, 68, 69, 71

Sensible, Captain, 152

Serkis, Andy, 88–9

Sewell, Grace, 323–6

'Sex & Drugs & Rock & Roll,' 81

Sex Pistols, 60, 62, 79, 101, 152, 319

Sham 69 (band), 277

Shanghai, 291–4

Shard, London, 285

Shields, Kevin, 191

Shinwell, Emanuel, 224

'Shipbuilding' (song), 106–10

Shirley, Jerry, 75

Shotton, Pete, 134

Silver Jubilee (1977), 60

Simons, Judith, 51

Simpson, N. F., *One Way Pendulum*, 302

Simpson, O. J., 177

Sinatra, Frank, 230

Siouxsie Sioux, 103

Sire Records, 125, 198

Skinner, Mike, 307–12

Skinner, Richard, 31

Slam (band), 223

Slits, The (band), 103

Small Faces (band), 164, 231

Smith, Adam, 88

Smith, Patti, 103, 152

Smith, Rick, 120, 121, 122, 199, 200, 203, 204, 205

Smiths, The (band), 152, 172

Social, the (club), 258, 263–6

Soft Cell (band), 125, 148

Soma records, 223

Sony Awards ceremony, 355

Soufrière Hills, Montserrat, 118–19

Sounds of the Seventies (radio programme), 7

Index

Index

Index